MW00574329

SCHISM

PAUL BLUSTEIN

SCHISM

CHINA, AMERICA AND THE FRACTURING
OF THE GLOBAL TRADING SYSTEM

Centre for International
Governance Innovation

© 2019 by the Centre for International Governance Innovation

ALL RIGHTS RESERVED. No part of this publication may be reproduced, stored in a retrieval system or transmitted by any means, electronic, mechanical, photocopying, recording or otherwise, without the prior written permission of the publisher, application for which should be addressed to the Centre for International Governance Innovation, 67 Erb Street West, Waterloo, Ontario, Canada N2L 6C2 or publications@cigionline.org.

978-1-928096-84-9 (hardcover)   978-1-928096-85-6 (paperback)
978-1-928096-86-3 (ePUB)   978-1-928096-87-0 (ePDF)

Library and Archives Canada Cataloguing in Publication

Title: Schism : China, America and the fracturing of the global trading system / Paul Blustein.

Names: Blustein, Paul, author. | Centre for International Governance Innovation, publisher.

Description: Includes bibliographical references.

Identifiers: Canadiana (print) 20190118229 | Canadiana (ebook) 20190118253 | ISBN 9781928096856 (softcover) | ISBN 9781928096849 (hardcover) | ISBN 9781928096863 (HTML) | ISBN 9781928096870 (PDF)

Subjects: LCSH: World Trade Organization. | LCSH: United States—Commerce—China. | LCSH: China—Commerce—United States.

Classification: LCC HF3128 .B68 2019 | DDC 382.0973/051—dc23

The opinions expressed in this publication are those of the author and do not necessarily reflect the views of the Centre for International Governance Innovation or its Board of Directors.

Printed and bound in Canada. This product is made of recycled materials and other controlled sources.

Cover design by Melodie Wakefield.
Page design by Brooklynn Schwartz.

Centre for International Governance Innovation and CIGI are registered trademarks.

**Centre for International
Governance Innovation**

Centre for International Governance Innovation
67 Erb Street West
Waterloo, ON Canada N2L 6C2

www.cigionline.org

TABLE OF CONTENTS

Acronyms and Abbreviations vii

Author's Note and Acknowledgements xi

1. Dispiriting History 1

2. The Wolf Is Coming 13

3. Maximum Concessions 45

4. China Opens Up, America Gets a Shock 71

5. Cheap Currency: If Only There Were Rules 91

6. Not an Exotic Version of Canada 111

7. China in the WTO Dock 141

8. Party Like It's 2025 169

9. Trans-Pacific Delusions 207

10. Might Unmakes Right 223

11. Make the WTO Great Again 259

ACRONYMS AND ABBREVIATIONS

5G	fifth-generation
AD	anti-dumping
APEC	Asia Pacific Economic Cooperation
APT1	Advanced Persistent Threat 1
ASEAN	Association of Southeast Asian Nations
CEO	chief executive officer
CFIUS	Committee on Foreign Investment in the United States
CIA	Central Intelligence Agency
CIGI	Centre for International Governance Innovation
CNR	China North Locomotive & Rolling Stock Corp.
COMAC	Commercial Aircraft Company of China
CPTPP	Comprehensive and Progressive Agreement for Trans-Pacific Partnership
CSIS	Center for Strategic and International Studies
CSR	China South Locomotive & Rolling Stock Corp.
CUSMA	Canada-United States-Mexico Agreement
CVD	countervailing duties
DRC	Development Research Center
FDI	foreign direct investment

GATT	General Agreement on Tariffs and Trade
GE	General Electric
IMF	International Monetary Fund
ISSI	Integrated Silicon Solutions
IT	information technology
JCCT	Joint Commission on Commerce and Trade
JV	joint venture
MERICS	Mercator Institute for China Studies
MFN	most-favoured-nation
MLP	National Medium- and Long-Term Plan for the Development of Science and Technology
NAFTA	North American Free Trade Agreement
NATO	North Atlantic Treaty Organization
NBER	National Bureau of Economic Research
NCSC	National Cyber Security Centre
NDRC	National Development and Reform Commission
NSA	National Security Agency
OECD	Organisation for Economic Co-operation and Development
PLA	People's Liberation Army
PNTR	permanent normal trading relations
PRC	People's Republic of China
RCEP	Regional Comprehensive Economic Partnership
RMB	renminbi
SASAC	State-owned Assets Supervision and Administration Commission
SED	Strategic Economic Dialogue
S&ED	Strategic and Economic Dialogue
SEI	Strategic Emerging Industries
SMEs	small and medium-sized enterprises
SOEs	state-owned enterprises
TAA	Trade Adjustment Assistance
TPP	Trans-Pacific Partnership
TRIPS	Trade-Related Aspects of Intellectual Property Rights
USITC	United States International Trade Commission
USTR	United States Trade Representative
WTO	World Trade Organization

To Sidney,

Who has inspired my fondest dream, namely that a few decades from now he will pull a yellowed copy of this book off his parents' shelf and think to himself, "Wow, the world sure was messed up when Grandpa wrote this. Good thing my generation fixed it!"

AUTHOR'S NOTE AND ACKNOWLEDGEMENTS

I suppose the first person I should thank is Donald Trump, since the idea for writing this book occurred to me during his presidential campaign when I heard some of his more outlandish statements regarding China's entry into the World Trade Organization. This was a subject I knew a thing or two about, having covered much of the process as a reporter for *The Washington Post,* and having also interviewed a number of the key players in the years after the accession. A more serious intellectual debt is owed to Mark Wu of Harvard Law School, whose seminal article "The China Inc. Challenge to Global Trade Governance" greatly helped me frame my approach to the book, as did an enjoyable conversation with Mark in Cambridge, MA.

So I was delighted when the Centre for International Governance Innovation (CIGI), where I'm a senior fellow, approved my book proposal and generously provided the necessary financial support. This was not an inexpensive undertaking: the research and writing spanned more than two years and required travel from my home in Japan to Beijing, Shanghai, Geneva, Brussels, Paris, Washington and Little Rock, Arkansas, home of the William J. Clinton Presidential Library.

Including conversations that took place before the project was launched, the book is based on interviews with well over 150 people — current and former officials of governments and international organizations, business executives, consultants, academics, attorneys and other experts. Only a fraction of those whom I interviewed are quoted or cited — that is partly because most of the conversations were on "deep background" to protect confidentiality, and partly because in writing my narrative I relied as much as possible on contemporaneous material rather than quoted recollections. But the interviewees know who they are, and I sincerely appreciate their sharing their knowledge and insight; every single interview shaped the book in one way or another. Books, articles, reports and news stories by people too numerous to name were invaluable in helping me piece together the tale. Footnotes will reveal most of the authors of such work, but no doubt some were inadvertently excluded; I noticed just as I was finishing the book that the people footnoted don't include Brad Setser of the Council on Foreign Relations, whose observations strongly influenced my thinking.

Since China is the main focus, I feel obliged to note that I have never received money or other emoluments, directly or indirectly, from any Chinese individuals or institutions. All the support for my research and writing came from CIGI, which takes justifiable pride in its independence and in its transparency about its own funders. As it happens, no Chinese individuals or institutions appear on CIGI's donor page; the biggest funding sources are public and private sources in Canada.

The necessity for such an emphatic avowal is unfortunate. The atmosphere surrounding the debate over China, especially in the United States, has become toxic, with serious scholars and organizations subject to smears and innuendos if they have financial relationships or entanglements of any sort with Chinese counterparts. To be sure, Beijing is making a determined effort to sway policy and public opinion in Western capitals, using its cash as a lubricant; exposing conflicts of interest is both legitimate and desirable. But cynicism about the recipients of Chinese funds is becoming unhinged.

That said, I can assure readers that this book is above reproach in that regard. Neither Chinese money, nor money from Beijing's opponents in the trade debate — the US steel industry, for example, or labour unions — played any part in funding my work. The book may be attacked by China hawks for being naive and by Chinese nationalists for casting a harsh eye on the nation's economic system. But my views, however wrong-headed, were come by honestly, without the slightest pressure or financial encumbrance whatsoever. I've called 'em as I've seen 'em.

I am immensely grateful to Rohinton Medhora, CIGI's president, for his backing, wisdom and encouragement. Bob Fay and Oonagh Fitzgerald, directors of the two CIGI programs that funded the book — the Global Economy Program and the International Law Research Program — reviewed the manuscript and provided extremely helpful criticisms and comments, as did two anonymous reviewers whose expertise saved me from embarrassing goofs. That said, the usual provisos apply about my sole responsibility for remaining errors and omissions. Jennifer Goyder was both meticulous and pleasant in handling the editing chores, under the capable supervision of Carol Bonnett, CIGI's publisher, whose work in managing publication and dissemination I also deeply appreciate. Heather McNorgan, the program manager for the Global Economy Program, was cheerful and efficient as always in dealing with logistical issues that arose. Last but not least, huge thanks go to my CIGI colleague Alex He for translating a portion of a book about China's WTO accession.

Since this is my sixth book, my wife Yoshie and our sons have become relatively inured to the privations necessitated by my absences from home and other inconveniences associated with this kind of work. Still, I would be remiss in failing to express my gratitude for Yoshie's devotion and support during yet another long project. Being Japanese, she prefers that my romantic sentiments be expressed privately, so suffice to say that I do.

On another note regarding family, ours expanded while this book was being written when Sidney, my first grandchild and apple of my eye, was born. I have dedicated this book to him in appreciation for entering the world, thereby providing a timely reminder of what is truly important in my life.

Paul Blustein
Kamakura, Japan
May 15, 2019

CHAPTER 1

DISPIRITING HISTORY

Five uninhabited islets and three barren rocks, known as Senkaku in Japan and Diaoyu in China, are claimed as sovereign territory by both countries, and as a result, the surrounding waters of the East China Sea are often the scene of confrontations between Japanese and Chinese vessels. Much to Beijing's aggravation, Tokyo maintains administrative control over the islands, using its coast guard to ward off incursions. In most cases, warnings bellowed over loudspeakers by Japanese coast guard officers suffice to resolve such encounters peaceably. But the clash that occurred on September 7, 2010, was different.[1]

That morning, the *Mizuki*, a Japan Coast Guard patrol boat, was cruising near the islands when urgent word came that a Chinese fishing trawler was acting more belligerently than usual — not only had it disregarded commands to exit the area, it had deliberately collided with a much larger Japanese cutter and sped away. Ordered to pursue the trawler, the *Mizuki* headed it off, together with another cutter, still within territorial waters claimed by Japan. To the consternation of the *Mizuki*'s crew, the trawler — clearly bent on another

---

1   A thorough account of the Sino-Japanese confrontation can be found in Michael Green et al., 2017, *Countering Coercion in Maritime Asia: The Theory and Practice of Gray Zone Deterrence,*" Center for Strategic & International Studies, May, chapter 3, case 2.

ramming — suddenly steamed toward the patrol boat's stern on the starboard side. A video[2] conveys the crew's mixed English and Japanese shouts, over the whooping of an emergency siren:

"Stop engine!"

"Stop engine!" *"Oi! Tomare!"* (Hey! Stop!) *"Oi! Tomare! TOMARE!"*

A loud bang resounded as the trawler plowed into the *Mizuki*, sending black smoke billowing from the point of impact. Although nobody was injured, the collision dented the patrol boat and damaged a railing. Shortly thereafter the trawler was chased down and boarded by Japan Coast Guard personnel, who took the crew and captain, 41-year-old Zhan Qixiong, into custody.

The events that followed sent a jarring message to the world about how China might wield the power accorded by its burgeoning economy. In foreign capitals where China's growth was beheld with a mixture of awe and disquiet, Beijing's response to the ship collision ratcheted up the level of anxiety.

At first, Chinese anger over Japan's actions manifested itself in sharp diplomatic protests and demonstrations by groups of citizens aroused by memories of Japanese imperialism. Contending that the trawler had the legal right to fish in waters deemed by China to be its own, Beijing denounced the detention of the ship and crew as "harassment" and demanded their immediate release. Although Japanese authorities allowed 14 crew members to return to China on September 13, Captain Zhan remained confined in an Okinawa police station. The possibility of Tokyo lodging formal charges against the captain drew Chinese warnings of "strong countermeasures" and the suspension of bilateral exchanges on issues ranging from aviation to coal. Then, two weeks after the collision, the stakes rose exponentially.

On September 22, *The New York Times* reported that Beijing was blocking exports to Japan of rare earths, over which China held a near-monopoly of the world supply.[3] These minerals, such as neodymium, samarium, praseodymium and cerium, are crucial in the manufacture of high-tech products including hybrid cars, smartphones, guided missiles, low-energy lightbulbs and camera lenses — and Japanese companies were almost totally dependent on Chinese imports. Industry sources told the *Times* that Chinese customs officials had notified exporters to halt shipments to Japan of pure rare earths

---

2   See www.youtube.com/watch?v=1ZbsmKrjxXk. The video was taken by a *Mizuki* crew member and posted on YouTube two months after the collision.

3   Keith Bradsher, 2010, "Amid Tension, China Blocks Vital Exports to Japan," *The New York Times*, September 22.

or rare-earth oxides and salts, although shipments to other countries were still permitted.

Chinese officials publicly denied that they were singling out Japan,[4] and some evidence indicates that supply problems afflicting Japanese companies stemmed from a more general policy that Beijing had adopted earlier in 2010 reducing rare-earth exports to all countries. But other news reports bolstered claims that Japan was being targeted for an embargo subtly orchestrated by powerful Chinese policy makers,[5] and US officials said later that they had received private confirmation.[6] Facing an apparent threat to strangle advanced sectors of its economy, Tokyo quickly backed down in humiliating fashion, releasing Zhan on September 24 to fly home on a chartered plane sent by the Chinese government.

Among the most influential alarms sounded abroad was that of economist Paul Krugman. "I find this story deeply disturbing," Krugman wrote in his *New York Times* column, noting similarities between Beijing's behaviour in this case and its increasing tendency for crafty manipulation to favour Chinese firms. "China…showed no hesitation at all about using its trade muscle to get its way in a political dispute, in clear — if denied — violation of international trade law."[7]

A chilling question thus arose: had the rule-making club for the global trading system admitted an economic superpower that was going rogue?

Nine years before the ship collision, China joined the World Trade Organization (WTO), a historic integration into the global economy of the world's most populous nation at a time when it was rapidly shedding vestiges of Maoist totalitarianism. The WTO, then as now a subject of considerable controversy, is the single most important institution in preserving and advancing economic globalization; it is the current embodiment of the system established after World War II to prevent a reversion to the protectionist horrors of the 1930s. WTO rules keep a lid on the import barriers of member

---

4   James T. Areddy, David Fickling and Norihiko Shirouzu, 2010, "China Denies Halting Rare-Earths Exports to Japan," *The Wall Street Journal,* September 23.

5   Agence France-Presse, 2010, "China blocked exports of rare earth metals to Japan, traders claim," September 24. Further evidence came from a survey of Japanese firms by Japan's Ministry of Economy, Trade and Industry, cited in Kristin Vekasi, 2018, "Politics, markets, and rare commodities: responses to Chinese rare earth policy," *Japanese Journal of Political Science,* December 5.

6   Richard McGregor, 2017, *Asia's Reckoning: China, Japan, and the Fate of U.S. Power in the Pacific Century,* New York, NY: Viking, chapter 12. McGregor's account corresponds with my own reporting.

7   Paul Krugman, 2010, "Rare and Foolish," *The New York Times,* October 17.

countries (which numbered 164 at last count), and members are expected to take their disputes to WTO tribunals for adjudication rather than engage in tit-for-tat trade wars. In addition, the WTO is the guardian of the "most-favoured-nation" (MFN) principle, under which member countries pledge to treat each other's products on a non-discriminatory basis — a valuable bulwark against the formation of hostile trade blocs.

To gain entry to the Geneva-based trade body, China had undergone 15 years of negotiations. US trade officials served as Beijing's chief interlocutors and tormentors, demanding measures to reform the state-dominated Chinese economy and open the nation's markets in ways that exceeded the requirements imposed on other nations. For example, China had to promise that it would reduce its tariffs on manufactured goods to an average of about nine percent by 2005 — less than one-third of the comparable figures for Brazil, Argentina, India and Indonesia.[8] Beijing also had to agree that for a number of years, its trading partners could use several unusual mechanisms that could restrict the inflow of Chinese products into their markets. The main reason Chinese officials accepted such severe conditions was that WTO membership conferred enormous potential benefits, in particular protection against the arbitrary imposition of sanctions on Chinese exports. After numerous fits and starts and near-collapses, the talks finally ended with China's formal admission at a conference of ministers from WTO member countries in November 2001. With the inclusion of China, a nation of 1.25 billion at the time, the "W" in the trade body's acronym attained validity that it previously lacked.

Transformative results ensued, as thousands of Chinese laws and regulations were changed or scrapped to conform with commitments Beijing had made to join. In response to the much greater openness and predictability of the market, foreign companies' China-based operations expanded dramatically. The economy, which had already grown robustly during the 1980s and 1990s, lifting hundreds of millions of Chinese out of poverty, surged on an even steeper upward trajectory during the first decade after entry into the WTO, as GDP quadrupled, while exports almost quintupled. Throughout the world, consumers saved tidy sums by buying more made-in-China products, and producers cranked up exports to satisfy booming Chinese demand. Economic liberalization and the adoption of reforms promoting the rule of law afforded hope in the early 2000s that China was on a gradual path toward true free

---

8   The figure refers to "bound" tariffs, meaning the maximum China and the other countries are allowed to impose under their WTO commitments. "Applied" tariffs — the duties actually imposed by law — are usually lower.

enterprise — if not fully unbridled then at least a form similar to that in, say, South Korea. In a 2002 book that he co-authored, WTO Director-General Supachai Panitchpakdi enthused: "The agreement signals China's willingness to play by international trade rules and to bring its often opaque and cumbersome government apparatus into harmony with a world order that demands clarity and fairness."[9]

But such optimism was rooted in a failure to anticipate how China's economic policies would evolve — and how those policies would flummox trading partners trying to identify rules that Beijing might be accused of violating.

Starting around 2003, and continuing for about a decade thereafter, China kept the exchange rate of its currency pegged at artificially low levels, bestowing significant competitive advantages on Chinese exporters. That exacerbated a phenomenon that has come to be known as the "China shock," which refers to the decimation of manufacturing companies in a number of American blue-collar communities.

Also in 2003, Beijing established institutions giving it tighter and more efficient control over the management of giant state-owned enterprises (SOEs) and banks, the setting of prices for key commodities and inputs, allocation of subsidies, enforcement of regulations and approval of investments. By the time of the 2010 ship collision, China's leaders were guiding the country in a new direction, variously dubbed "state capitalism," "techno-nationalism" and "China Inc." Although the private sector was vibrant and flourishing — by one estimate, it accounted for roughly two-thirds of China's GDP[10] — intervention by the government and the Communist Party was becoming far more pervasive than before. Foreign firms that had once been welcomed with open arms were fuming about falling victim to a bewildering array of obstacles and industrial policies aimed at promoting and protecting Chinese competitors favoured by the party-state. High on the list of gripes were tactics effectively forcing the handover of proprietary technology, or the purchase of inputs from domestic suppliers, as the price of access to the vast Chinese market. Concerns about these policies greatly intensified after the rise of Xi Jinping as China's paramount leader in 2012, notably when Beijing launched a plan called "Made in China 2025" aimed at fostering national self-sufficiency in critical sectors such as new-energy vehicles, biomedicine and robotics.

9   Supachai Panitchpakdi and Mark L. Clifford, 2002, *China and the WTO: Changing China, Changing World Trade*, New York, NY: John Wiley & Sons.

10 Nicholas R. Lardy, 2014, *Markets Over Mao: The Rise of Private Business in China*, Washington, DC: Peterson Institute for International Economics.

In theory, the WTO provides the means to remedy such problems — and in numerous instances, countries have brought complaints against China to the trade body and won; Beijing generally complies by changing its policies in accord with rulings by WTO tribunals. But China's system has become so opaque and uniquely structured that many of its practices fall beyond the scope of the trade body's rules and bedrock principles.[11] This challenge is of existential importance to the WTO given the outsize dimensions of China's market and external trade. (China is the world's largest exporter, with about 13 percent of the global total in 2017.) The administration of US President Donald Trump is dismissive of the WTO's efficacy with regard to China — that was one of Washington's main justifications for starting a trade war against Beijing — and for all the president's misconceptions about trade, he and his acolytes are by no means alone on this score. Their frustration is shared by trade experts across a broad swath of the political spectrum.

This book chronicles China's entry into the WTO and the profound changes that this development has engendered — for both good and ill — for China, for its trading partners (in particular, its most important, the United States) and for the trading system writ large. The rise of the Chinese economic juggernaut is traced, as is the deviation in Beijing's economic modus operandi from the expectations of other WTO member countries. Also recounted are the efforts by non-Chinese officials and political actors, chiefly Americans, to address China's most problematic policies; in addition, the book examines the parts played by multilateral institutions, specifically the WTO and the International Monetary Fund (IMF). The narrative culminates in the Sino-US trade war and related events of 2018-2019 that have brought the trading system to a breaking point.

The book proceeds along chronological lines with detours to explore major themes, as follows: Chapters 2 and 3 recount China's long quest to gain the rights and privileges of WTO membership. These chapters make clear that US negotiators, who have been criticized for striking the deal, were anything but lax in demanding concessions. Chapter 4 examines the period immediately after the 2001 inception of China's membership, when Beijing embraced the required reforms and market opening with apparent sincerity and even excitement. Events covered in this chapter also include the takeoff in Chinese exports and the China shock. Chapter 5 tells the tale of China's currency practices and provides a detailed account of the futile attempts by the IMF to rectify the alleged "misalignment" of foreign exchange rates.

---

11 A particularly cogent version of this argument can be found in Mark Wu, 2016, "The China Inc. Challenge to Global Trade Governance," *Harvard International Law Journal* 57 (2): 261–324.

China's increasingly statist economic approach under the presidency of Hu Jintao (2002–2012) is the subject of chapter 6, which also explores the sluggishness of the George W. Bush administration's response and mounting antagonism over Beijing's industrial policies. Chapter 7 presents a granular look at two WTO cases involving China, to illuminate the issue of whether the trade body is equipped to handle Beijing's economic practices. That is followed by an account in chapter 8 of Xi's reign, which started out appearing market-oriented but soon revealed itself to be significantly more interventionist than Hu's. In chapter 9, one highly touted initiative for countering China's trade policies — the Trans-Pacific Partnership (TPP) — undergoes critical scrutiny. The tenth chapter appraises the Trump administration's approach — the slapping of tariffs on $250 billion[12] worth of Chinese imports, to which China responded with retaliatory actions before the two sides agreed to try negotiating a settlement.

The book's conclusion, also presented in chapter 10, is that the huge challenge posed by China Inc. warrants a much more forceful response than the multilateral trading system has delivered so far — but rather than Trump-style bullying, the right way forward would be to double down on multilateralism. In support of this proposition, chapter 11 presents multilateral strategies that hold substantial promise for ameliorating China-related trade concerns. Because Trump and his team pursued unilateralism instead — bludgeoning countries with tariffs on no real authority but their own say-so — they ignored approaches that could have worked better and they inflicted damage on the WTO that is even more detrimental than the Chinese practices they can reasonably expect to stop. That conclusion will stand regardless of the outcome of the US-China negotiations, which were continuing as this book went to the printer in the spring of 2019.

This series of events is integral to the evolution of global capitalism in the twenty-first century — dispiriting history for those who believe, as I do, in the benefits of both free markets and robust international governance.

China's admission to the WTO was a capstone of US-led economic globalization, which had been on a roll in the 1990s with the approval of the North American Free Trade Agreement (NAFTA) and the international pact that included the WTO's creation. Comeuppance came in 2007-2008, when the outbreak of the global financial crisis brought glaring defects in the American model to the fore — and, as we shall see, the crisis also stymied efforts to modify China's policies. Increasingly confident in the virtues of its

---

12 All figures are in US dollars unless otherwise noted.

own model, Beijing diverged from the economic approach of its trading partners; in so doing, it undermined support for the WTO system abroad. Now the foundations of that system have been fractured by the capricious behaviour and contempt for international rules on the part of the current US president.

Further deterioration may well lay in store, in the form of a deepening US-China schism. That word, the title of this book, has one dictionary definition — "discord, disharmony" — that already applies to the world's two biggest economies, given their disparate economic models, toxic mutual distrust and conflicting interests. Incipient signs of a more full-fledged schism — meaning a major reversal of Sino-American economic integration or even a division of the global economy into separate and exclusive blocs — should be viewed as ominous.

That prospect arose during the trade wars of 2018-2019, amid the dislocation of multinational supply chains and rumblings from Washington about the desirability of a US-China "decoupling." The spectre grew more tangible in mid-May 2019, right at the deadline for finishing touches on this book, when a breakdown in negotiations led Trump to order a sharp increase in the tariffs already levied on $200 billion worth of Chinese imports and the initiation of plans to hit all the other goods shipped from China to the United States. (China vowed to "take necessary countermeasures.") The most serious potential for schism stems from the battle over next-generation telecommunications, which is fraught with tension over espionage and technological ascendancy. The US government has levelled criminal charges against Huawei, the world's leading telecom equipment maker, and sought to block Huawei and other Chinese firms from building networks in overseas markets. One all-too-plausible upshot of the strife over Huawei is a sundering of the global market for many high-tech goods and services.

Be not comforted, even if the US-China negotiations of 2019 end with a signing ceremony at which Trump and Xi jointly rescind tariffs and exchange vows of eternal friendship. In early April, Trump predicted a "very monumental" agreement, and a deal similar to the one that was reportedly taking shape then — assuming it is finalized — may alleviate strains. But the toll taken on the trading system has also been monumental, and any pact the two sides reach will fall well short of permanently resolving their differences. China's political and economic system is not about to change in fundamental ways, nor is the US political establishment about to alter its conclusion that China is America's most formidable strategic rival. With Cold War-like antagonism and suspicion on the rise, Washington and Beijing are contriving to minimize dependence on each other for key technologies. Schism will remain a clear and present danger, and conflict between China and its trading partners will be ongoing.

A proper grasp of China's WTO saga is therefore essential to arrive at informed opinions about the nation's trade regime; sound assessment requires understanding the historical background. Yet false and misleading interpretations of China Inc.'s evolution abound. One is that China was granted entry into the WTO on easy terms; here are others — uttered not by tub-thumping protectionists but by respectable commentators:

- "China astutely knew what it had to promise to gain access to the WTO club, and it made these promises, but its subsequent actions demonstrate that China had no real intention of keeping them."[13]

- "China is a member of the WTO. It's supposed to live up to certain requirements, and it lives up to virtually none of them."[14]

- "China is a trade cheat. [Its actions] directly contradict [its] commitments when it joined the World Trade Organization in 2001."[15]

Such assertions are not only historically inaccurate and unfair to the policy makers involved, they lead to poorly grounded conclusions and policy choices that can be encapsulated in arguments that run roughly as follows: "we've been weak against China — all that's needed is some backbone"; "let's give the Chinese a dose of their own medicine — they don't care about the rules, so we shouldn't either"; and "nothing but unilateral action will work."

It would be Pollyannish in the extreme, of course, to credit Beijing with honouring the spirit of the WTO's rules as faithfully as their letter. As later chapters will show, China's trade mandarins are ingenious at detecting loopholes in WTO texts and exploiting the system's weaknesses. Even more important is the Chinese system's singular lack of transparency. Nobody can tell for sure when orders are being surreptitiously given for state-controlled firms and banks to conduct business or negotiations in ways that promote Beijing's industrial policy goals and unfairly disadvantage foreign competitors, but

---

13 Stephen J. Ezell and Robert D. Atkinson, 2015, "False Promises: The Yawning Gap Between China's WTO Commitments and Practices," Information Technology & Innovation Foundation, September.

14 Testimony by Richard Ellings, professor at the University of Washington and executive director for the Commission on the Theft of American Intellectual Property, at a hearing of the US Trade Representative's Office, "Section 301 Investigation and Hearing: China's Acts, Policies, and Practices Related to Technology Transfer, Intellectual Property, and Innovation," October 17, 2017.

15 Fareed Zakaria commentary on "Fareed Zakaria GPS," CNN, April 8, 2018.

the evidence that such practices exist is persuasive if not conclusive in every instance. Foreigners often shrink from complaining for fear of retaliation by regulators wielding arbitrary power over corporate fortunes. Randal Phillips, a former Central Intelligence Agency (CIA) official in China who now heads the Asia offices of the Mintz Group, a consultancy for multinational companies, told me, "We've had clients who have literally been scared to even approach the US embassy, in case they were seen entering."

Comprehending these practices, the tale of how they developed and why they've proven so intractable is also crucial to the formulation of a sensible approach toward China. Turning a blind eye to their use by the world's second-largest economy is unthinkable; the schism that separates China's economic model from that of other nations must be squarely faced. But China's affront to the WTO's foundational tenets is not the same as absence of respect for the rules, and that is a distinction with a substantial difference. The distinction is especially important when it comes to deciding whether and how to defend the rules-based system.

The WTO's value — and limitations — are the subtext of the narrative that unfolds in chapters to come. Even to well-informed laypeople the trade body is a puzzlement, but there are few better backdrops for demystifying the system than the "enter the dragon" spectacle of the China story.

A few reminders of what the system is *not:* it is not "free trade," or "fair trade" or even "reciprocal trade," as those terms are commonly understood. All WTO members maintain some barriers to other countries' products, usually to accommodate the demands of narrow interest groups, thereby sustaining political support for the general openness that is necessary for economic dynamism. Unjust as it may seem, some countries are bigger "sinners" than others, by maintaining more and higher tariffs and other obstacles than their trading partners. And barriers lack "reciprocity" in the sense that tariffs are not equalized for like products in all countries. Different nations insist on protecting different producers — in Canada, as the world learned during the acrimonious Group of Seven summit in June 2018, dairy farmers have long been coddled, while in the United States, the most sheltered include sugar growers and pickup truck manufacturers.

But the system is pretty free, pretty fair and pretty reciprocal. In multilateral agreements reached over past decades, countries bargained based on reciprocity of concessions — that is, each would open its markets to the extent that it could extract enough from its trading partners to make a deal attractive. Many of the provisions involved issues other than tariffs, notably the protection of intellectual property; one reason the United States accepted the imposition of higher tariffs on certain items by other WTO countries was that Washington put top priority on securing legal guarantees abroad against copying of high-value products made in Hollywood and Silicon Valley. The resulting system doesn't end all protectionism, or eliminate all egregious conduct, but it does constrain those problems to reasonably acceptable levels.

The rules sometimes tilt too far in favour of corporate interests, reflecting the influence of lobbies, such as the pharmaceutical industry. But the WTO has kept global commerce from operating according to rule-of-the-jungle, might-makes-right principles. To the extent it continues to do so — an increasingly shaky assumption, in view of Trump's coercive tactics and threats to withdraw — it provides a global public good, from which all nations broadly benefit and no single nation can deliver alone. In the same way that a police force provides the public good of law enforcement at the local level, and a military provides the public good of defence at the national level, the WTO provides the public good of (relatively) open markets at the global level. The resulting stability and predictability of the business environment helps foster economic growth and investment; in the absence of such stability — with trade barriers rising and falling based on the whims of the powerful — corporate executives and entrepreneurs will naturally turn skittish about building or expanding their business operations.

That should be kept in mind while reading in chapter 10 about the actions Trump has taken, and about China's transgressions in chapters 5, 6 and 8. The system is obviously well worth preserving; on the other hand, how long can it survive if the rules inadequately address legitimate grievances about the actions of a major player? Also worth bearing in mind is what might be called the great counterfactual — that is, how China would have developed if it had been kept out of the WTO. Counterfactuals are by definition unamenable to proof, but having intensively reviewed China's development since 2001, I believe it is beyond dispute that WTO membership has made the Chinese economy more open and liberal than it would have been otherwise.

Nor should this book be read without due consideration to the sheer scale of human advancement that China has achieved during its WTO era. No one aware of the wretched conditions in Chinese villages and cities in the late twentieth century can fail to be inspired by the statistics on poverty reduction: in 2002, 409 million Chinese still fell under the international poverty line as defined by the World Bank; a dozen years later, that number had dwindled to 18 million, a mere 1.4 percent of the population.[16] Prosperity has made it possible for the nation to make great strides in cleaning up its air and water and contribute meaningfully to international progress on climate change.

Yet China's new-found wealth has also begotten many untoward consequences. It has helped legitimize the iron grip of the Communist Party and financed an aggressive military posture in the South and East China Seas. It is also funding the development of databases using facial recognition and other forms of high-tech surveillance to clamp down on dissent and induce Party-approved behaviour among the nation's citizenry, making a mockery of predictions by the likes of President Bill Clinton that WTO membership would enhance prospects for the Chinese people to attain political freedom.

This book makes no pretense to covering problems involving China's military or diplomatic policies, human rights, espionage or other non-trade issues except insofar as they relate to trade. I am well aware of the viewpoint that China has become a dangerous adversary to the United States and its allies, and I acknowledge that national security must take precedence over commercial interests, so schism is inevitable to some degree — keeping militarily valuable technology from falling into Beijing's hands being one obvious justification. But the deeper the schism, the greater the economic cost; unlike the circumstances during the Cold War with the Soviet Union, China is extensively intertwined with the global economy. This book's underlying assumption, therefore, is that to the maximum possible extent, trade with China should be grounded in policies and rules aimed at promoting mutual benefit and enrichment. Determining how best to do that is challenging enough without taking competing objectives into account. Worthy as it undoubtedly is to combat Beijing's oppression at home and threats to liberal democracy abroad, I leave those subjects to others, who can hopefully devise solutions at costs that liberal democracies are willing to bear.

China never promised to be America's ally, or anyone else's ally for that matter. Nor did it promise to become a Western-style democracy — hopes for such a development have proven to be an American conceit. China did give myriad undertakings, however, when it joined the WTO. The full ramifications of that agreement are still unfolding, and now is a particularly opportune time to take stock, in a story that begins in globalization's halcyon days.

---

16 See http://povertydata.worldbank.org/poverty/country/CHN.

CHAPTER 2

THE WOLF IS COMING

Inside Beijing's heavily guarded Zhongnanhai compound, where China's top leaders work, stands the Hall of Purple Light, a building with vermillion walls and a roof of green glazed tiles, which has been used for much of its 500-year history to receive foreign dignitaries. There, on January 12, 1999, Chinese Premier Zhu Rongji met Alan Greenspan, the chairman of the US Federal Reserve. After settling into plush chairs separated by a small table adorned with a floral bouquet, the two men opened their conversation with a fulsome exchange of congratulations for the role each had played in boosting their respective countries' economic performances. With a touch of jocularity, Zhu told Greenspan, "You've already gone from a human being to a god," and the Fed chief responded, "The Chinese economy has benefited from your tireless efforts."[1] Most of their chat was devoted to issues within Greenspan's remit — monetary policy, the risks of financial crises and banking regulation — but at the end the 70-year-old Zhu turned to another subject.

Noting that President Bill Clinton had invited him to the United States in the spring, Zhu said, "I hope that during my visit, our two countries will be able to

---

1   Zhu Rongji, 2015, *Zhu Rongji on the Record: The Road to Reform 1998–2003*, Washington, DC: Brookings Institution Press, chapter 15. (The chapter contains a transcript of Zhu's conversation with Greenspan and a photo of their meeting.)

reach an agreement on China's accession to the World Trade Organization."
He emphasized Beijing's readiness to undertake the necessary market-opening
measures, saying China would need a "timetable," but added, "that's not to
drag things out. The idea of a timetable might be one year or it might be three,
not exceeding five years at the most." He apologized for "talking about things
unrelated to you," to which Greenspan replied, "On the contrary, what you
said just now is very relevant to me."

This exchange was no happenstance; it had been carefully and stealth-
ily scripted for a purpose. Negotiations between the two sides' trade officials over China's WTO entry had become bogged down in 1998, leading
some American policy makers, in particular in the Office of the US Trade
Representative (USTR), to the discouraging conclusion that China lacked
the political will for a deal in the foreseeable future. Worried that a golden
opportunity for a pact was slipping away, a pair of US officials worked in
cahoots to ensure that the Zhu-Greenspan meeting would give the talks a
jump-start. Jeffrey Bader, a senior White House adviser on Asia, met with
Greenspan prior to his departure for the Far East, asking the Fed chief to use
his enormous credibility as a conduit by drawing Zhu out on the WTO issue
and then conveying word back to Washington. At the same time, William
McCahill, the number two diplomat at the US embassy in Beijing, tapped his
Chinese contacts, urging them to tell Zhu to be as forthcoming as possible.[2]

The scheme worked. Zhu's message came through loud and clear, as witnessed
by a discussion on January 21, 1999, among Clinton's senior advisers on international economic issues. "Greenspan got a major breakthrough," a deputy
US trade representative crowed, citing tantalizing indications from Zhu that
"they are eager for transition periods of one to five years," and key issues were
"back on the table," according to notes of the meeting taken by a participant.
The US-China negotiations were soon in high gear.

Thus began a year — culminating in a landmark accord — of tumultuous ups
and downs in China's bid for WTO membership, which this chapter and the
next will recount in detail. Now that the consequences have become a topic of
global controversy — and even the American policy makers involved admit

---

2   These details come from interviews with several people involved in the events. Most interviews for this
    book were on "deep background," meaning interviewees were assured of confidentiality unless they gave
    permission to be quoted. In cases where permission for quotation was requested and granted, interviewees
    will be identified to the extent they have permitted, but source information about other information
    obtained from interviews will not be disclosed. Interviews with numerous participants in the accession
    negotiations provided many of the details reported in this chapter and the next. A substantial amount of
    information also comes from news reports; documents such as internal White House memoranda on file
    at the Clinton Presidential Library in Little Rock, Arkansas; and other published material (for example, a
    book containing accounts of confidential Politburo meetings), all of which is footnoted.

that China's economic policies turned out much differently than they had hoped — the question must obviously be asked: what exactly happened back then?

Joining the WTO — "acceding," in WTO speak — is a lot more complicated than submitting an application form and paying dues. To get in, a country must negotiate bilaterally with any WTO member that wishes to obtain some changes to the prospective member's trade regime, and all changes that are agreed are extended to the entire membership in accord with the MFN principle. Any one member dissatisfied with the terms can block the accession. Striking a deal with the United States was therefore not the only hurdle China had to surmount. But it was by far the most important.

The major turning points are well known: in April 1999, Zhu met Clinton at the White House amid fevered expectations that an accord was imminent, but the president backed away at the last minute, damaging the premier's standing and fuelling predictions that momentum had been lost. The following month, relations between Beijing and Washington went into a deep freeze when US aircraft bombed the Chinese embassy in Belgrade instead of an intended Serbian target. Only in November 1999, after six days and nights of exhausting and acrimonious talks in Beijing, did the two sides finally sign on the dotted line, paving the way for a broader pact among all WTO members for China's admission in 2001.

In 2016, in his inimitable fashion, Donald Trump denounced this "disastrous, terrible agreement [that] enabled the greatest jobs theft in history,"[3] positing that it was accepted by US officials who lacked the savvy depicted in his book *The Art of the Deal*. As he put it in a newspaper interview during his presidential campaign: "Political hacks get appointed to negotiate with the smartest people in China. When we negotiate deals with China, China is putting the smartest people in all of China on that negotiation. We're not doing that."[4] Ludicrous as such bloviating may be, it is reasonable to wonder, with the advantage of hindsight, whether Washington got something approaching the best possible terms from Beijing in 1999, or whether its negotiators failed to address serious problems with Chinese economic policy, perhaps because of naïveté, or diplomatic considerations, or political pressure, or spinelessness or something else entirely. A report issued by Trump's trade representative

3   Donald Trump, 2016, "Declaring America's Economic Independence," speech at Alumisource, Monessen, PA, June 28.

4   Maggie Haberman and David E. Sanger, 2016, "In Donald Trump's Worldview, America Comes First, and Everybody Else Pays, *The New York Times*, March 26.

stated: "It seems clear that the United States erred in supporting China's entry into the WTO on terms that have proven to be ineffective in securing China's embrace of an open, market-oriented trade regime."[5]

Nobody can say with certainty how events would have played out if China had faced tougher demands during these negotiations. But a few overarching themes emerge from a granular look at the process. First, both sides played extreme hardball and, if anything, it was the Chinese who felt bruised and humiliated at a number of turns along the way. Second, the talks nearly came unravelled at several junctures, coming even closer to breakdown than is commonly realized, with US negotiators usually being the ones to leave the table (a tactic highly touted in *The Art of the Deal*).[6] Third, it is hard to imagine how Washington could have driven a significantly harder bargain on economic issues and still secured Beijing's acquiescence. Indeed, Chinese officials interviewed for this book still burn with resentment over the "second-class citizenship" they were obliged to accept on a number of issues — no small matter for a country that had endured demeaning oppression at the hands of Western powers and Japan throughout the nineteenth and early twentieth centuries.

Consider the verdict rendered by Nicholas Lardy, a veteran observer of the Chinese economy, in a book published shortly after Beijing's WTO membership was finalized: "China's market access and other commitments are not only more far-reaching than those that governed the accession of countries only a decade ago; they exceed those made by any member that has joined the WTO since [its founding in] 1995.... [The] terms imposed on China, although legally enforceable, are so onerous that they violate fundamental WTO principles."[7]

To be sure, a thorough look back at this period shows that a number of experts were warning about the incompatibility of China's economic and legal system with WTO precepts, and due note will be taken of those prescient insights. It is fair to conclude that US negotiators, for all their firmness on individual points of contention, were over-optimistic in their belief that China's transformation under WTO membership would be so comprehensive as to nullify such concerns. But the evidence also indicates that worries about the risks of

---

5   USTR, 2018, "2017 Report to Congress on China's WTO Compliance," January, executive summary, p. 2.

6   On July 27, 2011, Trump tweeted: "'Know when to walk away from the table.' The Art of the Deal." Donald J. Trump, Twitter post, July 27, 2011, 7:25 p.m., https://twitter.com/realdonaldtrump/status/96284991041974273?lang=en.

7   Nicholas R. Lardy, 2002, *Integrating China into the Global Economy*, Washington, DC: Brookings Institution Press, chapter 1, pp. 9-10.

a deal were just as intense, if not more so, among influential Chinese. As US negotiators formulated their strategy, they had to wrestle with the question of whether rejecting an agreement — i.e., blocking China from joining the WTO — would make it a better global citizen than if it were inside.

The heat of the confrontations that often marred the negotiations is unsurprising, given the magnitude of the stakes for both sides. For the United States, the talks represented the single best opportunity — and presumably the *last* opportunity — to set the terms of China's global economic integration and access for American companies to the fabled China market. In prior years, Washington had undergone wrenching battles over trade with countries such as Mexico and Japan, and now US officials were dealing with a much more populous country, whose workers earned even less than Mexicans and whose government intrusion in the economy was even more pervasive than Tokyo's. Once China had been granted admission to the WTO, the United States would no longer have easy recourse to methods it had used in the past, notably the threat of unilateral sanctions, to cow Beijing when disputes arose. The Chinese would enjoy all the privileges of membership in the trade body; Washington would be obliged to bring its complaints to WTO tribunals.

At that time, US-China trade underwent an annual ritual that aroused tensions on both sides. In accord with federal law, Congress conducted a review of China's human rights record over the previous year and then voted on whether Chinese goods should continue to enter the US market for the next 12 months on an MFN basis — in other words, with essentially the same access as goods from other WTO members. Those votes invariably went in favour of keeping the Sino-US economic relationship intact, as American companies profiting from the lucrative China market descended on Capitol Hill to make the case that punishing Beijing financially wouldn't help on the human rights issue and would only lead to a mutually harmful trade war. As a result, the US market was already effectively open to most of the goods China wanted to export. But even this limited tool of leverage over Beijing's policies would be forfeited if China joined the WTO.

From China's perspective, the negotiations loomed equally large in significance, for inverse reasons. Gaining entry to the WTO would rid Chinese exporters once and for all of major uncertainties afflicting their ability to ship goods abroad, the congressional vote being the most irksome. That, in turn, ensured that China would join the mainstream of the global economy and fully share the benefits, presumably including increased investment by multinational corporations. Diplomacy was also a consideration; China wanted to attain its rightful place in international fora and convey to the world that as a rule-abiding country its rise should be welcomed rather than feared.[8]

This did not mean that Beijing was so avid for WTO membership that it would pliantly accede to conditions set forth by US officials. On the contrary, a widely-used phrase — *lang lai le* ("the wolf is coming") — encapsulated Chinese anxiety that going too far in exposing the nation's companies, workers and farmers to competition from America's mighty multinationals and agribusiness could lead to financial ruin, unemployment and upheaval.

At the same time, pressure of the sort Washington was exerting came as a welcome boost for some Chinese policy makers who perceived the desirability of opening markets in furthering the nation's development. The benefits of acceding to the WTO served as a perfect incentive, these reform-minded individuals believed, for measures that China ought to adopt anyway.

The most visionary of these policy makers was Zhu. No individual would play a more pivotal role in the events of 1999. But before delving into those events, some context from further back in history is necessary.

As Chinese officials often noted, China's bid for admission to the WTO wasn't about joining. It was about re-joining a system of which their nation had been a co-founder five decades earlier.

China was one of the 23 countries participating in an international conference that opened on April 10, 1947, at the Palais des Nations in Geneva, with the aim of laying the cornerstone of a multilateral trading regime. The conference was part of a multi-year postwar exercise to build institutions capable of preventing the dynamics that had engendered economic catastrophe, fascism and bloodshed.[9] Memories were still fresh of the protectionist policies — notably America's Smoot-Hawley Tariff of 1930, which raised tariffs on foreign products to an average of about 55 percent of the value of dutiable goods and prompted retaliatory responses by France, Italy, Britain, Canada, Germany, Japan and other countries.

---

8 Wang Yong, 1999, "Why China Went for WTO," *China Business Review* 26 (4): 42.

9 This section about the establishment of the postwar multilateral trading system draws heavily on the account in chapter 2 of my 2009 book, *Misadventures of the Most Favored Nations*, New York, NY: Public Affairs.

Also haunting conference delegates was the splintering of the world during the 1930s into trade blocs in which nations established special economic arrangements with close allies and colonies using preferential tariffs, currency controls and bureaucratic allocations — Japan's Greater East Asian Co-Prosperity Sphere was a prime example. The resultant stifling of world commerce had deepened the Great Depression and fuelled hostility among major powers.

Playing the leading role at the Geneva conference was the United States, whose delegates drew inspiration from Cordell Hull, America's longest-serving secretary of state, a passionate believer in trade as a necessary condition for both prosperity and peace. The talks nearly foundered at several junctures with the Australians threatening to bolt over tariffs on wool and the British tangling with the Americans about the preferential trading arrangements that London maintained with its colonies and Commonwealth members.[10] But in the end, the delegates produced an accord with 38 articles, named the General Agreement on Tariffs and Trade (GATT), signed on October 30, 1947, which entered into force the following year.

The GATT was designed both to open markets and limit the ability of governments to restrict imports in the future. Participating countries (known formally as "contracting parties," because the GATT was a compact rather than a full-fledged organization) would lower their tariffs and also "bind" them, meaning the tariffs would remain below specified levels. Underpinning the system were commitments that participating countries would abide by principles of non-discrimination among themselves. MFN was one such principle; it required each GATT country to treat the imports of the other participating countries equally with imports from their "most-favoured" trading partners.[11] (If, for example, Chile imposed a tariff on cash registers from the United States at 15 percent, it would have to levy the same 15 percent tariff on cash registers from France or Canada.) Another key principle was "national treatment," which meant that within their domestic economies, countries had to treat imported and locally produced goods equally — tariffs could be imposed at the border, of course, but once foreign products had cleared customs, they could not be subject to discriminatory laws and regulations.

10 Douglas A. Irwin, Petros C. Mavroidis and Alan O. Sykes, 2008, *The Genesis of the GATT*, Cambridge, UK: Cambridge University Press.

11 Some exceptions were allowed, notably for free trade areas and for countries wishing to give especially favourable treatment to goods from their colonies and former colonies.

After setting up shop in Geneva, and adding dozens more countries, the GATT fostered a broad movement toward open commerce in the non-Communist world.[12] In a series of negotiations known as "rounds," countries agreed to lower some of their trade barriers (as per the reciprocality mentioned in chapter 1) based on the proviso that their trading partners would lower some barriers as well. Although some large sectors, such as agriculture and clothing, were exempt for political reasons, average tariffs imposed by industrialized nations on manufactured goods fell from roughly 35 percent to 6.5 percent by the mid-1980s as a result of GATT agreements. (Developing countries' tariffs were higher.) In addition to tariff cutting, GATT countries agreed on rules limiting the use of subsidies and regulations to tilt the competitive playing field. When disputes arose, countries were expected to bring cases to GATT tribunals (comprised of three to five trade law experts from neutral member states), and if found guilty of violating the rules, the losing country could be ordered to change its offending practices or face sanctions, usually in the form of punitive tariffs levied by the winning party.

China's status as a GATT contracting party, however, was short lived. The Chinese officials signing the compact represented the Nationalist government, which was driven from the mainland in the fall of 1949 by Communist revolutionaries under the leadership of Mao Zedong, who triumphantly proclaimed the founding of the People's Republic of China (PRC). From their base in Taiwan, the only Chinese province they controlled, the Nationalists formally withdrew China's GATT status the following year.[13] That was of little concern to Mao, who was forging a system almost fully isolated from global commerce.

Based on his theory of "permanent revolution," according to which society must undergo repeated bouts of mass activism, Mao plunged China into a series of campaigns that put all aspects of economic life in the service of Communism.[14] Having confiscated and redistributed private farmland to the peasantry (a process during which roughly one million landlords were executed), Mao embarked in 1958 on the "Great Leap Forward," abolishing private ownership and collectivizing not only land, but houses, livestock and food.

---

12 The system was not nearly as robust as the founders had hoped. A plan approved at an international conference in Havana for a strong institution, dubbed the International Trade Organization, fell apart when the US Congress, by then growing suspicious of global organizations, refused to approve it.

13 Raj Bhala, 2000, "Enter the Dragon: An Essay on China's WTO Accession Saga," *American University International Law Review* 15 (6): 1469–538.

14 For details on Mao, Deng and their economic policies, see Orville Schell and John Delury, 2013, *Wealth and Power: China's Long March to the Twenty-First Century*, London, UK: Little, Brown, chapters 9, 10, 11 and 12.

More than 30 million died of famine (caused largely by crop failures and local officials shipping their communes' harvests to meet government-imposed targets rather than allowing local consumption), but the Great Helmsman was far from finished. Under his reign, all manufacturing, mining, transportation, wholesaling and retailing was controlled by state-owned firms; nearly all prices were fixed by government decree; supplies of raw materials and intermediate goods were determined by government plan; and funding for machinery and buildings came from the government budget. If any remnants of the old order survived, they were targeted for eradication during the Cultural Revolution, unleashed in 1966, when millions of youthful "Red Guards" ferreted out and attacked "capitalist roaders," "reactionaries," "class enemies" and anyone else (even including the Red Guards' own parents and teachers) suspected of disloyalty to "Mao Zedong thought." Unsurprisingly, all of this turmoil only made China poorer than it already was, as its GDP per capita, which was fifty-ninth in the world in 1952, fell to 134 (out of 167 countries) in 1978.[15]

The government's all-encompassing economic controls eroded in the years following Mao's death in 1976, when Deng Xiaoping emerged from a power struggle as China's paramount leader. Deng had been purged as a "rightist" during the chaotic fanaticism of Mao's final years, and the policies he adopted in the late 1970s and early 1980s showed that his enemies had pegged him correctly, at least by the rigid standards of Maoist ideology. Retail prices for many consumer goods were liberalized in accordance with supply and demand, rural free markets for agricultural products were allowed to blossom, private firms were accorded freedom to operate in a growing number of sectors and millions of Chinese found work in those private enterprises. With the spirit of entrepreneurialism reawakened, economic output expanded at double-digit annual rates in the first half of the 1980s.

The legacy of Maoism continued to permeate much of the economy, however. The majority of workers remained employed at tens of thousands of SOEs, a classic example being the No. 1 Auto Plant, which I visited in 1993. Built in the northeastern city of Changchun during the early 1930s, the factory employed 100,000 people who assembled more than $1 billion annually of Liberation trucks, Red Flag limousines and other vehicles. With workers wielding wrenches and blowtorches swarming around as engines and doors were bolted into place, the assembly line bore greater resemblance to the one in Charlie Chaplin's 1936 comedy *Modern Times* than the automated ones I

---

15 Penn World Tables 8.0 database, cited in David H. Autor, David Dorn and Gordon H. Hanson, 2016, "The China Shock: Learning from Labor-Market Adjustment to Large Changes in Trade," *Annual Review of Economics* (8): 205–40. The ranks are of GDP at constant national prices (in 2005 US dollars).

had seen in Japan and the United States. Protected from foreign competition by steep tariffs, the plant was government owned and heavily subsidized. Its sprawling grounds encompassed a cradle-to-grave social welfare system, called the "iron rice bowl," for workers and their families, including tens of thousands of apartments and dormitories, a hospital, 22 elementary and secondary schools, dozens of stores, a library and a theatre.[16]

In the hope of modernizing such enterprises, Deng's reforms included an opening of the once-cloistered economy to foreign investors, who could provide capital and know-how, and that in turn sparked Beijing's interest in the multilateral trading system. In 1982, China obtained "observer status" in the GATT, and on July 10, 1986, it submitted an application seeking to resume its status as a contracting party.[17] Beijing's motivation was clear: it wanted the greatest and most secure access in overseas markets for its rapidly growing exports, which in the late 1980s consisted mainly of toys, clothing, textiles and shoes.

Negotiations over the terms of China's GATT entry, although time-consuming, went fairly smoothly — impoverished and backward as it was, the country was not perceived as a serious competitive threat. "I was in the meetings in the spring of 1989," recalled Tim Stratford, who was then a commercial officer in the US embassy in Beijing, and he added, holding his forefinger very near his thumb: "We were this close to having a deal with the Chinese government," on terms that would have been far less ambitious than the ones China ultimately accepted.

Within weeks, prospects for such an accord went from good to inconceivable. On the night of June 3-4, 1989, hundreds of students and other pro-democracy protesters, who had amassed in Tiananmen Square, were killed by military forces under orders from Communist leaders bent on squelching any challenge to the Party's control. This brutality so horrified the West that for a number of years, China was refused any opportunity to bargain for improvement in its trade status. Although Chinese exports retained access to the US market under MFN terms,[18] the "butchers of Beijing" (the term used by Clinton in his 1992 presidential campaign) were unwelcome at the international trade

---

16 Paul Blustein, 1993, "Can 'Half-Reformed' China Last? Hybrid Economy Is Neither Socialist Nor Capitalist," *The Washington Post*, August 29.

17 China contended that the "withdrawal" by Taiwan in 1950 had no legal force because as a matter of international law the 1949 revolution did not change China's legal status; therefore, China should be allowed to "resume" its former status as a GATT contracting party rather than apply for accession as a new one. But the United States and others maintained that it must undergo a regular accession process, and Beijing acquiesced. See Esther Lam, 2009, *China and the WTO: A Long March Towards the Rule of Law*, Wolters Kluwer, chapter 4.

18 The House of Representatives voted in 1990, 1991 and 1992 to revoke China's MFN status, but the Senate voted to maintain it, so the status quo prevailed.

negotiating table. This stance would continue in the early 1990s, even as capital from the world's biggest multinationals — Coca-Cola, Volkswagen, General Electric (GE), Fujitsu and Ericsson, to name a few — poured into China, which by 1993 accounted for almost one-quarter of all foreign direct investment (FDI) in developing countries.

Much of that investment was aimed at using low-wage Chinese labour for manufacturing goods that would be exported abroad. Per-capita income in 1993 was estimated at $380 a year,[19] and about 900 million Chinese — three quarters of the population — were peasants, migrating by the tens of millions each year from the rural interior in search of factory jobs affording better living standards than they could hope for in their villages. For multinationals, which were in the midst of a "supply chain revolution"[20] aimed at placing each stage of their operations (design, research and development, component manufacturing, final assembly, etc.) in countries with the greatest competitive advantage, China was often the obvious choice for labour-intensive final assembly. In addition, the Chinese domestic market was exploding, in particular in the rapidly industrializing urban centres along the coast, and the potential profits of selling to the burgeoning Chinese middle class proved irresistible for executives in boardrooms around the world, despite pitfalls including endemic corruption and primitive infrastructure. Motorola, Inc., for example, started making pagers in 1992 at a plant in the northern port city of Tianjin, and when its output of 10,000 pagers a week couldn't keep up with Chinese demand, the company added a $200 million facility to make pagers, computer chips and mobile phones. Honda Motor Co., capitalizing on a Chinese motorcycle market that blossomed into the world's largest in 1992, launched three joint ventures with Chinese partners that year and increased its locally assembled production of motorcycles by more than 50 percent, to 580,000 units per year.[21]

Also key to investors' optimism was the fact that Beijing's economic reforms showed every sign of proceeding apace. In 1992, at the age of 87, Deng took a highly publicized tour of special economic zones, where private firms enjoyed extra incentives to invest, in both Guangdong province and Shanghai. In speech after speech, he made clear to Party cadres that notwithstanding the crackdown on political dissent, his quasi-capitalist approach, which he called

---

19 Official per-capita income significantly understated living standards because most Chinese enjoyed benefits such as free housing and medical care. Adjusting for such factors, the IMF estimated per-capita income at around $1,300 on a "purchasing power parity" basis in 1993.

20 For an insightful history of this process and how it took off in the 1990s, see Richard Baldwin, 2016, *The Great Convergence*, Cambridge, MA: Belknap Press of Harvard University Press.

21 Paul Blustein, 1994, "Cracking China's Market: Profits, or Peril?" *The Washington Post*, January 30.

"socialism with Chinese characteristics," was irreversible. Frail as he was (he had officially retired from official positions), he still wielded vast influence. And his agenda was getting a forceful push from the ascendancy of another man — Zhu.

Like Deng, Zhu had been a skeptic of overzealous Maoism.[22] A 1951 graduate of Beijing's prestigious Tsinghua University, Zhu joined the State Planning Commission where he questioned the realism of production targets set during the Great Leap Forward — perspicacity for which he was expelled from the Communist Party. Although he managed a return to the planning body, he was the victim of another purge during the Cultural Revolution, and like many officials deemed to lack sufficient revolutionary ardour, he spent several years working as a manual labourer at a rural "re-education centre."

Zhu's rehabilitation coincided with that of Deng, who saw in the younger man a kindred spirit oozing both technocratic proficiency and natural leadership skills. In 1987, Deng named Zhu to become mayor of Shanghai, which Deng envisioned as a laboratory for his approach. In Shanghai, Zhu earned the nickname "One Chop Zhu" because of his willingness to approve development projects and investments, including those by foreign companies, without the bureaucratic hassles that tended to foster corruption. Under his mayoralty, Shanghai took its first major strides toward becoming the national showpiece that it is today. That progress marked Zhu for elevation in 1991 to vice premier, with chief responsibility for national economic policy.

The economy's state of semi-reformation, Zhu recognized, was not sustainable. Most of the largest SOEs were bloated behemoths like the No. 1 Auto Plant, soaking up scarce resources to the tune of billions of dollars a year in subsidies. They depended on loans coming mainly from giant state-owned banks, which did not lend based on the expectation of being repaid with interest; rather, banker-bureaucrats shovelled money out at artificially low rates based on government plans or the influence exerted by well-connected individuals. The system was depriving worthy private borrowers of needed capital, and the lack of market discipline over banks made the economy prone to up-and-down swings as lenders turned the credit taps on and off in accord with orders from on high.[23] Revamping the system was bound to be complex

---

22 For information on Zhu and his policies prior to becoming premier, see Schell and Delury, *Wealth and Power* (see footnote 14 in this chapter), chapter 13; John Pomfret, 2016, *The Beautiful Country and the Middle Kingdom: America and China, 1776 to the Present*, New York, NY: Henry Holt and Co., chapter 44; and James McGregor, 2012, *No Ancient Wisdom, No Followers: The Challenges of Chinese Authoritarian Capitalism*, Westport, CT: Prospecta Press, chapter 1.

23 Blustein, "Can 'Half-Reformed' China Last?" (see footnote 16 in this chapter).

because workers at SOEs depended on their employers for social services. Still, Zhu pressed on, determined to instill efficiency and eliminate the economic drag caused by the state sector as much as possible.

The result was an ambitious initiative, with the slogan "Grasp the big, let go of the small," that materialized in the mid-1990s. Small SOEs were relinquished — sometimes sold to employees, sometimes simply allowed to go under on the assumption that the workers would be able to find jobs elsewhere in a growing economy. Big ones were "corporatized," meaning that private investors would become part owners while the government held a majority stake, and management would become responsible for turning profits. (The schools, hospitals, pension commitments and other such services often went to local governments.) In some cases, private money was invested via purchases on the stock exchanges that were established in Shenzhen and Shanghai, or even in overseas stock markets, where investment firms, such as Goldman Sachs (then led by Henry Paulson, the future Treasury Secretary), provided underwriting services (for hefty fees, of course). The first Chinese company to go public in an international offering was the beer company Tsingdao on the Hong Kong exchange in 1993; many more followed.

It is important to recognize that these large SOEs were not privatized. Socialism with Chinese characteristics meant that major swaths of the economy would remain firmly under the control of the party-state; private funds would help with modernization, but the shares in private hands would not exceed those held by the government. Still, for a population accustomed to the iron rice bowl, the disruptive impact was immense. About 26 million jobs at SOEs, nearly one-quarter of the total, disappeared between 1996 and 2000, according to official figures.[24] Hardest hit by layoffs were three northeastern provinces (including the locale of the No. 1 Auto Plant) that were China's equivalent of the US rust belt. To the extent those laid off were able to find work in the booming private sector, many presumably earned less, and had to manage with stingier benefits.

Yet even as China reformed its economy, it was paying continued penance for the 1989 Tiananmen Square massacre. The global trading system was undergoing another transformation — the GATT was in serious trouble, losing-credibility and increasingly viewed as ineffective — but this time, Beijing would be relegated to the sidelines.

---

24 Joseph Fewsmith, 2001, "The Political and Social Implications of China's Accession to the WTO," *China Quarterly*, September.

Imagine a court in which a person could be accused of a crime and be found guilty but then could, before being imprisoned, stand up and announce, "I am exercising my right to void the verdict," and walk off scot-free. The GATT's system for settling disputes sometimes worked like that.[25] Countries could, and did, bring grievances against trading partners to GATT tribunals, but an odd loophole allowed losers to evade punishment. A tribunal's ruling could be rendered void if just one GATT country — including the one found to be violating the rules — lodged a dissent. Indeed, an accused country could stop a case from even being heard because full consensus among GATT participants was required at every step of the proceedings, including the referral of a dispute to a tribunal. These rules often led to absurdly long delays, in which countries would refuse for months or even years to allow cases against them to move forward.

So the GATT was in many ways toothless, and that fact helped inflame protectionist sentiment in Washington, especially as angst was arising during the 1980s about the apparent decline in US competitiveness and the seeming invincibility of Japanese industry. Trade hawks argued that the United States had to take matters into its own hands because the GATT was incapable of remedying the problems in foreign markets that disadvantaged US corporations and workers. Washington already had a potent weapon, bitterly resented abroad, commonly known as "301" (based on the section of US trade law in which it was encoded). With 301, the USTR could effectively act as police force, prosecutor and judge against countries that engaged in "unjustifiable and unreasonable" treatment of US exports. Legislation passed by Congress in 1988 toughened requirements for the imposition of sanctions on such countries — a unilateral approach to handling disputes that struck at the heart of the principles on which the GATT had been created.

Salvation for the multilateral system came in 1994 with the completion of the Uruguay Round — the eighth series of talks held under GATT auspices and by far the most sweeping. As with the initial creation of the GATT, the United States was taking a leadership role and stood to reap enormous gains in sectors where US producers enjoyed major competitive advantages. In agriculture — where European subsidies grievously distorted international markets — new rules and disciplines curbed the dumping of farm surpluses. Intellectual property — patents and copyrights — gained new protection

---

25 This section about the GATT's weaknesses, the Uruguay Round and the creation of the WTO draws on my book *Misadventures of the Most Favored Nations*, chapter 2 (see footnote 9 in this chapter).

throughout much of the globe, a prize eagerly sought by the American entertainment industry as well as pharmaceutical and computer software companies.

At the top of the round's achievements was the creation of the WTO, whose dispute settlement system instilled trade rules with much greater enforceability. The immunity from prosecution available under the GATT could not be invoked by WTO members. In exchange for giving up the right to reject rulings that they considered erroneous, countries could appeal to a newly established, seven-member appellate body, whose decisions were final. To be sure, the WTO could not force its members, which are sovereign nations, to do anything. A member found to be in violation of WTO rules could refuse to change its offending laws or practices. But the cost of defiance could be economically painful, because victorious complainants had the right to impose retaliatory measures against violators. With such a strict system in place, the United States effectively committed to stop resorting to unilateralism (although 301 and other such provisions remained in federal law).

Attaining entry into this new institution became a major focus of China's leaders, none more so than Zhu, who in March 1998 rose to the premiership, a position second only to Jiang Zemin, the nation's president and general secretary of the Communist Party. With the aim of preparing the way for further reforms he knew would be necessary, Zhu oversaw a radical reorganization of the government bureaucracy that managed the economy. Importantly, ministries holding responsibility for entire industries were subordinated to a new economic supervisory agency, the State Economic and Trade Commission. This diminished at least some of the clout of officials who were most likely to resist the measures required for a WTO deal.[26]

But Chinese economic policies were still sufficiently Mao-infused that drastic alterations were necessary before Beijing's trading partners could contemplate its admission to the WTO. Moreover, China was no longer the economic weakling that had first sought to rejoin the GATT in 1986; by 1996, it boasted the world's seventh-largest GDP. Exports in 1998 reached $184 billion, 10 times the 1980 level, and they now consisted not only of cheap toys, shoes and clothing but also higher-value goods, such as stereos, computer components, steel and electrical machinery. Made-in-China products filled practically every household throughout the United States and other economically advanced countries.

---

26 Wang, "Why China Went for WTO" (see footnote 8 in this chapter).

Agreement for WTO entry was therefore possible only on "commercially mean-ingful terms," rather than on the basis of diplomatic or political considerations. This was the conceptual formulation often uttered by US negotiators — one in particular, who by her own account repeated it until she was blue in the face.

Growing up in Chicago, a daughter of Eastern European Jewish immigrants who prized scholarly pursuits, Charlene Barshefsky could not have imag-ined the series of events that vaulted her to the role of dealing with China's top leadership. As a student at the University of Wisconsin, she planned to seek a graduate degree in political theory, the sort of intellectual distinction her par-ents favoured. Instead, given the poor job market for Ph.D.s, she opted for law school and upon graduation in 1975 joined Steptoe & Johnson, a high-powered Washington law firm. Then her career took more unexpected twists.[27]

Trade law was not Barshefsky's chosen specialty, as became evident when, at a luncheon for new Steptoe associates, the firm's head partner asked her whether she might be interested in working on a dumping case. Unaware that "dumping" meant the unloading of foreign goods in the US market at unfairly low prices, Barshefsky assumed she was being enlisted to represent a corporation that had improperly disposed of toxic waste, so she demurred, saying she wouldn't want to oppose environmental interests.

With that humorous introduction to the field, Barshefsky commenced work in Steptoe's trade practice, which turned out to be well-suited to her talents — so much so that over the next 18 years she rose to become chair of the firm's international division. In 1993, the incoming Clinton administration, impressed by her reputation as a legal combatant, offered her the post of dep-uty US trade representative with responsibility for Asia and Latin America, a job that came with ambassadorial rank.

The decision was an agonizing one for Barshefsky, then the mother of two young daughters, aged nine and four, because she knew the job would entail constant, gruelling travel that would crimp her family life. Moreover, she had never set foot in Asia. But since such opportunities come along rarely in a lifetime, she accepted, and was soon spending enormous amounts of time jetting to Tokyo, Beijing and other regional capitals. Administration colleagues nicknamed her "Stonewall" for the unyielding manner in which she dealt with foreign interlocutors, tartly deliver-ing arguments — and threats — in complete and orderly paragraphs.

---

27 This section about Barshefsky draws on my account in *Misadventures of the Most Favored Nations* (see footnote 9 in this chapter), chapter 4.

On November 7, 1995, after nearly 26 hours of travel from Washington, Barshefsky checked into the China World Hotel, then one of the few five-star hotels in Beijing, and was given the key to suite 1407, the same one she had occupied on a previous visit.[28] She knew Chinese agents would be monitoring as many of her conversations as possible; the coincidence of her suite assignment was an extra tipoff. So when her staff gathered in her suite for a meeting, she chose her words carefully, to convey the proper combination of flexibility and resolve. "I want them to understand two things," she said. "First, we would like them in the WTO. But second, the price is not cheap."

Officials in China's Ministry of Foreign Trade and Economic Cooperation understood who they were up against. A couple of years earlier, Barshefsky had taken charge of an initiative aimed at defending American intellectual property — chiefly movies, music and computer software — against the illegal copying that was then rampant in China. Warning that the US government would punish this piracy by imposing stiff duties on billions of dollars in imported Chinese goods, she had extracted an accord in which Beijing promised a crackdown. Now she was back, partly to admonish her Chinese counterparts that they needed to enforce that deal more aggressively or again face the threat of economic sanctions. Avoiding such unilateral bullying, of course, was one of the main reasons for China's interest in becoming a WTO member.

On the last day of her visit, Barshefsky met with Wu Yi, China's 57-year-old trade minister, one of the highest-ranking women in Beijing and a formidable presence in her own right, with grey hair swept into a bun. (Wu's nickname was "the Iron Lady.") This gathering was not confrontational; the purpose was for Barshefsky to present a document she had brought, which she called a "road map," for how China might enter the WTO. The road map did not spell out in specific detail or numbers the market-opening measures, such as reductions in tariffs, that would be required. Rather, it set forth fundamental concerns Washington had about the workings of the Chinese economy and rules that Beijing would have to follow if it wanted to join the trade body. Wu did not commit to using the road map — "Your demands in the paper are still very, very high," she told Barshefsky — but she didn't dismiss it, and as the two women parted in the ministry's lobby, Wu smiled and gave Barshefsky a hug.

One of the overarching WTO rules China would have to accept as a member was national treatment, which, as previously noted, means giving foreign companies operating inside the country the same legal rights and protections

---

28 A detailed account is provided in Elsa Walsh, 1996, "The Negotiator," *The New Yorker*, March 18. Walsh accompanied Barshefsky on the trip.

as domestic ones. The Chinese trade regime was riddled with myriad forms of discrimination against foreigners.[29] A major example was the distribution system — that is, wholesaling, retailing, transporting goods to market and providing after-sales service, such as repairs. Chinese state-owned firms largely controlled these networks; foreign companies could not conduct such operations unless their business licences granted them special permission.

Similar restrictions applied to trading rights — that is, the rights of firms to import and export. During the Maoist era, only 12 enterprises, all effectively controlled by the trade ministry, were allowed to buy or sell goods across the border, and although the government had permitted many more to do so by the mid-1990s, its practice of doling out licences was another inhibition on foreign companies' ability to operate. In the agricultural sector, foreign crops and food were often subject to much tougher quality inspection than Chinese equivalents. Other problem areas included requirements for foreign investors to buy components locally and export their production.

Moreover, Beijing often required foreign firms to hand over technology, and build sophisticated facilities in China, as the price of entry to the Chinese market. Foreign makers of telecommunications equipment, for example, were obliged to construct computer chip fabrication plants in China, a proposition that entailed outlays in the hundreds of millions of dollars. The Chinese authorities could impose such demands because all of the companies — France's Alcatel, Germany's Siemens, America's AT&T, Sweden's Ericsson, Canada's Northern Telecom and Japan's NEC and Fujitsu — were salivating over the bonanzas to be reaped in a country that by the year 2000 planned to install three times as many phone lines as existed in Britain.[30]

Those issues and many others concerning the Chinese market — including, of course, the lowering of tariffs — were subject to countless negotiation sessions, mostly in Beijing and Washington, in the years following Barshefsky's November 1995 trip. Details concerning these talks in 1996, 1997 and 1998 need not be recounted in this book because significant progress materialized only in 1999. But it would be grossly misleading to suggest that the negotiations were confined to topics concerning the openness of China's market. The Clinton administration was also insistent that Beijing agree to measures that would give the US market extra layers of insulation from penetration by products made with cheap Chinese labour.

---

29 Lardy, *Integrating China into the Global Economy* (see footnote 7 in this chapter).

30 Blustein, "Cracking China's Market: Profits, or Peril?" (see footnote 21 in this chapter).

These "defensive" measures (as opposed to "offensive" ones aimed at expanding access to China's market) are called "trade remedies." They will come up often in later chapters, so a brief explanation is in order.

Perfectly legal under WTO rules, trade remedies involve the imposition of duties on imports to address three types of situations. Anti-dumping duties may be imposed on imports that are being sold at "less than fair value" (as Barshefsky learned after joining her law firm's trade practice). Countervailing duties may be imposed on imported goods whose sellers are receiving government subsidies that injure domestic industry. And safeguard duties may be imposed to provide temporary relief to an industry whose survival is menaced by a sudden flood of imports.

Many economists view trade remedies, and the US government's enforcement of them, as thinly disguised forms of protectionism that are antithetical to America's professed support of free trade. If inexpensive foreign products are widely available to American consumers, the argument goes, so much the better for the US economy's long-term prospects; the money people save will be spent on other things and resources will flow into the economy's efficient, high-value sectors. And if a foreign country wants to squander its own citizens' tax money to subsidize exports, there is little economic justification in preventing Americans from enjoying the benefits and low prices of such goods. Similar logic applies to the many other countries that have adopted variants of US trade remedy laws.

Although trade remedies are beloved in Congress for ostensibly establishing a "level playing field" on which domestic and foreign firms compete, critics deride the process as tilted heavily in favour of US producers, in particular politically powerful industries such as steel and lumber. A foreign firm can be found guilty of dumping, for example, if its prices in the US market fall below its costs of production — a sensible-sounding rule, but the method for determining costs is far stricter in dumping cases than it is in predatory-pricing cases involving domestic firms. And where foreign companies can really get hung out to dry is if they fail to provide the US Commerce Department with sufficiently responsive and timely answers to the department's questions about their operations. Then the department's analysts are obliged to make their calculations using information furnished by the domestic industry or other sources that are likely to result in higher duties. The results are sometimes nonsensical on their face; in a mid-1990s case alleging dumping of Italian pasta, for example, the DeCecco brand — well known as one of the most expensive on supermarket shelves — was found to be sold at "less than fair value" and slapped with duties of nearly 50 percent.[31]

Defenders of trade remedies — including sincere, thoughtful free traders — counter that the system needs "safety valves" lest it lose public support entirely. In this view, persuading governments to open markets will be politically impossible unless they have the tools to protect their industries and workers against import competition that ordinary people deem unfair. Restraints on trade remedies may be necessary to prevent protectionist abuses, but if governments are hamstrung in using the laws, the constituency for free trade will dwindle.

In China's case, the United States would demand the right to use even more stringent trade remedies and other defensive measures than it applied to other countries. Washington wanted a "general safeguard" allowing it to slap duties on all imported Chinese goods in the event of an economy-damaging surge in such goods. Another safeguard that US officials sought, called "China product-specific," would make it easier to use the safeguard mechanism against surges of certain Chinese imports. In the textile sector, Washington wanted to keep quotas in place limiting Chinese imports until 2010, five years longer than other countries had agreed.

Most importantly, American negotiators insisted on China accepting that it would keep the legal status of "non-market economy" for decades after entering the WTO. That would make Chinese imports vulnerable to very high duties in anti-dumping cases because, under the rules for products from non-market economies, the methods used to calculate the degree of dumping are much more disadvantageous than for goods from market economies.

Bridging differences over these issues was hardly easy. But it helped that one nettlesome topic had been removed from the trade negotiators' agendas.

The evening that Bill Clinton conducted the People's Liberation Army (PLA) band may go down in history as the high-water mark of Sino-American relations in recent decades. The occasion was a state dinner at the Great Hall of the People on June 27, 1998.[32] Festivities got off to a warm start as Clinton, hand-in-hand with First Lady Hillary Rodham Clinton, ascended a long, scarlet-carpeted staircase where Chinese President Jiang Zemin and his wife

31 Paul Blustein, 1996, "Italy Loses the Pasta Wars," *The Washington Post*, July 31.

32 Paul Blustein, 1998, "Little Stick Diplomacy," *The Washington Post*, June 29. I was one of the pool reporters covering this state dinner.

were waiting at the top to welcome them and strike chummy poses for photographers. With his stout build, thick-framed glasses and slicked-back hair, Jiang did not command the aura of a strongman — he was often mocked as a "weathervane" for following prevailing opinion among his Politburo colleagues — but he had consolidated his position as the nation's supreme leader and relished playing the role.

After exchanging friendly toasts in the cavernous banquet hall and dining on coconut-flavoured chicken soup with bean curd, shark's fin in soy sauce and grilled beefsteak, the leaders' buoyant mood seemed to intensify. Accompanied by their wives, Clinton and Jiang made their way to the back of the hall to meet the PLA band, which had been serenading diners with a variety of American and Chinese tunes. A commotion ensued as the leader of the band engaged in an animated discussion with Jiang, who was modestly declining an invitation to conduct, but Clinton egged him on, saying, "You can do it, Mr. President! Go for it!" And so Jiang did, waving the baton for a few bars of "Song for the Motherland" to the amusement of the cabinet ministers and other notables in attendance. Then Clinton gamely led the band in "Hands Across the Sea," a John Philip Sousa march, as people clapped to the beat.

This display of leader-to-leader bonhomie was emblematic of a remarkable turnaround by Clinton, who early in his presidency chilled relations with Beijing by making human rights the central focus of his China policy. A few months after taking office in 1993, he signed an executive order linking China's MFN status to "overall significant progress" on human rights issues, such as the free emigration of dissidents and release of political prisoners. This was a dire threat; withdrawing MFN status would have severed nearly all Sino-US trade by raising the average tariff on Chinese goods to 37 percent — on some items, as high as 70 percent.[33] But that approach didn't last long. Chinese leaders manifested utter contempt for US economic pressure, jailing activist Wei Jingsheng shortly before a 1994 visit by Secretary of State Warren Christopher and bluntly telling Christopher that the issue was "none of your business."[34]

As a result, Clinton abandoned his hard line in favour of "constructive engagement," which meant pursuing trade with China for mutual economic gain without preconditions regarding human rights. The president came around

33 Douglas Irwin, 2017, *Clashing Over Commerce: A History of US Trade Policy*, Chicago: University of Chicago Press, chapter 13.

34 For an excellent overview of the Clinton administration's changing views on the human rights issue, see Pomfret, *The Beautiful Country and the Middle Kingdom* (see footnote 22 in this chapter), chapter 42.

to the view that economic progress offered the best hope for effecting political change in such a powerful and proud country, especially given the deep
grievances the Chinese harboured over the subjugation the nation had suffered at foreign hands. The more Chinese joined the middle class, the more
they would presumably agitate for political freedom and other privileges of
democratic societies.

The administration did not drop discussion with China about human rights —
on the contrary, the president himself raised the subject in an extraordinarily
direct way during his June 1998 visit. A joint news conference with Jiang, which
was televised live and uncensored to Chinese viewers, turned into a dramatic
debate over Tiananmen Square, oppression of Tibet and other delicate issues.
"I believe, and the American people believe, that the use of force and the tragic
loss of life [at Tiananmen Square] was wrong," Clinton said. "I believe, and the
American people believe, that freedom of speech, association and religion are,
as recognized by the UN Charter, the right of people everywhere and should
be protected by their governments." To this, Jiang retorted: "With regard to
the political disturbances in 1989, had the Chinese government not taken the
resolute measures, then we could not have enjoyed the stability that we are
enjoying today."[35]

Still, US-China trade was to be encouraged, as far as the White House was
concerned, rather than used to reward or punish China's human rights record.
Cynics could charge — and many did — that Clinton was embracing the US
business community's position in a bid to curry favour and garner corporate
donations for Democratic candidates. China was by far the fastest-growing
destination for investment by American multinationals, so CEOs had an obvious interest in preserving the access of their Chinese subsidiaries to the US
market. But the administration had been chastened by the failure of its initial
efforts to push China around, and the engagement policy enjoyed support from
many independent scholars and experts.

Moreover, engagement with China followed logically from the zeitgeist of the
era, which held that the world was on an inexorable march toward a future
modelled on American-style free markets and democracy. Recent historical
events — the collapse of the Soviet bloc and the democratization of previously
authoritarian states, such as South Korea and Taiwan — reinforced this world
view, as did the inception of the internet and US companies' domination of it.
Within China itself, people enjoyed far greater personal liberty in the late 1990s

---

35 John M. Broder, 1998, "Clinton in China: Clinton and Jiang Debate Views Live on TV, Clashing on
   Rights," *The New York Times*, June 28.

than in prior decades, even if outright defiance of the Communist leadership was prohibited.

The amicability of the Clinton-Jiang summit would prove fleeting, however. By early the next year, China's critics in Congress were up in arms over allegations of Chinese espionage at US nuclear laboratories. The White House was already on the defensive over a scandal involving illegal campaign contributions from foreigners with ties to Beijing, and although the evidence in the spying case was flimsy (it later fell apart), Republicans milked it for all it was worth in a bid to portray Clinton as cravenly cozying up to a malevolent regime. Powerful Democratic politicians, too, were stepping up denunciations over China's persecution of dissidents and vowing to oppose legislation that would grant Beijing "permanent normal trading relations" (PNTR), the term the White House had started to use instead of MFN, since the latter misleadingly connoted especially favourable treatment for Beijing. Prominent among these anti-PNTR Democrats were the party's two top leaders in the House, Richard Gephardt of Missouri and David Bonior of Michigan, long-time allies of organized labour.

For the man spearheading China's drive for WTO membership, this deterioration of the atmosphere in Washington was unpropitiously timed.

The woodenness typical of Chinese leaders' public personas did not afflict Zhu Rongji. On March 15, 1999, two months after his meeting with Greenspan in the Hall of Purple Light, the premier held a press conference at which his capacity for brusque, self-deprecating humour was on full display. Responding to the recent rise in hostility toward China in the United States, Zhu cited a critical article in an American business magazine and joked, "I myself was also victimized by this anti-China trend. My picture on the cover of [that] magazine looks like a dead man."[36]

The premier was soon to embark on his visit to the United States, scheduled for April 6–14, for which his chief aim was clear — sealing a WTO pact. "Black hair has turned grey" during the 13 years since China had first applied to join the GATT, Zhu lamented. "It's high time to conclude the negotiations." To do so, he added, "China is prepared to make the biggest concessions within its abilities."

Enthusiasm for his venture among the Chinese leadership was anything but unanimous. Entrenched interests who stood to lose from market liberalization

---

36 A state television account of the press conference is available at www.cctv.com/lm/980/718/82299.html.

were battling Zhu and his pro-reform allies at every turn. Although secrecy shrouds the deliberations that transpire behind the walls of Zhongnanhai, an account titled *Zhu Rongji in 1999*, authored by a confidant of the premier, provides remarkable insight into the internal wrangling, including extensive quotations from meetings of the Politburo and other official bodies.[37] Notable among the supporters of the old planned economy was Zhu's predecessor as premier, Li Peng, a hardliner widely vilified for his role in the Tiananmen massacre, who still exerted influence as a high-ranking Communist Party official. "We must stand on principle and ensure the development of [our] state-owned enterprises and national industries," Li argued at one Politburo meeting. "The United States bullies the fainthearted but fears the stouthearted. If they insist on putting pressure on us, we can wait another 13 years."

But resolute in his conviction that reform should proceed faster rather than slower, and that a WTO deal would help, Zhu forged onward, with the cautious Jiang offering sufficient backing. The news media was abuzz in March with accounts of unprecedented Chinese flexibility on a host of issues. Tariffs on more than 1,000 items would be lowered, including those on autos, electronics and agricultural products; sectors previously walled off to foreign firms — banking, insurance, telecommunications — would be opened to at least some extent; restrictions on distribution and import-export business would be eased. Although details were still secret, "China's proposals represent an about-face from just a few months ago, when talks were stalemated and China seemed years away from joining the WTO," *The Wall Street Journal* reported on March 25.[38]

All eyes were on Barshefsky, who was now the US trade representative, having been promoted to that cabinet-level post three years earlier. She and her top aides were alternately flying to Beijing and meeting their Chinese counterparts in Washington. US business associations whose officials had been briefed on some of the terms under discussion were extolling the prospective benefits of China's WTO membership. Large multinationals, such as Caterpillar

---

37 Zong Hairen, 2002, "Zhu Rongji in 1999," *Chinese Law and Government* 35 (1), translation by M.E. Sharpe Inc. from the Chinese text. Zong Hairen was a pseudonym for a staff member (or perhaps several staff members) close to Zhu, and China scholars in the West view Zong's account as authoritative despite the lack of certainty regarding Zong's identity. In a guest editor's introduction to the English translation of the book, Andrew Nathan of Columbia University explains that "Zong…is a person or persons with high-level access in Zhongnanhai, who belongs to the reformist wing of the Party, and who has chosen the unconventional but not unprecedented method of publishing information outside mainland China as a means of trying to influence the distribution of power and the direction of policy within the [Party]." Nathan also writes that he is unable to share further information about Zong's identity "for the security of the people involved."

38 Ian Johnson and Leslie Chang, 1999, "China Offers an Array of Reforms," *The Wall Street Journal*, March 25.

and General Motors, were proclaiming themselves pleased with what they had heard they would get.

A week before Zhu's visit, Barshefsky made one last trip to Beijing to see him, spending a total of five hours on March 30 with the premier and separate meetings with Wu Yi, who was now in a more exalted position herself as a member of the State Council. According to an internal administration memo about the meetings that day, "the general [Chinese] line was, 'You said you wanted a commercial deal, not a political deal. If that's true, let's close out the market access package.'"[39] But Barshefsky had to admit that for all the American avowals to evaluate the accord strictly on economic merits, politics was intruding heavily into White House calculations over whether to reach a pact during Zhu's visit. Indeed, according to Barshefsky, one of the reasons for her trip was to make sure the premier understood the possibility of a failure in April, so as to preserve chances for an agreement later.

Upon leaving the meetings, she stopped outside the car she was taking to the airport for a confidential chat with Robert Cassidy, the assistant US trade representative for China affairs, since sensitive conversations were not supposed to take place inside vehicles, which might be bugged. Both she and Cassidy were delighted on the whole with the progress they had made; they were certain that the business community would deem the package enormously attractive once a few more gaps were closed.

"Bob, I want you to know I'm doing everything I can do to make sure there's support inside the administration to sign this deal," Barshefsky said, according to Cassidy, who reacted with astonishment over the idea that anyone in the administration would oppose it. "I said, 'Do you know what we have here? All hell will break loose in the private sector if this isn't signed,'" he recalled.[40]

The pros and cons of the deal as it then stood were thrashed out on April 2 at a White House meeting among Clinton's top international economic policy makers, who were deeply split. Secretary of State Madeleine Albright, National Security Adviser Sandy Berger and other members of the foreign policy team were eager, for the sake of improving Sino-US ties, to see an agreement emerge from the Clinton-Zhu summit. So was Barshefsky, provided that some last Chinese concessions were forthcoming. In their view, rejecting an economically

---

39 "Read-out from Beijing," March 30, 1999, on file at the Clinton Presidential Library in Little Rock, Arkansas, File 2014-1039-F, Box 2.

40 Cassidy later expressed deep regret over the failings of China's accession agreement, especially the inability to curb Beijing's currency manipulation. See Economic Policy Institute, 2009, "Remarks by Robert B. Cassidy," January 27, www.epi.org/publication/20090127_cassidy/.

meritorious accord would inflict a serious blow on Zhu and the reform movement that he represented. Their worry was that if he returned home without having attained his chief goal, the anti-reform forces might gain the upper hand in Beijing, possibly leading to a change of heart about China's readiness to open up.

But a more politically attuned group in the US administration argued against finalizing a pact at that point, for fear of arousing fresh accusations that Clinton was going soft on Beijing — which in turn might doom the legislation needed for China to get PNTR status. This faction included White House Chief of Staff John Podesta, National Economic Council Director Gene Sperling and Commerce Secretary William Daley — and it had the support of administration heavyweight Robert Rubin, the Treasury secretary. As for Clinton, he needed no convincing that China ought to join the WTO, but in the colourful words of one of his top advisers, he had been "Lewinsky-ized" — that is, weakened by the scandal over his affair with White House intern Monica Lewinsky. During his impeachment ordeal, Democratic members of the House and Senate had stood loyally by him, and having just won acquittal in mid-February, the president was loath to push those members of his own party to take a politically damaging vote on China.

In economic terms, numerous "wins" were on offer, according to an internal administration memo summarizing the April 2 meeting.[41] The US high-tech industry "will be enthusiastic" about the tariff reductions and changes in control over distribution China was willing to make; "many export-oriented manufacturing sectors, including much of chemicals and wood and paper, will be strong supporters of significant tariff cuts, trading rights, distribution rights and quota phaseouts"; and the deal China was proposing to open its agriculture market "will garner strong support" in the farm belt although "there might be isolated complaints from rice, others," the memo said.

Not all industries were so positive, the memo noted. Hollywood was dissatisfied with the number of US movies China would allow in its theatres; foreign companies would not be permitted to hold majority stakes in telecommunications firms serving the Chinese market; and the cut in auto tariffs that China was offering, from 100 percent to 35 percent, was sufficient for General Motors and Ford but not enough to overcome opposition from Chrysler and the United Auto Workers union. Moreover, China was balking at a number of US demands on defensive issues — that is, protections for the US market, in

---

41 "POTUS meeting with international economic advisers," April 2, 1999, on file at the Clinton Presidential Library, file 2014-1039-F, box 2.

particular the extension of quotas limiting Chinese textile imports for five years longer than other countries' imports.

The group debated several options, according to the memo. One was "Go for a deal: negotiate hard and be prepared to accept China's bottom line." That would be the "best option for China relationship, Zhu stature, [and] preserving existing market access concessions," but it "would encounter intense opposition from organized labor and congressional members," as well as "allegations we accepted a weak deal" for the sake of capping Zhu's visit with a success.

Another option, labelled "Keep talking," was the preferred approach of the politically minded faction including Podesta and Sperling. It meant the administration would "announce we are close to a deal but there can be no deal until all elements are completed" and "provide assurances we want China in by the end of the year." This option "risks undermining Zhu" and "losing some market accession concessions," the memo said. On the other hand, it would be the "best demonstration we are holding out for a tough deal" and "offers best optics for [an] ultimate congressional vote."

Clinton reserved judgment pending Zhu's arrival, and in the ensuing days he emitted so many positive signals that some of his advisers felt certain he would "go for a deal." But as the memo shows, the "keep talking" option was well-formulated in advance and, in retrospect, it appears clear that the president was strongly inclined to adopt it.

China's chief negotiator, Long Yongtu, arrived in Washington a couple of days ahead of the premier and immediately plunged into talks with his US counterparts that generated encouraging results. A flurry of Chinese concessions were announced on April 7 in aviation, insurance and software piracy.[42] The two sides were still at loggerheads over several key issues, with textiles and apparel the most intractable. Anxious to show that he would protect the interests of the Carolinas and other textile-producing states, Clinton was holding out for the right to limit imports of Chinese clothing over a prolonged period, all the way to 2010. To Zhu, surrendering on this point would negate one of his most compelling justifications for WTO membership — obtaining global market access for China's apparel makers sooner rather than later.

Still, on the morning of April 7, as Zhu was flying from Los Angeles (his first stop) to Washington, Clinton gave a speech stating: "The bottom line is,

---

42 Chad Bowman and Gary G. Yerkey, 1999, "Chinese negotiators push for a deal as Premier Zhu lands on U.S. soil," *BNA International Trade Reporter*, April 7; Helene Cooper, Bob Davis and Anna Wilde Mathews, 1999, "U.S Claims Broad Progress in Trade Talks With China," *The Wall Street Journal*, April 8.

if China is willing to play by the global rules of trade, it would be an inexplicable mistake for the United States to say no."[43] Business groups drafted press releases and fact sheets for issuance as soon as an accord was announced. The ground was being laid for a mutually acceptable compromise — or so it appeared; operating on that assumption, USTR staffers were spending long hours poring over fine print.

That evening, Clinton welcomed Zhu to the White House for what was billed as a social call and brought him to the Yellow Oval Room, an elegant chamber in the presidential residence used for small receptions. After showing Zhu the view from the balcony, the president sat down with the premier and broached the subject of the WTO, stating first of all that he and his team were united in support of China's entry. But then he delivered the "no" that he had described hours earlier as an "inexplicable mistake."[44]

Citing his political and legislative advisers, Clinton said they believed closing a deal right away would look hurried and staged for the media, which might mean Congress would reject the necessary legislation. On the other hand, his foreign policy team feared that failure to forge a pact during Zhu's trip would enfeeble him back home. So Clinton said he would leave it up to Zhu — if the foreign policy camp's worries were correct, the president would call Barshefsky immediately and instruct her to negotiate the remaining differences between the two sides; hopefully a settlement could be reached while Zhu was still in town.

Zhu had no difficulty recognizing Clinton's gist — the president wasn't ready at that point to close a deal that would be acceptable to China — so he replied that he was willing to wait for a more opportune time. But he would soon be accusing the president of lacking courage. His own political flanks were now dangerously exposed, and although he didn't know it that evening, his imperilment was about to deepen.

It was only natural that Barshefsky's staff would prepare a document summarizing the terms on which Chinese and American negotiators had tentatively agreed. If Clinton and Zhu reached an accord, after all, the list of provisions, which had previously been kept confidential, would have to be publicly

43 William Clinton, 1999, "Troublesome Times; Staying the Course," speech at the United States Institute of Peace, Washington, DC, April 7.

44 A number of versions of the meeting in the Yellow Oval have been published; this account, which differs only in some minor detail, is based on my interviews with participants and people who were briefed on the details immediately afterward.

disclosed. With the aim of trumpeting the economic boons in store for nearly every American industrial and agricultural sector, therefore, the USTR compiled 17 pages of information about the Chinese commitments that had been hammered out over the previous days and weeks.

But the two leaders had stopped short of a final handshake; technically China had committed to nothing. Shock and fury was thus the reaction among Chinese officials when, on the afternoon of April 8 — the day after the Yellow Oval meeting — the White House press office released the document on the internet for all the world, including Chinese netizens, to see.

Administration officials depicted the release as a sort of accident — a premature disclosure that had been made without approval by anyone in a position of authority. It was nothing of the kind. Having spoken with many of the participants, I can report that it was a tactical decision, at Barshefsky's instigation, based on the concern that China would start retracting some of its concessions. If the document were public, she reasoned, affected American interest groups would see what they were supposed to get, which would make it difficult for the Chinese to roll those provisions back. The move risked enraging Beijing so much that it might backfire, so Barshefsky cleared it with top White House colleagues. But she believed it to be a calculated risk, well worth taking.

Some on the US side were dismayed, seeing the likely downside as far outweighing any benefits. "Zhu was deeply skeptical about his trip — he saw it as potentially a lose-lose proposition," recalls Kenneth Lieberthal, who was senior director for Asian affairs on the National Security Council and wasn't involved in discussions about the document release. "Either he would be accused of failing to get a deal, or he would be accused of having given away the store — he had made a lot of concessions. Turned out it was even worse. Since someone published the draft on the White House website, he was accused of both failing and giving away the store."

Key items in the "store giveaway," as specified in the 17-page document, included the following[45]:

- Tariffs on industrial goods would be reduced from an average 24.6 percent to 9.44 percent, with most of the cuts implemented by 2003. For some items of particular interest to US industry, tariffs would be even lower — the duty on soda ash, for example, would be 5.5 percent. In

---

45 USTR, 1999, "White House Documents Summarizing China's WTO Commitments," Press Release 99-34, April 8.

the auto sector, China would cut its existing tariffs on vehicles from 80–100 percent to 25 percent, and for auto parts, the tariff would be an average 10 percent.

- In agriculture, tariffs would drop to levels below those of most US trading partners, to an average 17 percent, by 2004. Of special benefit to American farmers and ranchers were a three percent tariff on soybeans, which would take effect immediately upon accession to the WTO, and a phased-in cut in beef tariffs from 45 percent to 12 percent.

- Restrictions on foreign companies' distribution and trading rights would be eliminated over three years.

- China's telecommunications services sector, from which foreign involvement had long been restricted, would be opened up, with foreign firms allowed to invest up to the 49 percent level in most services and a majority stake in a few.

- A minimum of 40 foreign films would be allowed for theatrical release in China immediately upon accession, and five additional films would be allowed in each of the following two years.

- Requirements that foreign investors use local inputs for their manufacturing would be eliminated. As for technology transfer, it would no longer be required of foreign investors except insofar as the requirements were consistent with WTO agreements.

- Foreign banks and insurance companies would be permitted to operate much more freely in China than before.

- The United States could continue to deem China a "non-market economy" for purposes of calculating duties in anti-dumping cases, although the duration of this status was still under negotiation.

- To protect its industries against surges of imports of certain Chinese products, the United States could use special rules to levy safeguard duties that would be easier to apply than for imports from other countries.

Chinese ire over the lack of agreement and the document's publication was manifest in Zhu's public comments over the next two days. The premier vented his frustration that Clinton "did not dare" complete the deal, and he warned an American audience, "If you want too much too soon…you may end up with nothing." He also indicated that Beijing might well backpedal from some of the items on the list of supposed commitments. "Yesterday the American side made public all the relevant documents and papers and said that the Chinese had agreed to all of these," he said in a speech on April 9. "But we had not agreed to all of these."[46]

His underlings soon made it clear how high Chinese dudgeon was, in meetings between the two parties that lasted an entire night on the eve of Zhu's April 10 departure from Washington.

The Clinton administration was still hoping to salvage one major "deliverable" from the summit — a pact on agricultural inspections that would dismantle Chinese barriers on the importation of American wheat, citrus fruit and meat. The terms had been negotiated, and agreed, on a trip to Beijing by Peter Scher, Barshefsky's deputy for agricultural issues — Congress was insisting on it as a precondition for China's WTO entry — and the White House had looked forward to trumpeting it at a signing ceremony on Friday, April 9. Instead, to the alarm of US officials, their Chinese counterparts were threatening to scuttle the accord.[47] Cancelling their Friday evening plans, Barshefsky, Lieberthal and several other US policy makers rushed to Blair House, the presidential guest quarters, in an effort to persuade Trade Minister Shi Guangsheng and his colleagues to relent. Surely, they argued, it wouldn't be in anyone's interest for the summit to end with a serious breach. But the release of the 17-page document had soured Chinese attitudes. "You don't do this to people," Long Yongtu seethed at Scher.

Talks dragged on well past midnight — also at issue was a memorandum of understanding about the provisions of the 17-page document — and at around 3:00 a.m. the parties trooped to the Willard Hotel where Wu Yi was staying to see whether she could break the impasse. Rousted from her bed, the Iron Lady's first words to the US officials concerned how upset she was about the document release; a sincere apology from Lieberthal appeared to mollify her. After some more time negotiating in Wu's suite, the Chinese grudgingly came around on the agriculture agreement, much to the Americans' relief, and at 7:00 a.m., signatures were finally affixed. Shortly thereafter, a joint statement was released on the status of the WTO talks, with wording to placate the Chinese side. It hailed the "significant consensus" that had been achieved "on a broad range" of issues and added: "The United States strongly supports

46 Chad Bowman and Mark Felsenthal, 1999, "USTR defends rejection of China WTO offer, denies politics, protectionism drove decision," *BNA International Trade Reporter*, April 14.

47 The episode is recounted in Paul Blustein, 1999, "Clinton Scrambles to Appease Diverse Critics on China," *The Washington Post*, April 15.

the accession of the People's Republic of China to the WTO in 1999," a goal toward which Clinton and Zhu were instructing their trade ministers to continue negotiating.

Predictably, the US business community liked what it saw in the 17-page document and was appalled that such a juicy deal had been foregone. Gathered on April 12 for a briefing in the Old Executive Office Building next to the White House, executives from Washington-based business associations — who knew perfectly well about the divisions in administration ranks — gave a standing ovation to Barshefsky, while greeting Sperling with a stony silence. When Sperling urged the attendees to wait patiently for a bulletproof deal, insisting, "We're all in agreement here," a chorus of invective erupted. "No, we're not!" shouted Robert Kapp, president of the US-China Business Council.[48]

Clinton, meanwhile, was stricken with second thoughts, having been showered with criticism that he had shrunk from a sensible agreement for political reasons. On April 13, he called Zhu, who was then visiting New York before heading to Canada. The president offered to dispatch Barshefsky promptly, anywhere in North America that Zhu chose, to resume negotiations. But Zhu declined, saying that the United States was welcome to send its representatives to Beijing after his return.

Hoping to pick up the pieces, Cassidy flew to Beijing on April 21, and met with Long. "He yelled and screamed at me," Cassidy recalled adding that regarding the 17-page document, "He said, 'No way we're going to live up to this! It's not even accurate!'"

The two were at least able to draft a plan for how negotiations should proceed. Upon returning to Washington, Cassidy told Barshefsky that for face-saving reasons, the United States would have to give way on a few issues in the 17-page document, to which Barshefsky replied that he should make sure nothing important was sacrificed. A memo proposing this strategy went to the White House, and on May 7, it was approved.

That very day, however, the plan would go up, quite literally, in smoke — and blood.

---

48 Paul Blustein, 1999, "U.S. Tries to Placate China on WTO Talks," *The Washington Post*, April 13; David E. Sanger, 1999, "How Push by China and U.S. Business Won Over Clinton," *The New York Times*, April 15.

CHAPTER 3

MAXIMUM CONCESSIONS

Ever since the Gulf War of 1991, when video showed "smart bombs" devastating Iraqi targets with pinpoint accuracy, American military technology has awed the world. The same lethal efficiency might therefore have been expected of the mission launched on May 7, 1999, when a B1-B bomber took off from Whiteman Air Force Base in Missouri armed with five GPS-guided precision bombs on a mission to a target more than 8,000 km away. The aircraft, which was participating in a North Atlantic Treaty Organization (NATO) campaign against Serbian forces in the war over independence for Kosovo, was supposed to destroy a warehouse used for military purposes in Belgrade, the Serbian capital. Instead the bombs slammed into the Chinese embassy in that city, killing three employees and injuring two dozen more.[1]

Word of the bombing, which came on Friday evening in Washington, plunged White House officials into frantic efforts to find out what had happened and minimize the damage to Sino-American relations. Together with others in the administration, Ken Lieberthal, the Asia senior director at the National Security Council, soon discovered that the fault lay with the CIA, where someone had used a flawed methodology to identify the location of the warehouse,

---

1 See https://en.wikipedia.org/wiki/United_States_bombing_of_the_Chinese_embassy_in_Belgrade.

and failed to realize that the embassy actually stood on that spot — incorrect information that had been programmed into the bombs' guidance systems. It was therefore crucial to convey to the Chinese leadership that the bombing was a tragic accident, nothing more; American bombs hit what they are aimed at, but in this case, they had been mistakenly aimed at the wrong building.

Lieberthal drafted a personal president-to-president letter from Clinton to Jiang, which after intensive wordsmithing over 30-plus hours within the White House, was approved and ready early Sunday morning for hand-delivery to the Chinese embassy in Washington. "I was so exhausted by then, I was afraid to drive," Lieberthal recalled. "My wife drove me to the White House, I picked up the letter, and we started to go up 17th Street to go to the Chinese embassy, but I yelled at her to pull over — I just threw up on the curb. She drove me home, and I basically collapsed. So we had my wife going to the embassy and telling the people there, 'This is a genuine letter from the President of the United States.'"

Lieberthal's physical exertions notwithstanding, the US explanation did not satisfy China's leaders, who decided that the bombing must have been delib-erate, aimed at testing their resolve and perhaps destabilizing the country by making them appear weak. The fact that the bomber took off from US soil, instead of a NATO base in Europe, bolstered the theory of an American plot to maintain global hegemony. However erroneous the Chinese leaders' conclusion might have been, they weren't about to back down. Throngs of anti-American demonstrators surrounded US diplomatic facilities in Beijing, Shanghai, Guangzhou, Chengdu and Shenyang, hurling rocks and setting fire to the residence of the US consul in Chengdu. The US ambassador, James Sasser, was essentially trapped in the Beijing embassy. Only after several days had passed did Chinese authorities allow Clinton's apology to be broadcast and issue orders for police to restrain the demonstrations.

Now it was China's turn to treat a deal on WTO entry as politically impossible to consummate in the near future. Prospects for an agreement had suffered an incalculable blow.

To the vast majority of trade specialists around the world, the desirability of a WTO accord for China was almost an unassailable proposition. The central argument of the Clinton administration — that the rigours of membership in the trade body would open China both economically and politically, to the benefit of the United States and its allies — was widely shared in academic and policy circles. Although labour and environmental activists were vehemently opposed, on the grounds that the Chinese government suppressed collective bargaining and allowed industry to pollute the air and water with impunity, those problems were common throughout the developing world. Trade experts had a seemingly persuasive answer to the activists' objections: China's treatment of its workers and its sensitivity to environmental degradation would improve as the wealth of its citizens increased, so fostering good trade relations with Beijing offered the greatest hope for bettering the country's labour and environmental standards.

It would be wrong to conclude, however, that mainstream intellectual opinion was unanimous on this score. Even among experts favourably disposed toward free trade in general, some voiced qualms about China's WTO entry that are worth recalling at length because they look remarkably farsighted in retrospect. Many of the concerns these economists and scholars expressed hinged on unique features of the Chinese economy and legal system that are often cited in current debates about the nation's trade policies.[2]

Among the earliest was a paper published in November 1997 by University of California, Los Angeles law professor Richard Steinberg, who wrote:

> China is fundamentally different from other WTO members, partly because of its size…but also because of its particular political-economic structure: a continuing large role for state enterprises; a lack of transparency of some domestic rules and rule-making processes; a lack of meaningful competition policy rules; a judicial system which, on commercial matters, is in the early stages of development and is not always perceived as independent of politics…These are differences that are not accounted for by WTO rules. And if the political friction associated with these differences can not be addressed in another manner — through WTO constitutional procedures or China's Protocol of Accession — then China's accession is likely to weaken the WTO institutionally.[3]

---

2   Robert Lighthizer, who later became USTR in the Trump administration, is often credited for warning about the economic pitfalls of China's WTO accession. But a careful reading of his commentary prior to accession shows that his opposition was based mainly on human rights and national security grounds. See, for example, Robert E. Lighthizer, 1999, "A Deal We'd Be Likely to Regret," *The New York Times*, April 18. In one much-cited op-ed he wrote mentioning the dangers to American workers, the full passage reads as follows: "If China is allowed to join the W.T.O. on the lenient terms that it has long been demanding, virtually no manufacturing job in this country will be safe." (Robert E. Lighthizer, 1997, "What Did Asian Donors Want?" *The New York Times*, February 25.) However, China didn't join on those terms; the Clinton administration insisted on much greater stringency.

3   Richard Steinberg, 1997, "Institutional Implications of WTO Accession for China," Berkeley Roundtable on the International Economy Working Paper 110, November.

Also striking for its sagacity was this analysis by Canadian economist Sylvia Ostry: "The multi-layered complexity of the evolving Chinese legal system — including several administrative laws — make it impossible to conform to WTO transparency. Chinese laws at present lack specified procedures to constrain bureaucratic discretion and include no mandatory right of comment. Finally, the requirement for judicial review…faces the basic problem that there is no separation of powers in the constitution and therefore no concept of an independent judiciary. Indeed the Chinese Communist Party has the final say on judicial appointments."[4]

Perhaps the most clairvoyant of all was Robert Herzstein, a former US undersecretary of commerce for international trade:

> The WTO calls on its member countries to recognize a bright line between business and government. Businesses respond to market forces and engage in transactions on the basis of commercial considerations; governments make rules for businesses to protect the public interest, but normally are not authorized to interfere in individual transactions.

> China's economy has been built on a different assumption, that commerce is a state responsibility…Key commercial decisions have been determined not by market forces but by government officials implementing a plan….

> Suppose you are an executive of an American company eager to enter the Chinese market. You have been successful in other foreign markets, so when you learn that China has promised to eliminate the tariff on your product you aggressively look for customers and distributors there. You find that, despite the zero tariff, you can't make headway in competition with established Chinese producers,[5] for one or more of these reasons:

> • Some of your prospective customers are state enterprises, run by managers attuned to goals other than company profits and shareholder value. They deal with your Chinese competitors because this helps achieve planning goals, or because of custom, reciprocal business arrangements, personal friendships or other relationships.

---

4   Sylvia Ostry, 1999, "WTO Membership for China: To Be and Not to Be: Is that the Answer?" www.csls.ca/events/slt01/ostry.pdf.

5   Many other countries, of course, have non-tariff barriers — Japan, with its tight networks among major companies, is a classic example — but Herzstein's point was that the problem would likely prove particularly acute in China's case.

- Other prospective customers, though owned by private entrepreneurs, are responding to suggestions or mandates they have received from government officials at the local or provincial level, or in ministries with little interest in China's WTO obligations. These officials may have personal or political reasons for steering business to your competitors.

- Your Chinese competitor is enjoying a hidden subsidy from a government entity, in the form of cheap raw materials, transportation, electricity or other resources, which gives it an unfair advantage....

Until businesspeople on the ground feel confident that they can sell goods and services on their competitive merits, free of politics, cronyism and other noncommercial influences, the benefits of China's [WTO] membership will be asymmetrical, giving it opportunities in cleaner markets than it offers its trading partners.[6]

Warnings about the implications of China's WTO accession were not confined to Westerners fearful about the consequences for the trade body. The aforementioned expression "the wolf is at the door" reflected anxiety among many prominent Chinese about the impact on their country's economy. But in the case of China's apprehensions, the forecasts look, in hindsight, to have been highly overblown if not absurdly misplaced.

According to a 2001 survey of elite Chinese opinion by sinologist Joseph Fewsmith, "Many worry that China's industries will be exposed to crippling competition, that farmers will be hurt by the import of cheap (and better quality) foreign wheat and corn, and that China as a nation will become entangled in a global capitalist network that will erode the country's sovereignty and, in the worst case scenario, reduce China to an 'appendage' of the West, particularly the United States."[7]

Among the evidence cited by Fewsmith was a book titled *Pengzhuang* ("Collision"), the cover of which consisted of a red circle with a line through it over the letters "WTO." Authored by economist Han Deqiang of Beijing Aeronautics and Space University, the book argued that "as soon as American agricultural products can push open the door to China's market, China's

---

6   Robert Herzstein, 1999, "Is China Ready for the WTO's Rigors?" *The Wall Street Journal,* November 16. Reprinted here with permission.

7   Joseph Fewsmith, 2001, "The Political and Social Implications of China's Accession to the WTO," *China Quarterly,* September.

farmers are likely to be unable to afford to buy oil, salt, soy and vinegar, and even more of the rural population will flow into the cities." Another Chinese scholar, Cui Zhiyuan, a leading figure in a movement critical of capitalism called the "New Left," argued that China's ability to develop a high-tech sector would be crippled by acceptance of the WTO's protection of intellectual property rights for US and other foreign technology companies. Even analysts who favoured liberalization were wary about the short-term costs; the Unirule Institute of Economics, a Beijing think tank, estimated that China's productivity and efficiency would increase in the long run but only after five million industrial jobs had been lost.[8]

Incredible as it now seems, some Western experts took the view that China was risking something akin to industrial suicide by joining the WTO. "China's large-scale industries will face immense difficulties on 'the global level playing field' which is about to arrive in China," predicted Peter Nolan, a professor of Chinese management at Cambridge University, in an essay written shortly before Beijing's WTO accession.[9] "None of China's leading enterprises has become a globally competitive giant corporation, with a global market, a global brand, and a global procurement system." After examining major industries in turn — aerospace, pharmaceuticals, electrical equipment, oil and petrochemicals — Nolan heaped scorn on China's prowess and concluded that "few Chinese enterprises are in a position to compete with the world's leading companies in each sector." He ended on an apocalyptic note, deriding assertions that China had no alternative but to gamble on the WTO: "These sentiments echo in eerie fashion the comments a decade earlier on the need for dramatic system change in Russia and Eastern Europe.... The Soviet economy collapsed...Human welfare deteriorated drastically, with a massive increase in death rates and rise in poverty."

Such pessimism about China may merit ridicule in light of subsequent events, but the purpose of citing it is to put in context the uncertainty that prevailed in Beijing about the costs and benefits of a WTO deal. Members of the coterie of policy makers working closely with Zhu Rongji recall feeling besieged and lonely in their belief about the gains China would reap from joining the trade body. No less an authority than Jiang, who once worked at the No. 1 Auto Plant, sometimes heard from his former colleagues that WTO entry would doom the Chinese auto industry; the president did not hesitate in conveying

---

8   Clay Chandler, 1999, "China Braces for Open Trade Bid," *The Washington Post*, September 11.

9   Peter Nolan, 2002, "China and the WTO: The Challenge for China's Large-scale Industry," in Heike Holbig and Robert Ash (eds.), *China's Accession to the World Trade Organization: National and International Perspectives*, London and New York: Routledge, chapter 3.

those messages to Zhu's team. Needless to say, the spines of Chinese negotiators stiffened as a result.

A barrage of insults and accusations of traitorous behaviour cascaded upon Zhu in the late spring and summer of 1999 as China's leadership mulled over how to proceed on the WTO issue. His enemies — primarily policy makers overseeing agriculture, telecommunications and SOEs — were on the offensive, attacking him for having betrayed the country by offering such generous concessions as the ones the Americans had revealed in the 17-page document. Among the most stinging barbs came from a Communist leader who likened the document to the "Twenty-one Demands" sent by Japan to China in 1915 in a bid to expand Tokyo's imperial domain; Zhu's acceptance was therefore tantamount to surrender of national honour.[10] Those who were eager for a WTO deal, notably chief negotiator Long Yongtu, fired back that the opponents were motivated by self-interest in wanting to protect bureaucratic fiefdoms that afforded opportunities for corrupt enrichment.[11] But ominously, Jiang appeared to be distancing himself from the premier, remarking that he thought the delegation sent to Washington might have exceeded the mandate bestowed by the Politburo.[12] Zhu himself dropped out of public view; rumours periodically surfaced, causing sell-offs in the Hong Kong stock market, that he had offered to resign over the failure of his April visit to Washington.

Weakening Zhu's position further was the embassy bombing, since he was perceived as overly close to the United States. Negotiations with Washington about the WTO were out of the question until a decent interval had passed and the White House showed adequate contrition, which included the dispatching of envoys to Beijing, sending of more letters and delivery of a $4.5 million "voluntary humanitarian payment" to the families of those killed and injured. In response to US requests for a resumption of WTO talks, grudging Chinese assent came only in late August, followed by a serendipitous opportunity for Clinton and Jiang to meet face-to-face on September 11 at a summit both were attending in Auckland, New Zealand, among leaders from the Asia Pacific Economic Cooperation (APEC) forum.

---

10 Zong Hairen, 2002, "Zhu Rongji in 1999," *Chinese Law and Government* 35 (1), translation by M.E. Sharpe Inc. from the Chinese text (see footnote 37 in chapter 2).

11 Ian Johnson, 1999, "China, with Economy Slowing, Renews its Push to Join WTO," *The Wall Street Journal*, June 4.

12 Zong, "Zhu Rongji in 1999" (see footnote 10 in this chapter).

A peculiar gift was in store for Clinton at the Auckland meeting, the first time he had met with Jiang since their jolly conducting of the PLA band 15 months earlier. The Chinese president handed his US counterpart a book on a subject that obsessed him — the Falun Gong, a meditation sect regarded by Beijing as a subversive cult, but viewed sympathetically by some Americans.[13] Clinton politely but persistently directed the conversation to the WTO, urging Jiang three times to join him in instructing their negotiators to resolve remaining differences as soon as possible. "It's not going to get any easier," he said, since the 2000 presidential elections were looming, which would make an agreement more politically fraught. In the end, Jiang shifted his focus from Falun Gong to the WTO, the meeting got Sino-American relations back on track and trade minister Shi Guangsheng accepted an invitation from Barshefsky to come to Washington in the last week of September.[14]

But Chinese officials were not through avenging the ill treatment they felt they had received at US hands, as became evident when Shi arrived. To the dismay of Barshefsky and company, the Chinese delegation didn't include chief negotiator Long Yongtu, who had a volcanic temper but combined spontaneity with good English (he had a degree from the London School of Economics). That meant the Americans would have to endure the lectures and rehearsed speechifying for which Shi had a penchant. Shi admonished Barshefsky to "objectively and realistically" evaluate China's ability to concede more than it already had; if the Americans' asking price was too high they would again miss an opportunity for a deal and would end up with the opposite of what they wanted, he declared. Over dinner with Shi on September 27 after a day of talks, Barshefsky complained about the number of "clarifications" and "problems" raised by Chinese officials about concessions they had previously made, which was causing the gap between the two sides to widen rather than shrink. To this Shi retorted that such an assertion depended on what basis of comparison was used. If it was the 17-page list released in April, China had not fully agreed to that list anyway, so claims of a widening gap were invalid, he said.[15]

---

13 Associated Press, 1999, "Clinton Given Falun Gong Book," September 12. Titled *Li Hongzhi and His 'Falun Gong,': Deceiving the Public and Ruining Lives*, the book contained photos of Chinese allegedly driven to suicide by following the sect's preaching.

14 Helene Cooper, Bob Davis and Ian Johnson, 1999, "To Brink and Back," *The Wall Street Journal*, November 16.

15 Shi Guangsheng (ed.), Zhang Xiangchen and Suo Bicheng (co-authors), 2011, *A Reader for the Knowledge of China's Accession to the World Trade Organization* (in Chinese, portions translated by Alex He), section 5.

A more encouraging development, which both US and Chinese participants recall as pivotal, came in late October — Zhu's first meeting with a US official after his months in apparent purdah. The official was Larry Summers, the Treasury secretary, who was in Beijing to confer with his counterparts on macroeconomics and structural issues. Summers was told initially that Zhu was unavailable because he was travelling in China's far northwest, but when offered a meeting with the premier in Lanzhou, the capital of Gansu province — two-and-half hours by air from Beijing — Summers seized the opportunity, and a flight was arranged.

Over a long lunch at a state guesthouse, Zhu told Summers bluntly that he had suffered an enormous setback in the wake of the April meeting in Washington — "You guys really pulled the rug from under me," is how one attendee summarized the premier's lament. As Treasury secretary, Summers wasn't authorized to negotiate on WTO issues, but he asked Zhu what was necessary for a deal to be struck. Zhu had a list, including some issues that Chinese officials had been raising for weeks, which was promptly conveyed to Washington. Soon thereafter he received word from the US embassy in Beijing that a letter from Clinton would be on its way to Jiang providing satisfaction on most of the items of greatest concern to the premier.[16]

First, Zhu wanted a virtual guarantee that as part of the WTO deal, Congress would approve PNTR legislation. Second, Zhu wanted US negotiators to drop the idea of subjecting China to a "general safeguard" that would give Washington the right to impose tariffs on all Chinese imports if a surge materialized. Those two demands were fairly easy for Clinton to offer soothing assurances on. The president had long since come around to favouring an end to the annual congressional vote on China's human rights record, and he expressed confidence that Capitol Hill would go along provided the final terms of the deal included the vast majority of items the two sides had agreed to in April. As for the general safeguard, US trade officials recognized that invoking it would be a "nuclear option" — essentially a declaration of trade war on China — that would never be used anyway. Clinton agreed to withdraw it.

A third item on Zhu's wish list was much more intractable — an easing of US controls on exports of high-tech products to China. Washington regarded this as a matter of national security, utterly separate from the terms of China's WTO membership, and Zhu relented when he was told the White House

16 "Talking Points for [William] McCahill," on file at Clinton Presidential Library in Little Rock, Arkansas, file 2014-1039, box 6.

couldn't give way on that subject. But the premier won concessions on other issues of major concern to him. Clinton agreed to withdraw Washington's demand for a 10-year period of maintaining quotas limiting Chinese clothing and textile imports; the length of time would be shorter. He also promised to negotiate a time limit on the "China product-specific" safeguard and on China's "non-market economy status" in anti-dumping cases. In other words, Chinese imports would be subject to stricter trade remedies than products from other countries but not indefinitely.

The stage was now set, following a series of phone calls between Clinton and Jiang, for the most frenzied act in China's WTO accession saga.

For the trip that Charlene Barshefsky took to Beijing in November 1999, bottles of Perrier, packages of Swiss cheese and bags of M&M's were procured in sizeable quantities, with the purpose of ensuring that she and her staff would have plenty to munch and sip on without fear of digestive troubles. "Do or die" was the much-bandied cliché applied to the trip, which was billed in advance as a two-day visit — the idea being that either a deal on China's WTO membership would be reached during that time along the lines of the one discussed in April, or the issue would be deferred indefinitely, perhaps years. Barshefsky was immersed in preparing to host a major meeting of WTO trade ministers in Seattle at the end of the month, so to underscore that time was of the essence, she had packed only two days' worth of clothing when she boarded the flight on November 8, and she apprised the Chinese of that fact. Just in case additional time was required, she brought a couple of extra scarves to avoid giving the appearance that she was wearing the same clothes day after day — a wise decision, as things turned out.

Among the half-dozen administration officials accompanying her was Gene Sperling. Chinese negotiators soon had a name for him — "Party representative" — because he reminded them of the Communist Party members assigned to monitor and meddle in goings-on at Chinese factories, universities and other institutions. Everyone knew he had favoured rejecting the April agreement because of political considerations, and that was exactly the reason Barshefsky saw some advantage in bringing him. As long as Sperling accepted the terms of a deal she had negotiated, her Chinese interlocutors would not need to worry about the risk that the president might turn around and veto it.

As talks got under way, lobbyists in Washington reported getting calls from the Commerce Department asking how far the administration could diverge from the terms in the 17-page document without losing their support.[17] A similar process was going on among Chinese policy makers. At a special Politburo meeting, Zhu made an impassioned plea for flexibility. "Under the premise of not harming our country's fundamental interests, we should be mentally prepared to make the maximum concessions," he said, according to the book by his confidant, adding:

> We must cast away two illusions: The first is that the United States will make concessions and take a step backward at this meeting if we adopt a tough stance. The second is that the United States and European Community will lower their terms somewhat if [we] join [the WTO] at a later date. Such thinking is completely unrealistic.

> Opening up to the outside is a fundamental state policy, and practice has long since proven that the earlier we open up, the more rapid will be our development. Many of our present enterprises have grown and become stronger in the course of setting up joint ventures. After we join the WTO, we may suffer impacts, some of which may be severe, but in the long run the advantages outweigh the disadvantages.[18]

As before, others favoured a less forthcoming stance, including Jiang, who said, "We will by no means sacrifice our basic interests in order to join the WTO." That may explain why the negotiations went poorly for most of the first two days, November 10 and 11. Once again, Barshefsky faced off against the bombastic Shi Guangsheng, sparring to little effect over issues that the Americans maintained had been agreed in April and the Chinese insisted were still not settled. The biggest bones of contention included the schedule for lowering tariffs on autos, foreign investment in telecommunications, opportunities for foreign banks to open branches and the length of time that Chinese exports would be subject to a special safeguard in the United States.[19]

After consulting with Washington — Barshefsky spoke with Clinton every night on a secure line from a room at the US embassy called "the refrigerator" — she agreed to extend her visit, but she told the press, "We are discouraged. The clock has nearly run out."[20] And when talks on Friday, November 12,

---

17 Steven Mufson and Robert G. Kaiser, 1999, "Missed U.S.-China Deal Looms Large; Near-agreement in April May Prove Pivotal in WTO Talks," *The Washington Post*, November 10.

18 Zong Hairen, "Zhu Rongji in 1999" (see footnote 10 in this chapter).

19 Shi, *A Reader for the Knowledge of China's Accession to the World Trade Organization* (see footnote 15 in this chapter).

20 Ian Johnson, 1999, "Growing List of Trade Disputes Looms as China and U.S. Work on WTO Deal," *The Wall Street Journal*, November 10.

still produced scant progress, tempers flared. To some extent, the eruptions were theatrical; the Americans agreed beforehand that when an impasse was reached, Sperling should exploit his position as a close associate of Clinton's, and he did, shouting that the president would "never, never never, never, never, never, never, never" accept an agreement without China's agreement on certain provisions. In other cases, the exasperation was genuine, as when Barshefsky told Shi she was sick of spending so much time, after having come such a long distance, listening to "bullshit." Upon hearing the word translated, Shi pounded the table, called her an "imperialist," and snarled, "the days when China could be intimidated by foreigners are over!" — a riposte that he delighted in recounting to underlings long thereafter, even if its impact may have lost something in translation.

On Friday night, the US delegation announced plans to return to Washington the following day, with Barshefsky stating, "there are no positive developments to report at this stage."[21] But she demanded to see Zhu, indicating that she remained open to further bargaining, and at around 3:00 a.m., a call came to the US delegation inviting her to meet the premier later in the morning. If the intent was for him to play "good cop" to Shi's "bad cop," Zhu performed the role magnificently.

The meeting took place in the Hall of Purple Light, with Barshefsky and Zhu occupying the two chairs of honour. Off to the side sat Sperling, who was waiting for the interpreter to translate as Zhu began speaking in Mandarin. To Sperling's surprise and discomfiture, he heard his name mentioned a couple of times, while at the same time the Chinese officials present were breaking into uproarious laughter. Wondering what the hilarity was about — these same officials had sat so stony-faced through previous meetings that they seemed incapable of amusement — Sperling finally understood when he heard the translation of Zhu's words, which went roughly as follows: "I'm sorry I haven't been at the negotiations, but I've read the transcripts, even the part where Mr. Gene Sperling used the word "never" eight times in a single sentence. We do not teach our children to say a word eight times in a sentence!"

On a more serious note, Zhu expressed appreciation for Clinton's recent easing of US demands regarding issues such as the general safeguard and textile quotas, and he assured Barshefsky that the Chinese leadership, all the way up to Jiang, wanted to see the negotiations succeed. To that end, he agreed to open China's market to non-bank companies offering financing for auto

---

21 Mark Suzman, 1999, "US breaks off trade talks with China," *Financial Times*, November 13.

purchases, a move Washington hoped would spur sales of foreign autos, in return for a longer period to reduce auto tariffs.

But in the afternoon, with Shi again leading the Chinese team, the atmosphere deteriorated anew. On one of the major issues — investment in telecommunications companies operating in China — Barshefsky had conceded that foreign investors could be capped at less than majority ownership, but she wanted written guarantees that foreigners could obtain management control. Barshefsky also insisted on a 20-year period for non-market economy status to apply to China in anti-dumping cases. Neither demand was acceptable, Shi retorted,[22] and the Americans again began preparing for a breakdown. A press release was drafted announcing Barshefsky's departure, quoting her as saying she was "disappointed we were not able to make significant progress in our talks with the Chinese leadership."[23]

Although that press release wasn't issued — the US team decided there was still some glimmer of hope for a deal — the negotiations that took place the next day, a Sunday, were the worst yet, with officials on both sides exhausted and cranky. As a prearranged tactic to show the Chinese that the US delegation was serious about the shortness of time remaining, Lieberthal interrupted the talks mid-morning to announce that he had a plane to catch, and he left for the airport even though he in fact had no reason to be back in Washington urgently.

In the evening, the Americans found themselves sitting in a room alone at the trade ministry, and when more than an hour went by without any word from the Chinese, Barshefsky decided it really was time to leave. Convinced that the Chinese knew their whereabouts, and suspicious that Beijing might be setting them up for humiliation (to settle the score after the mistreatment of Zhu in April), she and Sperling went to the embassy "refrigerator" to call Clinton again. According to her recollection, she said, "It would be unseemly for the United States for us to stay any longer," to which the president responded with disappointment but also agreement. Sperling likewise recalls telling Clinton, "It's been several hours, nobody's contacted us, and we've got to tell you, Mr. President, it looks like it just won't happen.' I love Bill Clinton for this — he was so nice; he said, 'Look, I know how you've thrown your hearts into this.'" Suitcases were ostentatiously loaded onto vans outside the US delegation's hotel, and mobile phones switched off.

---

22 Shi Guangsheng, *A Reader for the Knowledge of China's Accession to the World Trade Organization* (see footnote 15 in this chapter).

23 US Trade Representative, 1999, "Draft Press Release," November 13, on file at Clinton Presidential Library, File 2010-1024-F, Box 8.

Chinese officials who were involved in the negotiations assert they never intended to embarrass anyone; they were embroiled in intensive consultations about the WTO and other issues at an annual gathering of representatives from many of China's biggest companies. Even so, the talks came perilously close to rupturing at this point. Having lost track of the Americans, Chinese negotiators figured the US walkout was a bluff — this was not Barshefsky's first departure threat, after all.

During the middle of the night, officials on both sides made phone calls in a bid to restore contact. Most importantly, Jiang called Shi, and when told that the Americans were out of pocket, the president ordered the trade minister to find them, according to Chinese officials who recall Shi's account of the conversation. This was a clear signal that Jiang had come down in favour of a deal. And when the Americans arrived at the trade ministry around 7:45 a.m. on Monday, November 15, for one last meeting, an even clearer signal awaited.

At first, both sides were looking daggers at each other. Shi appeared as if he had slept in his clothes; Sperling, who had also been up much of the night, exploded upon hearing that the media was gathering for photos. Then, suddenly, the atmosphere changed, when the matronly face of Wu Yi appeared at the door, cheerfully beckoning William McCahill, the embassy's number two official, to convey startling information: Premier Zhu was coming to the ministry, and would meet the US negotiators in a conference room on the eleventh floor. Incredulous that a premier would travel to a ministry building to meet foreigners — an unheard-of step for the protocol-sensitive Chinese — McCahill whispered to Barshefsky and Sperling that Zhu would not be coming if he was planning to leave them hanging.

In the conference room, where he was joined by Wu, Shi and Qian Qichen, a vice premier specializing in foreign affairs, Zhu started by asking why the Americans had walked out of the previous night's meeting without giving notice. Sperling replied that because he and Barshefsky had been left alone for such a long period, they had assumed the Chinese side was abandoning the talks. After a couple of more back-and-forths over who had walked out on whom, Barshefsky passed a note to Sperling: the argument, she wrote, sounded like an episode from *Seinfeld*[24] — meaning it was inconsequential, and the time had come to discuss substance.

Regarding the issues still outstanding, Zhu gave in — on some of them, at least. He stood firm regarding the control that foreign investors would be

---

24 An American television comedy that calls itself "a show about nothing."

allowed to hold in telecommunications operations; he said he had no leeway to offer majority stakes, and since this involved the flow of information — an issue on which the Communist Party pinned its survival — Barshefsky concluded that he wasn't bluffing. But on the product-specific safeguard, Zhu was sufficiently forthcoming that Barshefsky and Sperling concluded they had gotten what they needed. And on the final issue, China's non-market economy status in anti-dumping cases, Zhu agreed that the provision could stay in force for 15 years. That wasn't as long as the 20 years the US side had demanded, but it was long enough to be acceptable to Washington. Handshakes were exchanged all around.

A touch of indignity marred the moment of triumph that followed. Barshefsky and Sperling needed to call Clinton, who was in Ankara, Turkey, on a visit to southern Europe, but the only place in the ministry they could find that was sufficiently private was the anteroom of a women's bathroom. Then, upon getting patched through, they were told that Clinton was in the shower. To their relief, he quickly came out to get on the phone. "Mr. President, the world's greatest trade negotiator has some very good news for you," Sperling recalls telling Clinton before handing the phone to Barshefsky, an episode they dubbed "bathroom-to-bathroom diplomacy."

Decorum was fully restored at a signing ceremony later in the afternoon, during which Barshefsky and Shi raised a champagne toast in the presence of the news media, and in the evening, Jiang hosted a celebratory gathering for the US delegation at a pavilion in Zhongnanhai.

The splashy treatment the deal received in the news media the next day is the subject of a memory enshrined in Barshefsky's family lore. Her husband, Edward Cohen, showed their daughters *The New York Times* and *The Washington Post* and announced: "Look, Mama got her China deal!" — to which ten-year-old Devra replied, with the savvy peculiar to certain Washington schoolchildren: "Oh, good — above the fold!"

In the years since striking that agreement, Barshefsky, now back in private law practice, has outspokenly criticized the direction of China's economic policies. "The environment in China has shifted negatively for foreign businesses," she said at a 2016 event on the fifteenth anniversary of China's WTO accession. "Multinationals saw enormous gains in China...from roughly 1999 to 2007-08. But at that juncture, opening began to sputter...and in the place of reform and opening, increasingly what is seen [are] zero-sum, mercantilistic policies. These are counterproductive…and they have the potential to desta-bilize the US-China relationship as a whole."[25]

But Barshefsky is unapologetic about the deal she negotiated in 1999. "Not a single member of Congress, nor a single industry person, came to me and said, 'I need more,'" she told me. "People were astonished at what we got. Even labour. Not one labour person said to me, 'I have to have more on spe-cial safeguards,' or, 'I have to have more on this mechanism or that.' Were the labour people happy? With any trade deal? No. Could they say, 'You didn't get what we asked for?' In every instance, what labour asked, I got what they asked for, or more than they asked for. In that sense, we were as comprehen-sive as we could have been at the time."

That may be an overstatement. If organized labour had had its full druthers, China would have been required to go much further — sharply raise the Chinese minimum wage, for example, and give Chinese dissidents, especially labour activists, the same rights that their American counterparts enjoy. But none of that was even remotely negotiable as far as Beijing was concerned, and the numerous trade experts whom I interviewed for this book were vir-tually unanimous in assessing the 1999 pact as achieving pretty much every-thing that could have practically been demanded of China.

Recall Zhu's comments to the Poliburo as the November talks got under way — especially his warning that it would be an "illusion" to expect a hardline Chinese negotiating position to produce US concessions. That indicates how credible Barshefsky was in presenting a resolute stance. Noteworthy, too, is the fact that the November pact included most of the provisions specified in the 17-page document released in April, one exception being the cap on foreign investment in telecommunications firms at a less-than-majority stake. (Chinese officials insisted that US claims of an agreement in April on 51 per-cent foreign ownership must have been based on a misunderstanding.)

Perhaps the best evidence for the deal's scope and breadth is a summary of the terms, which were spelled out in a 250-page document several inches thick.[26] All WTO members were to get the same benefits as the United States, of

25 Center for Strategic & International Studies (CSIS), 2016, "China's 15th WTO Anniversary: Assessing the Record and Charting the Path Forward," December 16, www.csis.org/events/ chinas-15th-wto-anniversary-assessing-record-and-charting- path-forward.

26 A summary is contained in US Trade Representative, 1999, "U.S.-China Bilateral WTO Agreement," November 15. Detailed and informative discussions of the terms can also be found in Raj Bhala, 2000, "Enter the Dragon: An Essay on China's WTO Accession Saga," *American University International Law Review* 15 (6): 1469–538 and Nicholas R. Lardy, 2002, *Integrating China into the Global Economy*, Washington, DC: Brookings Institution Press.

course, under the MFN principle. Following are the highlights, starting with the "defensive" provisions that Barshefsky negotiated to protect the US market. These were the most salient parts of the pact that relegated China to a sort of second-class citizenship.

Safeguards

If imports of Chinese goods were adversely affecting a US industry, Washington could impose duties on those specific Chinese products. This "China-specific safeguard" provision, which was to remain in force 12 years after China's accession to the WTO, was a remarkable deviation from the WTO's non-discrimination principle. Under normal circumstances, WTO rules require a country levying safeguard duties on problematic imports to impose them on such products from all foreign countries, not just one; China had accepted that its products could be singled out.

Moreover, this provision set a much easier standard for imposing safeguard duties on Chinese imports than on imports from other countries. WTO rules normally require a country levying safeguard duties to show that increased imports have "caused or threaten to cause serious injury" to a domestic industry. But under the terms of the 1999 deal, safeguard duties could be imposed on Chinese imports that were causing "market disruption."

Anti-dumping

For 15 years after China's accession to the WTO, the United States could continue to apply non-market economy status to China in anti-dumping cases. This too marked an acceptance by Beijing of discriminatory terms; no other country had agreed to such treatment for such an extended period.[27]

In anti-dumping cases, as previously noted, imports from a non-market economy are much more likely to be found guilty of being sold at "less than fair value" and therefore hit with high duties. That is because prices and costs in a non-market economy are assumed to be distorted rather than reflective of supply and demand, so calculations of the degree of dumping can be quite arbitrary, based on prices and costs in other countries.

Textiles and Apparel

Although the Clinton administration backed off from insisting that imports of Chinese clothing remain capped until 2010 (compared with 2005 when

---

27 As shall be seen in chapter 8, this provision has become a matter of hot dispute. When the 15-year deadline passed in 2016, the United States and some other WTO members insisted on continuing to apply non-market economy status to China on the grounds that it had not yet become a market economy; Beijing has filed a complaint contending that this violates the terms of its accession.

such caps would expire for other countries), a special safeguard mechanism applicable only to Chinese imports would be created, remaining in effect until December 31, 2008.

The following are the "offensive" provisions.

Goods

In line with the 17-page document released in April, Chinese tariffs would be lowered significantly over a few years, to an average 9.4 percent for industrial goods and 17 percent for agricultural products. Tariffs on autos would remain relatively high, at 25 percent, and fall only gradually to that level by 2006, but that was still drastically below the 80 to 100 percent tariffs that applied pre-deal, and tariffs on auto parts would be cut to 10 percent. Foreign firms seeking to produce autos in China for the local market would have to do so in joint-venture partnerships with Chinese companies, with the foreign shares limited to 50 percent. That provision stemmed from Beijing's worries that in a fully open market, foreign automakers would crush Chinese competitors. (US automakers already had joint ventures with Chinese partners, which conferred some advantages.)

Most import quotas on industrial goods — which applied to products such as medical equipment, fertilizers, polyester fibre, distilled spirits and beer — would be eliminated by 2002, and all others by 2005. For bulk farm commodities, such as barley, corn, cotton, rice and wheat, China agreed to a major liberalization by allowing large quantities of imports to enter the market at very low duties before high tariffs would kick in.

Distribution and Trading Rights

Foreign firms would be able to establish their own retail and wholesale networks, and after-sales services (for example, repair) without Chinese intermediaries, for both agricultural and industrial goods, within three years of China's WTO accession. (There were a few exceptions, such as gasoline, salt and tobacco.) The same would go for the right to import and export goods.

Telecommunications

Although China refused to allow foreigners to own majority control in telecommunication service companies, such as mobile voice and internet service providers, foreign investors could obtain up to a 49 percent stake in joint ventures, rising to 50 percent in some cases. (Foreign equipment makers, such as Motorola and Nokia, had long maintained extensive operations in China, but the burgeoning telecommunications service market had been closed to foreign firms.) Moreover, China pledged changes in its regulatory regime that would give newcomers realistic opportunities to compete with the monopolistic China Telecom.

Financial Services

Numerous foreign banks and insurance companies had established operations in China during the 1990s, but a tangle of laws and regulations severely restricted the types of business they could conduct — and the terms of the 1999 deal envisioned a dramatic change.

After long being barred from doing business in domestic currency with Chinese clients, foreign banks would be able to conduct such business with Chinese enterprises two years after Beijing's WTO entry and with Chinese individuals three years after that. Geographic restrictions on foreign bank branches would gradually be lifted. As for insurance, where foreigners were confined to operating in Shanghai and Guangzhou, there too geographical limitations would gradually end, along with many restrictions on the types of insurance that foreign firms could offer.

Government Procurement and SOEs

In one respect, this issue was left uncovered by the 1999 deal and created a major loophole that allows Chinese government agencies to favour domestic firms in their purchasing decisions.

A separate WTO pact (not part of the overall WTO agreement) covers purchases by government agencies, with the benefits limited to countries that sign. In other words, a country that agrees to open its government procurement market sufficiently to the other signees' products can qualify to sell to the other signees' governments; countries that aren't part of this deal don't enjoy similar access to those other markets. China didn't join in 2001 — one major reason being that Washington was loath to offer Beijing reciprocal access to the US government procurement market. Instead, China promised to negotiate terms to join in the near future. But that pledge remains unfulfilled to this day, which means that Chinese authorities still have the right to discriminate in favour of domestic firms — and against foreign firms — when their government agencies make purchases.

On the other hand, Beijing agreed to a US demand that purchases and sales by SOEs should not be considered government procurement. In other words, normal WTO rules would apply to the massive SOE sector.

Cultural Imports

As per the April 17-page document, China would allow the importation of 40 foreign films for theatrical release in the year after WTO entry, increasing to 50 films a couple of years thereafter.

Major Rules

Upon entering the WTO, China would abide by the trade body's key agreements including the Agreement on Trade-Related Aspects of Intellectual Property and the Agreement on Trade-Related Investment Measures. That would cement China's obligations, already undertaken in bilateral agreements with the United States, to honour patents and copyrights and crack down on piracy. It would also severely limit Beijing's long-standing practice of imposing local content requirements on foreign investors and conditioning approval of foreign investment on the transfer of technology.

Developing Country Status

China maintained that it should deem itself a developing country in the WTO, which meant it would be entitled to "special and differential treatment" that the trade body grants to developing countries for certain purposes, such as the length of transition periods for implementing market-opening measures. US negotiators gave way on this point based on the recognition that in China's case, developing country status was of symbolic rather than substantive importance, because Beijing was agreeing to much more stringent terms for entry than other developing countries.

All in all, this array of commitments gave the White House potent ammunition when, in the spring of 2000, Congress weighed the legislation for China's PNTR status. On March 8, Clinton submitted the bill to Capitol Hill, arguing that forgoing the annual vote on Beijing's human rights record was a small price to pay for the benefits to be gained. "Economically, this agreement is the equivalent of a one-way street," the president asserted. "It requires China to open its markets — with a fifth of the world's population, potentially the biggest market in the world — to both our products and services in unprecedented new ways. All we do is to agree to maintain the present access which China enjoys."[28]

Mobilized against the bill were groups such as Human Rights Watch, Amnesty International and organized labour, which cited China's rock-bottom wages (25 cents an hour, on average, for manufacturing workers[29]) as grounds for the

---

28 *The New York Times*, 2000, "Full Text of Clinton's Speech on China Trade Bill" (as recorded by Federal News Service), March 9, https://archive.nytimes.com/www.nytimes.com/library/world/asia/030900clinto n-china-text.html.

29 Congressional Research Service, 2000, "China and the WTO: Labor Issues," July 21.

prediction that massive numbers of American jobs would disappear as a result of intensified Chinese competition. But political and economic forces were now working strongly in the president's favour. The lustre of the US economy was at levels not seen since the 1960s, with growth at boom rates for five consecutive years and Silicon Valley wizards ginning up dazzling new technologies. Approval of NAFTA in 1993 had not led to a "giant sucking sound" of US jobs to Mexico as opponents had prophesied; instead, unemployment among American workers was hovering in the four percent range. Japan, the would-be usurper of America's economic primacy, was struggling to eke out minimal rates of growth following the bursting of its real estate and stock market bubble. In many emerging countries of Asia and Latin America, a number of which had been ravaged by financial crises during the 1990s, the superiority of the American way was being preached, from its rule of law to its shareholder-oriented corporate governance to its reliance on vibrant securities markets for funding the growth of industries.

In his March 8, 2000, speech, Clinton therefore indulged in what sinologists call America's "missionary complex" — the belief that China would and should become more like the United States. "By joining the WTO, China is not simply agreeing to import more of our products; it is agreeing to import one of democracy's most cherished values: economic freedom," he said. "And when individuals have the power, not just to dream but to realize their dreams, they will demand a greater say." The transcript of his remarks continues with words that, so far at least, have poorly withstood the test of time:

> We know how much the Internet has changed America, and we are already an open society. Imagine how much it could change China. Now there's no question China has been trying to crack down on the Internet. (Chuckles.) Good luck! (Laughter.) That's sort of like trying to nail jello to the wall. (Laughter.)

"WTO membership," the president acknowledged, "is not in and of itself a human-rights policy. But still, it is likely to have a profound impact on human rights and political liberty."

Corporate America — represented by the National Association of Manufacturers, the Business Roundtable, the US Chamber of Commerce, the National Retail Federation and countless other lobbying groups — pulled out all the stops to secure support in the House of Representatives, where the vote was expected to be close. Former presidents Gerald Ford, Jimmy Carter and George H. W. Bush, as well as former secretaries of state from past administrations, joined Clinton in making a bipartisan pitch that the trade measure would have a salutary impact on China's human rights behavior.[30]

As the House vote began on May 24, 2000, Barshefsky invited staffers who had worked on the China deal to watch on her office television. Both sides had launched lobbying blitzes and television ad campaigns in previous days. An organized labour ad featured Wei Jingsheng, who had been imprisoned 18 years for his pro-democracy activism; business groups' spots portrayed China's burgeoning market as a prize other countries would exploit if America forewent the opportunity.[31] Furious horse-trading was under way until the last minute, with the White House promising lawmakers money for pipelines, weather stations and defence plants.[32] In the end, the margin of victory was wider than expected, 237 to 197. The Senate followed suit in the fall.

Still, China was not yet in the WTO. To paraphrase Zhu's joke about "black hair turning grey" during the 13 years after China's application for readmission to the GATT, membership would come only after grey hair had turned a bit whiter.

Nestled on the shores of Lake Geneva, with the Alps on the horizon across the lake, stands the WTO's headquarters, an Italianate villa named the Centre William Rappard (in honour of the Swiss diplomat). There a "working party" on China's accession, which had first convened at the time of Beijing's 1986 GATT application, stepped up its activity in 2001 as the final stages of the process approached. Consisting of representatives from a number of China's trading partners, the working party was racing to meet a deadline — the planned formal approval of China's accession at a meeting of trade ministers from WTO member countries, scheduled to begin on November 9, 2001, in Doha, Qatar. A couple more moments of drama lay in store.

The United States was only the fourth country to reach a bilateral agreement with China on the terms of accession, and about 40 more countries were lined up for their turn to negotiate. Since Washington had done the heavy lifting in terms of extracting broad market-opening concessions, which would be "multilateralized" under the MFN rule, Beijing's negotiations with other trading

---

30 Charles Babington and Matthew Vita, 2000, "All-Star Cast Promotes Trade Bill," *The Washington Post,* May 10.

31 Charles Babington, 2000, "As Tight Vote Nears on China Trade, Backers and Foes Flood TV," *The Washington Post,* May 22.

32 Matthew Vita and Juliet Eilperin, 2000, "On the Fence and in Demand," *The Washington Post,* May 19.

partners involved issues of particular interest to those trading partners rather than global importance. Canada, for example, sought greater market access for barley and wheat, and the European Union wanted Chinese tariffs for scotch and cognac lowered to a level comparable to the tariff on bourbon that had concerned the Americans.[33] But in addition to bilateral deals, China was obliged to negotiate a "protocol of accession" with the WTO as a whole. The protocol would incorporate the commitments made in the bilaterals, but also spell out detailed plans for changing Beijing's laws, regulations and policies to conform with WTO rules. All of this would take considerable time — nearly two years from the date of "bathroom-to-bathroom diplomacy."

The issues at stake in the protocol were hardly trivial; among them, for example, was how China would fulfill WTO requirements regarding judicial review. Under the Uruguay Round agreement, the trade body's members are supposed to maintain tribunals that can pass judgment on trade-related actions by customs authorities, and those tribunals are supposed to be independent so that an aggrieved party can obtain a fair resolution by filing a complaint. China was pressured, and ultimately agreed, to go further than other WTO members, by pledging to establish impartial and independent tribunals not only for narrowly defined trade and customs issues but other issues relating to WTO agreements. This marked the first time that "impartiality" and "independence" were legally required for Chinese judicial bodies.[34]

By early September, only one major issue remained, but it had to be resolved quickly. The Doha meeting was looming, and only after all issues were settled could the WTO staff implement the necessary bureaucratic and translation procedures, which would take several weeks. The final issue involved US efforts to gain special access in the Chinese insurance market for American International Group, whose chief executive officer (CEO) Maurice "Hank" Greenberg was an influential donor to powerful Washington politicians. The European Union, which had its own insurance giants to protect, was objecting that all foreign insurers should be treated alike, in accord with WTO principles. The parochial nature of this dispute exasperated the other participants, as did last-minute efforts by China to add a handful of products to lists of items that could be subject to price controls and trading restrictions.

---

33 Hans-Friedrich Beseler, 2002, "The EU-China Negotiations: Breaking the Deadlock," in Holbig and Ash (eds.), *China's Accession to the World Trade Organization: National and International Perspectives* (see footnote 9 in this chapter).

34 Nicholas R. Lardy, 2002, *Integrating China into the Global Economy*, Washington, DC: Brookings Institution Press, chapter 3. China's compliance with the provisions regarding judicial independence and the establishment of special courts for WTO-related issues turned out to be mixed at best, as can be discerned in chapters 4 and 8, where Beijing's record on rule of law and related issues is covered.

Still, when the working party met at WTO headquarters on the afternoon of September 11, a compromise was expected that would wrap up China's accession terms. "The legal procedures for China to enter the WTO might be wholly completed tomorrow," Finance Minister Xiang Huiaicheng told a group of US government officials and journalists that morning in Beijing.[35]

But note the date — September 11. Shortly before 4:00 p.m. Geneva time, Keith Rockwell, the WTO's chief spokesman, burst into the negotiating room with news of the terrorist attack on the World Trade Center in New York. Pandemonium ensued, as phones began ringing and members of the US delegation gaped in teary disbelief at televised broadcasts of hijacked planes crashing into the twin towers and the Pentagon. Despite his eagerness to finish the business at hand, Long Yongtu, who was heading the Chinese team, acknowledged that it would be inappropriate to continue and requested a two-day suspension in the talks. For a while, uncertainty reigned about whether the US delegation would be ordered home, and whether they might be unable to receive negotiating instructions from Washington, which could have resulted in significant delay.[36]

Given the chaotic state of air travel, the Americans had little choice but to stay in Geneva, and over the following six days the outstanding differences were finessed. On September 17, the working party announced plans to forward some 900 pages of legal text regarding China's accession for formal acceptance by the 142 WTO members at the Doha ministerial, a development hailed by WTO Director-General Mike Moore as a "defining moment in the history of economic cooperation between nations."[37]

For the finale of China's tension-filled accession odyssey, Doha afforded a fittingly stressful milieu. Only two months had passed since September 11, and fears of more terrorist attacks were weighing heavily on the 2,600 official delegates, 800 journalists and 400 representatives of business and non-governmental organizations who were attending. Machine gun-toting Qatari police and military personnel in purple camouflage protected miles of roads surrounding the Sheraton Resort and Convention Hotel, where the meeting was taking place, and security officials wearing *thobes* (traditional white robes) and *kaffiyeh* headdresses manned metal detectors at every point of entry. Many

---

35 Clay Chandler, 2001, "China Close to Agreement on WTO Membership, Official Says," *The Washington Post*, September 12.

36 Daniel Pruzin, 2001, "WTO China Meeting Postponed as New Problems Surface in Final Stages," *BNA WTO Reporter*, September 13.

37 Daniel Pruzin, 2001, "Insurance Agreement Ends Stalemate on China's Accession to WTO," *BNA WTO Reporter*, September 18.

delegates had stayed home; American citizens (including journalists like me) were quietly given a password — "paging Mr. Black" — which, if broadcast over the public address system, would mean that some type of threat was materializing, and they were to gather at the hotel pool for evacuation by helicopter to US Navy ships patrolling offshore.[38]

The meeting was a focus of anxiety in world capitals because leaders around the globe, US President George W. Bush chief among them, wanted a deal to demonstrate solidarity among the international community in the wake of 9/11. The main agenda item was a proposal to launch a new global trade round, which would be the first since the system's rules were overhauled in the Uruguay Round in 1994. There was broad concurrence that the top priority of the new round should be to lower trade barriers in ways that would bestow more of the gains from global commerce on developing nations. But battles raged over the specific issues that would be on the negotiating agenda, and consensus was necessary. Only on the sixth day — 20 hours past the self-imposed five-day limit — did the last holdout, India, join the consensus to initiate what was officially called the "Doha Development Agenda" or, more commonly, the "Doha Round."

China's accession terms were scheduled for ministerial approval on the conference's second day, November 10. That too was the subject of wrangling because Taiwan was slated to join the WTO at the same meeting in the Qatari capital, and Beijing could not countenance the "renegade province" gaining membership first. In accord with a meticulously crafted timetable allowing both new entrants to obtain approval within the same 24-hour period, the chairman of the meeting, Qatari Trade Minister Youssef Hussain Kamal, read a brief summary of the working party report on China's accession and, hearing no objection, banged his gavel, declaring, "the ministerial conference so agrees." On the dais, Shi Guangsheng, who led the Chinese delegation, received a congratulatory hug from Moore.[39] A similar ceremony for Taiwan followed within hours, and one month later, on December 11, China's WTO membership became official.

Shortly after returning to Beijing from Doha, Shi was a guest of honour at the annual Government Appreciation Dinner held by the American Chamber of

---

38 Paul Blustein, 2009, *Misadventures of the Most Favored Nations*, New York, NY: Public Affairs, chapter 1.

39 Joseph Kahn, 2001, "World Trade Organization Admits China, Amid Doubts," *The New York Times*, November 11; Paul Blustein and Clay Chandler, 2001, "WTO Approves China's Entry," *The Washington Post*, November 11.

Commerce in China, whose chairman, Tim Stratford, congratulated him on completing the accession.

"I told him, 'Mr. Minister, some people say China's not serious about these commitments,'" Stratford recalled. "I said, 'I don't agree, because otherwise China wouldn't have spent 17 years negotiating. But based on my experience practicing law in China for a couple of decades, I think you're going to use every grey area and loophole to greatest advantage.' And he looked at me and said, 'You really understand China.'"

Does that mean admitting China to the WTO was a mistake? Would, say, the imposition of unilateral sanctions by the United States have been more effective against China's trade policies than WTO rules and WTO tribunal rulings, which carry the imprimatur of the international community? Such a conclusion strikes me as far-fetched. This much is certain: especially in the first few years after joining, China would treat the WTO with the utmost gravity.

CHAPTER 4

CHINA OPENS UP, AMERICA GETS A SHOCK

A t the National Museum of China on Tiananmen Square, visitors can gaze at artifacts from all of the country's epochs — jade burial suits from the Han Dynasty (206 BC–AD 220), for example, or pastel porcelain vases from the Qing Dynasty (1644–1911), or a painting of Mao's 1949 speech inaugurating the People's Republic, or the cowboy hat that Deng Xiaoping wore on his 1979 visit to Texas. And prominently displayed in a large glass box, denoting its status as a major historical milestone, is an official signed copy of China's protocol of accession to the WTO.

The exhibition of the protocol is just one illustration of the enthusiasm with which China welcomed its 2001 entry into the trade body. In bookstores around the country, books about the WTO — several thousand were published in China — filled the bestseller display tables. The government established "WTO centres" in major cities, and newspaper ads touted private seminars for business people seeking to understand what international rules would mean for their enterprises. A government-sponsored contest on WTO knowledge in 2003 attracted a reported five million entries. The finals were broadcast on China Central Television and the winning prize was a trip to Geneva to meet Director-General Supachai Panitchpakdi.[1]

Of more substantive import was the devotion manifest in the thorough dissemination of WTO rules and principles to people holding the levers of government policy. Even before accession, in June 2000, the trade ministry dispatched 23 lawyers, academics and officials from major domestic economic ministries to Washington for a two-week seminar at Georgetown University Law Center. The seminar's organizer was Georgetown Professor John Jackson, who is widely regarded as the WTO's intellectual father for a 1990 book he wrote envisioning the replacement of the GATT with a stronger trade body.[2] That seminar was followed several months later by a symposium in Beijing at which Jackson, WTO secretariat staffers and other experts spoke about the WTO's history and jurisprudence before an audience of more than 100 Chinese government officials. Jiang and Zhu themselves addressed a one-week training course in February 2002 for senior officials at the ministerial and provincial levels, the goal being to convey the top leadership's admonition that laws and regulations must align with WTO rules. That spurred the establishment of the regional WTO centres, whose staff reviewed local government actions for WTO consistency, offered information to companies facing trade barriers overseas and trained thousands more officials.[3]

The idealism that permeated these activities should not be underestimated. Among the most deeply involved — he helped coordinate the Georgetown seminar and spoke at more than 100 training courses in China — was Yang Guohua, a trade ministry official who had received a Ph.D. in law in 1996 from Peking University, where he specialized in international economic law and read Jackson's treatises. Such was Yang's reverence for the multilateral system that, in a memoir of his experiences, he wrote of the Georgetown seminar: "I was shocked that most lecturers criticized the WTO...while I came with this hallowed and enigmatic feeling about the WTO. Just imagine that the Monk Tangseng was shown some shortcomings of the Buddha when arriving in [India] after years of tremendous sufferings!"[4]

1 Sun Zhenyu, 2011, "China's Experience in 10 Years in the WTO," in *A Decade in the WTO: Implications for China and Global Governance*, Ricardo Meléndez-Ortiz, Christophe Bellmann and Shuailhua Cheng (eds.), Geneva, Switzerland: International Centre for Trade and Sustainable Development.

2 John Jackson, 1990, *Restructuring the GATT System*, New York, NY: Royal Institute of International Affairs, Council on Foreign Relations Press.

3 Yang Guohua, 2015, "China in the WTO Dispute Settlement: A Memoir," *Journal of World Trade* 49 (1): 1–18.

4 Ibid.

Yang served on the trade ministry teams that negotiated the US-China bilateral deal and also in the Geneva negotiations for the multilateral phase of China's accession. Having revelled in the thrill of travelling to distant locales and representing his country in international fora, he was initially crushed when, at year-end 2000, his boss ordered him to stay home and head a new project. But he gradually warmed to his assignment in view of its potential significance for effecting change in Chinese policy and institutions.

Over a two-year period, Yang's office scrutinized more than 2,300 laws and regulations. Their mission was to check for conformity with WTO rules — including, of course, commitments China made to accede — and, when inconsistencies were found, amendments were drafted or, in some cases, abolition or entirely new versions were required. Was a subsidy prohibited? Was a regulation discriminatory? Did a government practice violate China's commitments? As Yang later wrote:

> The result of this work, inter alia, was the amendment of the Foreign Trade Law to abolish the requirement on foreign trade rights, so that all companies could enjoy the rights of import and export automatically without approval by the authority. It also amended the foreign investment laws to abolish the local content and export performance requirements.
>
> Companies were no longer required to purchase domestic raw materials first in their production and export most of their products later. Many other laws and regulations were amended and numerous articles from these documents were abolished. At the same time some new articles — such as transparency and judicial review — were added. Dozens of new regulations were published, providing China market access, for example, on telecommunications, banking, insurance, legal services and education.[5]

As Yang and others saw it, this exercise was not merely about gaining and conceding commercial advantages; it was about using a rules-based international institution to instill rule of law in China. To appreciate the profundity of this transformation, it is important to recognize that rule of law had been an alien concept throughout nearly all of China's history. During the imperial dynasties, when Confucian philosophy held sway, law consisted mainly of decrees issued by emperors for the purpose of serving the interests of the state

---

5   Yang Guohua, 2016, "WTO and Rule of Law in China: A View Based on Personal Experience," *Global Trade and Customs Journal* 11 (6): 252–58.

and controlling society rather than protecting individual rights. In criminal cases, torture was common in extracting confessions, and for ordinary people, pressing a claim in court carried a taint of disreputability and often involved humiliating treatment; disputes were typically resolved informally by village elders. An effort to draft a legal code in the early twentieth century ended with the 1949 revolution, when Communist Party pronouncements and slogans replaced imperial decrees as instruments for mandating obedience, and during the Cultural Revolution, the legal system was essentially decimated, with lawyers and judges derided as capitalist lackeys. Even after Deng launched reforms and new codes were drafted for corporations and private property, many judges were former military officers who lacked legal training and, because they were poorly paid, were prone to corruption. Moreover, government officials maintained extensive power to dispense licences and other permission necessary to engage in all manner of business activities, another source of corruption and caprice that contravened rule of law.[6]

The years immediately following WTO accession took China in a new direction. "Joining the WTO has enabled China to reform its legal order towards a system that incorporates major rule of law principles," wrote Esther Lam, a Geneva-based journalist and researcher, in a 2009 study of the topic. "The WTO has provided an external impetus that guides Chinese legal reform in a way that domestic forces alone could neither achieve nor sustain."[7]

Transparency, a bedrock principle of any rule of law regime, was a perfect example. Some Chinese laws were known only to the authorities, who could invoke them when they saw fit. China promised, however, that upon accession, "only those laws, regulations and other measures pertaining to or affecting trade…that are published and readily available to other WTO members, individuals and enterprises shall be enforced."[8]

The overhaul of the Foreign Trade Law (cited above by Yang) was another important part of this process. Still another was the enactment in 2004 of a statute called the Administrative Licensing Law — which, according to Lam, "represents a remarkable philosophy shift for the Chinese government's regulatory role in society," because "the government can no longer arbitrarily interfere with market activities and peoples' daily lives through licensing. The previous assumption had been for Chinese citizens to ask for permission

---

6   Randall Peerenboom, 2002, *China's Long March Toward Rule of Law*, Cambridge, UK: Cambridge University Press, chapters 1-2.

7   Esther Lam, 2009, *China and the WTO: A Long March Towards the Rule of Law*, Wolters Kluwer, chapter 8.

8   WTO, 2001, "Protocol of the Accession of the People's Republic of China," Part I, Section 2-C.

and licensing for everything unless otherwise stated. Under the new law…
everything is permitted and no prior approval or license required unless it is
proscribed by law."[9] A related manifestation of this shift was a huge increase
in lawsuits — some 640,000 between 2000 and 2006 — brought by citizens against government authorities. Plaintiffs won about 30 percent of these
cases, an example being a suit filed by 12 farmers who contended that their
provincial government had inadequately and illegally set a low value on their
land for purposes of requisitioning it.[10] Judges stopped wearing military
uniforms in 2001, donning Western-style black robes instead and wielding
gavels.

Rule of law would suffer setbacks in later years, as shall be seen in chapter 8, and even in the early 2000s, the degree of reform was limited. Judicial
appointments remained subject to Party approval, and many lawyers earned
their fees based on *guanxi* (connections) with officials rather than their litigation skills. Still, in the period following WTO accession, law was "becoming
a significant tool in policy making, incrementally replacing crude political
power," Lam's study found, and as a result, "Pronouncements by political
leaders…are no longer sufficient. Both foreign investors and Chinese citizens
nowadays routinely demand whether actions and policies are based on and
prescribed by law."[11]

The effect on business in China, and consequently on Chinese living standards, was salutary, erasing worries among the nation's elite about wolves at
the door.

Foreigners who spent time in Beijing in the early 1990s, as I did, were bound
to become regular customers of the "Friendship Store," which was virtually
the only purveyor in town of goods from abroad, such as wine, chocolate bars
and peanut butter, and Western-style toiletries, cosmetics, shoes and clothing.
Friendship Stores, which also existed in other major cities, were off-limits to
Chinese — a passport was required to gain entry — and Chinese people who
had developed tastes for exotic luxuries (American or European cigarettes,
for example) had to rely on foreign friends and acquaintances for supplies. It
was a vivid illustration of how closed China remained to the outside world
even after a decade and a half of Deng's reforms. Only later, in the 1990s, were

9   Lam, *China and the WTO* (see footnote 7 in this chapter), chapter 6.
10 Ibid., chapter 8.
11 Ibid., chapter 6.

restrictions on entry to Friendship Store loosened as imported goods became more widely available.

Then came WTO accession — and the opening-up process went into overdrive. Tariffs were reduced from 2002 to 2006 as per China's commitments, together with the elimination of import quotas on products such as air conditioners, cameras, watches and motorcycles; foreign enterprises took advantage of their newly bestowed rights to establish their own distribution networks. With barriers down and distribution channels formed, goods from abroad poured in. In 2002, China's merchandise imports totalled nearly $300 billion, topping 20 percent of GDP for the first time, and over the following five years, imports more than tripled in dollar terms, to $956 billion in 2007, or 27 percent of GDP. (By comparison, US imports were only 13.9 percent of GDP in 2007.)[12]

Beneficiaries included American and European airplane manufacturers, Brazilian and Canadian farmers, and Japanese and German machinery makers. Shipments of US goods to China rose from $16 billion in 2000 to nearly $70 billion in 2008; aerospace products and parts, semiconductors and other electronic components were particularly fast-growing sectors.[13] Commodity producers in South America, Africa and other emerging parts of the globe enjoyed huge spikes in prices for metals such as tin, nickel, lead and zinc, for which China contributed all or nearly all of world consumption growth during 2002–2005; for copper, aluminum and steel, China contributed about half of global growth during that period.[14] Another sector that flourished was agriculture. As more Chinese became better able to afford meat in their diets, and the raising of livestock in China turned to mass-production techniques, demand skyrocketed for soybean meal, which is used in animal feed — one result being that in America, roughly one in four of the acres planted in soybeans went for export to China.[15]

Thanks to China's easing of limits on the operations of companies based abroad, inflows of direct investment (spending on plant and equipment) by foreign firms also soared, from $47 billion in 2001 to $92 billion in 2008;[16]

12 World Bank data, available at: https://data.worldbank.org/indicator/TM.VAL.MRCH. CD.WT?locations=CN&view=chart.

13 US Census data, available at: www.census.gov/foreign-trade/balance/c5700.html.

14 IMF, 2006, *World Economic Outlook*, chapter 5, Washington, DC: IMF.

15 Joseph Glauber, 2017, "Likely Effects of a Trade War for US Agriculture? Sad!" Institute for the Advanced Study of Food and Agricultural Policy, University of Guelph.

16 Ken Davies, 2013, "China Investment Policy: An Update," Organisation for Economic Co-operation and Development (OECD) Working Papers on International Investment, 2013/01, OECD Publishing. http://dx.doi.org/10.1787/5k469l1hmvbt-en.

in 2002, China surpassed the United States as a destination for FDI, the first country since the 1980s to do so.[17] Many of those investment decisions were paying off handsomely. A survey of about 200 companies by the American Chamber of Commerce showed that nearly two-thirds were profitable, *The Wall Street Journal* reported in 2003, citing the following examples:

> China is now Eastman Kodak Co.'s second-biggest film market after the U.S., and sales here are growing faster than in any other major market, the film firm says. Food conglomerate Groupe Danone SA of France has in the past six years built a $1.2 billion business in China that is profitable in all its divisions.

> Germany's Siemens AG, selling everything from washing machines to high-speed railways, saw double-digit profit growth last year in China, now its No. 3 market after the U.S. and Germany. Procter & Gamble Co. has invested $1 billion in China and says its operation here is profitable. The KFC restaurant chain, owned by Yum Brands Inc., opens a new store every other day in China, all funded by its Chinese profits. "China is an absolute gold mine for us," Yum's chief executive David Novak told analysts recently.[18]

Not all foreign companies were so delighted; makers of movies, musical recordings, computer software and the like complained that the Chinese government was failing to rigorously enforce intellectual property laws against the copying of their products, despite promises that it would faithfully do so in accordance with WTO rules.[19] Even makers of old-line industrial goods were victimized, one example being Gormon-Rupp, a Mansfield, Ohio-based firm whose sewage pumps were reverse-engineered by a Chinese copycatter so brazen that customers buying knockoff Gormon-Rupp pumps even received authentic-looking Gormon-Rupp brochures.[20] Still, on the whole, Beijing got credit for adhering to most of its WTO commitments.[21] "The

17 Kenneth Lieberthal and Geoffrey Lieberthal, 2003, "The Great Transition," *Harvard Business Review*, October. China's status as the number one recipient of FDI didn't last long; in subsequent years it slipped to number three, behind the United States and the United Kingdom.

18 Leslie Chang and Peter Wonacott, 2003, "Multinationals Crack Market in China by Adopting Customs," *The Wall Street Journal*, January 9. Reprinted here with permission.

19 Charles Hutzler and Phelim Kyne, 2004, "U.S. Businesses Urge China to Rein in Piracy," *The Wall Street Journal*, September 17.

20 US Senate Governmental Affairs Committee Subcommittee on Oversight, 2004, "Written Statement of the Gorman-Rupp Company," Hearing on "Pirates of the 21st Century," April 20, www.hsgac.senate.gov/imo/media/doc/042004Gorman589.pdf. In fairness to China, Gormon-Rupp accused Brazilian pirates of similar offences.

21 Hutzler and Kyne, "U.S. Business Urge China to Rein in Piracy" (see footnote 19 in this chapter). The article noted that the American Chamber of Commerce in China "said Beijing was generally in compliance with its commitments... The outstanding exception: protection of intellectual property."

combination of China's pre-WTO and post-WTO reforms is making it arguably the most open large developing economy," scholars Lee Branstetter and Nicholas Lardy wrote in 2006.[22]

Such a drastic augmentation in market access had been regarded with dread by some Chinese, as noted in chapter 3. But far from sapping China's economic vitality, the opening-up coincided with a growth spurt of unprecedented dimensions. China's GDP, which in 2002 was sixth largest in the world in US dollar terms, leapt another couple of notches by 2006 to fourth place, behind the United States, Japan and Germany — and four years after that, China's output of goods and services surpassed Japan's to become number two. To be sure, in per capita terms, China's GDP still lagged far behind advanced countries (at $4,524 in 2010, GDP per capita in China was only about one-tenth of the Japanese and US levels). But GDP per capita was rising fast, as witnessed by auto sales, which swelled from one million in 2002 to 9.4 million vehicles in 2008.[23] Whereas only 11 Chinese companies ranked in the *Fortune* 500 list of top global firms by revenue in 2003, 89 of them made the list a decade later.

The pace of change rendered me goggle-eyed when, on a trip to Beijing in 2007 after a few years' absence, I stepped out of my hotel into a department store next door with white marble floors and gleaming counters tended by fashionably attired salespeople. The Chinese shoppers I saw there would have been barred from Friendship Stores in the early 1990s, but they were plunking down cash for items well out of my price range — Swiss watches, English bone china, German espresso machines and French perfume. Next to the department store stood a Mercedes-Benz dealership bustling with customers. The E-Class cars were made by a joint venture in Beijing, a salesman told me, but the other models on the floor were imported from Germany.

The real force driving the Chinese economy during this period, however, was to be found far from the glitz of that department store.

---

22 Lee Branstetter and Nicholas R. Lardy, 2006, "China's Embrace of Globalization," National Bureau of Economic Research (NBER) Working Paper 12373, July.

23 Facts and Details, "Automobiles Sales in China," http://factsanddetails.com/china/cat13/sub86/item314.html.

Atop former rice paddies and duck farms, hundreds of factories sprang up during the 1990s and early 2000s in the southern Chinese city of Dongguan, which became a town of "construction and motion, jackhammers and dust" where "migrants walk along the shoulders [of wide highways] carrying suitcases or bedding, while buses and trucks bear down from behind," according to *Factory Girls*, an illuminating account about the lives of young women who comprised the bulk of these labourers.[24] The factories — many of which were owned by Taiwanese and Hong Kong investors — assembled goods for export, such as alarm clocks, cameras, sweaters, shoes, televisions, disk drives, desktop computers, furniture, bicycles, stuffed animals and mobile phones. The story was much the same in Shenzhen, Guangzhou, Shantou and dozens of other cities in the Pearl River Delta and further north along China's coast. The migration from interior provinces that provided the workforce of these plants has been described as the largest peacetime movement of people in history — a *liudong renkou* (floating population) totalling some 150 million, about 10 million of whom made Dongguan their temporary home in the early 2000s.

Among the women whose life is chronicled in *Factory Girls* is Lu Qingmin, who left her village of 60 households in 2003 and joined the 1,000 employees at a Dongguan electronics plant where the workday stretched from 8:00 a.m. until midnight (13 hours on the assembly line and two meal breaks). Her pay was the equivalent of about $50 per month, with the opportunity to earn close to double that depending on overtime. "Workers slept twelve to a room in bunks crowded near the toilets; the rooms were dirty and they smelled bad," author Leslie Chang writes. "The food in the canteen was bad, too: A meal consisted of rice, one meat or vegetable dish, and soup, and the soup was watery." Most workers, including Lu, changed jobs often, in pursuit of better pay and working conditions, and many returned to their villages, but new migrants were constantly arriving to take their places.

Small consolation though it may have been for the workers enduring such hardship, the surge in goods they were manufacturing for customers abroad was the key factor fuelling China's growth during the early years of the country's WTO membership. China's exports shot up at a rate of about 30 percent annually from 2001 to 2006, more than twice the growth rate of the previous five years, and also far outstripping the growth of imports.[25]

24 Leslie Chang, 2008, *Factory Girls: From Village to City in a Changing China*, New York, NY: Spiegel & Grau.
25 World Bank data, https://data.worldbank.org/indicator/NE.EXP.GNFS.CD?locations=CN.

Just as WTO accession helped increase the amount of imports flooding into China, so did it increase the torrent of exports going out. The US granting of permanence to China's MFN status ended the uncertainty surrounding the annual vote on human rights. That, in turn, encouraged foreign investors to build plants in China, which were often aimed at the export market — foreign-invested enterprises accounted for roughly half of China's exports during the era following WTO accession.[26] And yet another major export-boosting factor was China's reduction in its own tariffs under the terms of its WTO protocol, which made inputs (machinery, raw materials and so on) cheaper for Chinese manufacturers, thereby enhancing their competitiveness on world markets. The Chinese industries with the largest growth in exports were those that had large reductions in their input tariffs, according to a study published by the Federal Reserve Bank of New York.[27]

In no sector was WTO entry more important — and China's export performance more formidable — than textiles and apparel. A complicated system of worldwide quotas had governed trade in this industry since 1974, specifying how much fabric and how many items of clothing (blue jeans, pajamas, brassieres, men's jackets and so on) an individual country could export to the lucrative markets of the United States and Europe. These quotas hampered China's exports, but under WTO-agreed rules the quota system was due to be completely phased out by 2005, and since China had joined the trade body, it would also benefit at that time. (This didn't mean Chinese textile and apparel exports would be completely unconstrained by trade barriers. Fairly steep tariffs, averaging 16 percent in the United States, would continue to be levied, and a special safeguard mechanism, applicable only to Chinese products, would remain available until 2008 for the United States and other countries to limit Chinese imports.)

By 2004, in anticipation of the day when quotas would expire, the Chinese textile and apparel industry was in fighting trim, having shed millions of surplus workers and invested heavily in a full array of operations — the spinning, weaving and dyeing of fabric; the cutting and stitching of clothing; and manufacture and attachment of buttons and zippers. China accounted for the lion's share of worldwide purchases of advanced weaving machines known as shuttleless looms. Brother Industries, the Japanese sewing machine company, was doubling its sales in China year after year. Highways and ports in coastal China allowed delivery to the United States in as few as 18 days, compared

---

26 Davies, "China Investment Policy: An Update" (see footnote 16 in this chapter).

27 Mary Amiti, Mi Dai, Robert C. Feenstra and John Romalis, 2017, "How Did China's WTO Entry Benefit U.S. Consumers?" Federal Reserve Bank of New York, Staff Report No. 817, June.

with 28 to 45, for example, for Sri Lanka. In Japan and Australia, two nations that had no quota restrictions, China already captured 70 percent of the textile market by 2004, and in the United States, when quotas were lifted in 2002 on products such as baby clothes and robes, China's share in this market jumped from 11 percent to 55 percent in a matter of months.[28]

China's textile industry workers — 18 million strong in 2004 — were not the lowest paid in the world. Their average wage, estimated at around 68 cents an hour, compared favourably with the less than 50 cents an hour paid to textile workers in places such as India, Pakistan and Bangladesh. But China enjoyed an edge in cost competitiveness not just because of its new investments and better infrastructure, but also because Chinese employees were forbidden from organizing independent unions and were sometimes victimized by bosses violating overtime and minimum-wage laws. As Ling Li, a Chinese technician working at a garment factory in Cambodia, told my *Washington Post* colleague Peter Goodman: "Here, you have Saturday and Sunday off. In China, there's no such thing as Sunday. We work every day."[29]

To labour-rights activists in the United States and other wealthy countries, the success of China's textile and apparel industry, and the lives of Dongguan's factory girls, were classic illustrations of the "race to the bottom" — a shift in production to countries with the lowest labour costs and laxest regulations, which would inexorably drag down living standards as well as environmental quality around the globe. Viewing the phenomenon from the standpoint of pure economics, however, China was simply taking its place in a long historical progression of industrial development, a look at which suggests that the race-to-the-bottom theorists have got the directionality wrong.

The first "loser" in the race, after all, was Britain, home of the original Dickensian factories, which churned out cotton textiles cut and stitched by people in the most desperate stratum of the nation's society, mainly women from rural areas and children from poorhouses. Taking jobs from the British in the early 1900s were mills along rivers in Massachusetts and New Hampshire where thousands of young women from the New England and Canadian countryside toiled at similarly repetitive drudgery, often for more than 70 hours a week, until the industry moved to southern US states to take advantage of farm girls (and many *were* girls, 13 years old and younger) willing to work for wages half those paid in the north. Meanwhile, by the 1930s,

---

28 Peter S. Goodman and Paul Blustein, 2004, "A New Pattern is Cut for Global Textile Trade," *The Washington Post*, November 17.

29 Ibid.

millions of young Japanese women, living in squalid company boarding houses and working 12-hour days for substantially less than their American counterparts, were producing a large portion of the world's cotton goods. And although Japan's industry revived after World War II — expanding into shoes, toys and other products — it fell prey to competition from Hong Kong, South Korea and Taiwan in the 1960s and 1970s. In this "race" — whose latest "marathoner" was China — each "defeat" was undoubtedly anguishing for the factory workers displaced. But that was simply part of the process by which these countries became modern, diversified industrial economies, as their buying power created demand for new goods and services, leading, in turn, to new industries and jobs.[30]

Pure economic theory also points to the conclusion that the explosion of China's exports would provide important benefits for economies abroad, in the form of lower prices. Any American shopper knows that many of the bargains on the shelves at Walmart or Target are made in China, and a number of studies have calculated the impact with some precision. Xavier Jaravel and Erick Sager, two economists who dug deep into US price and import data, found that Chinese competition generated substantial price reductions for US consumers — specifically, every one percentage point increase in the share of spending on Chinese goods in a given industry would lead to an average three percentage point fall in prices for that industry. The overall result of increased trade with China, this study concluded, was an abatement in inflation shaving nearly two percentage points from the US consumer price index between 2000 and 2007.[31]

Lower prices in US stores, of course, means more money in American pockets, which translates into more income that helps buoy US economic growth. American consumers saved a little more than $202 billion from 2000 to 2007 thanks to the low cost of Chinese imports, according to the Jaravel-Sager study.

For certain parts of the United States, however, the bonanza of Chinese goods flowing abroad was no blessing. Pure economic theory has its limits.

---

30 In summarizing the historical evidence against the race-to-the-bottom theory, I am indebted to the excellent discussion in Pietra Rivoli, 2005, *The Travels of a T-Shirt in the Global Economy: An Economist Examines the Markets, Power, and Politics of World Trade*, Hoboken, NJ: Wiley.

31 Xavier Jaravel and Erick Sager, 2018, "What are the Price Effects of Trade? Evidence from the U.S. and Implications for Quantitative Trade Models," BLS Working Paper 506, U.S. Bureau of Labor Statistics, September.

In the years prior to China's WTO accession, America's furniture makers thought they had little to fear from Chinese competition. The thinness of profit margins in the business, plus the cost of shipping bulky items across the Pacific, seemed certain to keep imports at bay, as did the difficulties of crafting the high-quality tables, chairs, beds and dressers that American consumers demanded. US towns with large numbers of furniture factories were thriving in the late 1990s as home purchases went on the upswing. One of the most prosperous — in 1997, it was the hub of the fastest-growing manufacturing metropolitan area in the country, with an unemployment rate that dipped below two percent — was Hickory, North Carolina, population 40,000, where the local community college offered courses in furniture production to help ease labour shortages at nearby plants.[32]

By the turn of the millennium, the US industry was reeling from an onslaught of imports, mostly from China, whose factories proved astoundingly adept at producing furniture close to the designs of the most prestigious brands at much lower cost. In the furniture showrooms of the retailer Rooms To Go, for example, "For $2,500...you can buy the six-piece Island Treasures II solid-oak bedroom set that includes a king-size, four-poster bed in a rich tropical-brown finish with hand-carved pineapple and tobacco-leaf patterns," *Businessweek* reported in 2003. "Such prices are possible because Rooms To Go, based in Seffner, Fla., has the furniture made in China," where wages were as low as 50¢ an hour — a fraction of the North Carolina level of $16 an hour.[33]

Between 2001 and 2005, at least 230 furniture plants were closed in the United States, and 55,000 jobs lost, as China's share of the US wood furniture market — a mere three percent in 1994 — reached 42 percent in 2002 and 60 percent in 2005. Across the Carolinas, Virginia and Tennessee, where the industry was concentrated, the landscape was scarred with vacant factories that had once produced brands such as Henredon, Ethan Allen, Drexel Heritage and La-Z-Boy. In Hickory, the jobless rate was headed into the double digits — it would peak at 15 percent in 2010 — and the number of people on disability benefits rose by half, while poverty rates doubled.

---

32 Information about the impact of Chinese imports on the US furniture industry comes from Michael K. Dugan, 2009, *The Furniture Wars: How America Lost a Fifty Billion Dollar Industry*, Conover, NC: Goosepen Studio & Press; Bob Davis and Jon Hilsenrath, 2016, "How the China Shock, Deep and Swift, Spurred the Rise of Trump," *The Wall Street Journal*, August 11; Howard Schneider, 2016, "Away from spotlight, U.S. manufacturers battle back from 'China shock,'" Reuters, August 4; Jon E. Hilsenrath, Peter Wonacott and Dan Morse, 2002, "Competition from Imports Hurts U.S. Furniture Makers," *The Wall Street Journal*, September 20; and Dan Morse, 2005, "Coping with the Asian Invasion," *The Wall Street Journal*, January 31.

33 Pete Engardio and Dexter Roberts, 2004, "Wielding a Heavy Hand Against China," *Businessweek*, June 21.

Scrambling to save their companies as orders shrivelled, industry executives outsourced much of their production — in some cases, all of it — to factories such as Dongguan's Lacquer Craft Manufacturing, which described itself as an "aircraft carrier for wood furniture" and whose Taiwanese owner started in the pool cue manufacturing business.

"American visitors to China could not help but be amused at first," recalled Michael Dugan, the former president of Henredon, in his 2009 book *The Furniture Wars*. "The roads were terrible; the drivers used to drive trucks for the Red Army; the factories were a mess, and some were owned by the government and run by the army." He continued: "On your next trip, you would be astonished at the progress. New hotels, super-highways, public transportation, expanded port facilities, and more furniture factories — all completed since your last visit….Gradually it dawns on you — yes, lower labor costs are a huge factor in China's expansion into the furniture industry, but it is more than that. Modern factories, technology, machinery, low front-office costs, and relentless energy helped fuel this fabled growth."[34]

The furniture industry was at the epicentre of a jolt to the US economy that diverged significantly from economists' understanding about the way trade affects jobs and living standards. Only later did the economics profession diagnose and label what had happened with the publication in 2016 of an article titled "The China Shock: Learning from Labor-Market Adjustment to Large Changes in Trade," by David Autor of the Massachusetts Institute of Technology, David Dorn of the University of Zurich and Gordon Hanson of the University of California, San Diego.[35] Building on an accumulation of research, the article presented evidence showing that in the years following China's WTO entry, Chinese imports had an impact on US employment, especially in manufacturing, that exceeded anything traditional economic models predicted.

The invasion of US markets by Japanese companies starting in the 1970s, and intensified competition from Mexico following the approval of NAFTA in 1994, had deprived many Americans of jobs. But the US economy generated a reasonable amount of new employment for those adversely affected, especially in the 1990s, a decade of unusually healthy job growth. Both economic theory and evidence indicated that most laid-off workers would readily find jobs at expanding firms in their areas or perhaps relocate to more prosperous parts of

---

34 Dugan, *The Furniture Wars* (see footnote 32 in this chapter), chapter 14.

35 David H. Autor, David Dorn and Gordon H. Hanson, 2016, "The China Shock: Learning from Labor Market Adjustment to Large Changes in Trade," *Annual Review of Economics* 2016 (8): 205–40.

the country. This experience reinforced the conventional wisdom among economists that trade, despite severely disrupting some workers' lives for periods of time, wasn't a major contributor to either joblessness or rising wage inequality.

Then, around 2000, "just as the economics profession was reaching consensus on the consequences of trade for wages and employment, an epochal shift in patterns of world trade was gaining momentum," Autor, Dorn and Hanson wrote. "China, for centuries an economic laggard, was finally emerging as a great power and toppling established patterns of trade accordingly."

What distinguished the China shock was, first of all, China's economic size, speed of growth and import penetration — an order of magnitude different from the previous episodes of foreign competitive pressure. Imports from China swelled from 1.0 percent of US GDP in 2000 to 2.6 percent in 2011, almost a full percentage point more than the highest comparable figure for Mexico or Japan. Second, and in some ways more important, was the impact on communities with concentrations of manufacturers that competed with Chinese producers. Employment in these areas stayed depressed for years as laid-off factory workers proved unable or disinclined to seek jobs elsewhere. In addition to Hickory, another hard hit furniture-making town was Tupelo, Mississippi; other affected communities included Providence, Rhode Island (jewellery), San Jose, California (electronics), West Plains, Missouri (shoes) and Murray, Kentucky (toys).

Together with other economists, the Autor-Dorn-Hanson team scrutinized employment and layoffs in the industries most exposed to Chinese competition. The increase in Chinese imports, they calculated, resulted in the direct loss of 560,000 manufacturing jobs from 1999 to 2011 — roughly one-tenth of the total decline in manufacturing jobs in the United States during that period. But the job losses that could be attributed to China were greater because of knock-on effects, which were also likely to have concentrated impacts. For example, "rising import competition in apparel and furniture — two sectors in which China is strong — will cause these 'downstream' industries to reduce purchases from the 'upstream' sectors that supply them with fabric, lumber, and textile and woodworking machinery," the economists wrote, adding that this will affect the same communities "because buyers and suppliers often locate [near] one another." Beyond that, employment will fall because of other linkages, such as reduced spending by laid-off workers on goods and services. Using "input-output" analysis and other methods to estimate the linkages, the economists concluded that the employment impact of Chinese imports during 1999 to 2011 was a net loss of 2.4 million US jobs, including about 985,000 manufacturing jobs.

In interviews after the term "China shock" got wide circulation in the media, the economists involved in these studies emphasized that their findings shouldn't be construed as contradicting the argument in favour of trade. Overall benefits to the US economy will still exceed costs, they contended, and the China shock was not a permanent phenomenon — indeed, it was already abating by the time the studies were published. Chinese imports were no longer rising as a share of the US economy, in part because Chinese workers were earning higher wages, and even towns like Hickory were finally bouncing back. But the devastation that had occurred was indisputable and, to economists at least, novel. As Hanson explained:

> The stunning thing was a decade out, the regions that specialized in the same industries in which China was exporting products hadn't really recovered. We had a sense coming out of analysis of labor markets in the '60s and '70s and '80s that the US economy is a pretty dynamic place. If workers lose their jobs in one industry, they're going to find jobs in another industry tomorrow or the week after or the next quarter. And if they don't, then they'll just move somewhere else. Labor will follow capital in terms of where the opportunities are.
>
> And what we found was that simply wasn't the case. These regional labor markets that were in direct line of competition with China didn't recover quickly. In fact, they didn't even recover over the medium term. And perhaps the most surprising thing was that as economic conditions deteriorated in these locations — so this is, you know, the places in Southern Ohio and the northern South which are part of the manufacturing belt — workers just didn't leave.[36]

To keep the China shock in perspective, it is important to recognize that the estimated job loss of 2.4 million attributed to Chinese imports occurred during a period of time when total US employment rose by 2.1 million, to 132.9 million. And although the loss of manufacturing jobs in particular causes much hand-wringing, the United States is far from the only country in the world to suffer such a fate — pretty much the same has happened

36 James Pethokoukis, 2017, "We've had the 'China trade shock. What now? A Q&A with Gordon Hanson," *AEIdeas* (blog), the American Enterprise Institute, January 18.

over the past half-century to Germany, a country whose manufacturers and supporting government policies enjoy a sterling reputation. Manufacturing employment in Germany has fallen by more than half since 1971, as economic historian Brad DeLong pointed out in a critique of the China shock analysis, while manufacturing jobs in America fell about 62 percent over the same period.[37] The main reason is rising productivity (output per worker) stemming in large part from advancing technology and automation; in the early 1950s, a halcyon era for factory jobs in the United States, "lower productivity (compared with today) meant that many more workers were required to make each car, each refrigerator, each chair. That kept US manufacturing large in terms of employment," De Long wrote. A shrinking manufacturing workforce, in other words, is not necessarily indicative of economic decline — on the contrary, it is an inevitable part of economic advancement. As countries rise from poverty to wealth, their labour forces shift from agriculture (which accounted for nearly half of US jobs in 1870)[38] to manufacturing and then to services and technology.

The cliché that trade produces both winners and losers applies to the China shock as well, and not only because the cheapness of Chinese imports gave Americans more money to spend. Even as leading US furniture companies were closing manufacturing plants and outsourcing production to China, they were opening a number of retail stores around the country to sell their imported wares — which required the hiring of sizable sales staffs. Based on US manufacturing and trade data for the period 1991–2011, Robert Feenstra of the University of California, Davis, together with a team of colleagues, showed that the impact on manufacturing jobs from trade wasn't entirely negative in the United States. Companies that exported manufactured goods globally added enough new jobs to "largely offset job losses due to China's imports," according to the Feenstra-led study (although it should be noted that the export figures in the study were for sales abroad to all countries whereas the import figures pertained only to China).[39]

But it's also a trade cliché that the winners and losers are not the same people, and the safety net for trade's losers in the United States is notoriously tattered. The main federal government program, Trade Adjustment Assistance (TAA),

37 J. Bradford DeLong, 2017, "NAFTA and other trade deals have not gutted American manufacturing — period," Vox, January 24, www.vox.com/the-big-idea/2017/1/24/14363148/trade-deals-nafta-wto-china-job-loss-trump.

38 Patricia A. Daly, 1981, "Agricultural Employment: Has the Decline Ended?" *Monthly Labor Review*, November.

39 Robert Feenstra, Hong Ma, Akira Sasahara and Yuan Xu, 2018, "Reconsidering the 'China shock' in trade," Voxeu.org, January 18, https://voxeu.org/article/reconsidering-china-shock-trade.

is supposed to provide job training and transitional support to Americans who become unemployed due to foreign competition. But TAA has long suffered from underfunding and bureaucratic red tape that has kept eligible workers from getting benefits or even trying. Other countries devote much greater resources to such programs — Denmark, a particularly outstanding example, spends two percent of GDP helping unemployed workers back into the workforce, which is roughly 20 times the amount spent by the United States.[40] And regarding the China shock, here's the punchline: Autor, Dorn and Hanson found that in areas most heavily affected by Chinese imports, the type of federal aid that many laid-off workers turned to was Social Security Disability Insurance, which provides recipients with government payments and Medicare benefits if a doctor certifies that they are unable to work — a virtual guarantee of permanent withdrawal from the labour force. Incredibly, per-capita Social Security disability payments increased 30 times more than TAA payments in China-shocked regions.

Other countries were also hit by some variant of the China shock, as shown in studies of labour markets in Spain, Britain, Norway, among others.[41] Turkish textile companies shed about one-tenth of their workforce in 2005-2006 due to Chinese competition,[42] and in 2007, Brazil announced plans to raise duties on apparel and footwear, from 20 percent to the bound rate of 35 percent, in response to intense pressure from the country's clothing and shoe manu-facturers. They employed 1.6 million Brazilians and were clamouring for relief from imports, which had more than doubled over the preceding three years, with China supplying about half of those foreign goods.[43]

The casualties even included "sweatshops" in some of the world's poorest countries. Consider the tale of Danubia Rodriguez, a Honduran version of Dongguan's factory girls. The mountain village where Rodriguez grew up picking coffee beans with her family required a one-hour hike to reach from the nearest dirt road. She attended school only up to sixth grade, since the village had no school for higher grades, and left in 1998 to work in an apparel

40 Edward Alden, 2017, *Failure to Adjust: How Americans Got Left Behind in the Global Economy,* Lanham, MD: Rowman & Littlefield Publishers, chapter 5. According to Alden, "France and Germany spend five times as much [of their GDPs on these sorts of programs, compared to the percent of GDP spent by the United States]. Every other major economy spends at least twice what the United States does."

41 *The Economist,* 2016, "Coming and Going," September 29; see also Stefan Thewissen and Olaf van Vliet, 2018, "Chinese imports and domestic employment across 18 OECD countries," VOX CEPR Policy Portal, September 6, https://voxeu.org/article/chinese-imports-and-domestic-employment-across-18-oecd-countries.

42 Helen Murphy, Christopher Swann and Mark Drajem, 2007, "China's Power Erodes Free-Trade Support in Developing Nations," Bloomberg News, April 2.

43 Cited in Paul Blustein, *Misadventures of the Most Favored Nations,* New York, NY: Public Affairs, chapter 11.

plant. By 2004, when I met her for an article I was writing, Rodriguez was one of more than 130,000 Hondurans who had gotten jobs at new plants, or *maquilas*, and the $1.50 an hour she earned stitching Hanes brand sports shirts enabled her to afford luxuries not dreamed of in village life — a cinder block house with a gas stove, indoor plumbing, television and the electricity to power it and a diet that had moved beyond rice, beans and tortillas to include regular portions of meat, fish and fresh vegetables. But she was out of the job that made her rise in living standards possible. A few weeks earlier, the company that owned her *maquila* shut it down, depriving her and her co-workers of their incomes — the chief reason, company officials confided, was competition from China.[44]

Another victim of China's industrial machine — the damage could aptly be called "collateral" — was the WTO's Doha Round. When the round was launched in 2001, rich countries had anticipated that in exchange for granting more trade benefits to poor nations, they would secure ambitious market-opening commitments from fast-growing and populous emerging markets, such as Brazil, India, South Africa and Egypt. Wealthy nations already have very low tariffs on most manufactured goods, and in industries where they were especially competitive — chemicals, machinery and medical equipment, for example — they wanted barriers lowered significantly world-wide. But at a time when China was bestriding the manufacturing world like a colossus, the idea of cutting tariffs wasn't going over well in parts of Latin America, Africa and developing Asia, where company executives were trembling at the prospect of decimation at the hands of Chinese imports. In July 2008, the Doha Round broke down after nine days of fruitless meetings in Geneva, and although a number of factors were involved, one of the most often-cited by participating trade ministers was "the elephant in the room" — Chinese competition, which made many shrink from offering concessions.[45] No previous global trade round had ended in failure; efforts to revive the Doha talks in subsequent years repeatedly came up short.

So it goes in the jungle of global trade. China should not be begrudged the competitive success that was attributable to the hard work of its people, its investment in modern equipment and its building of efficient infrastructure. Furthermore, in the process of becoming the lean and mean exporter

---

44 Goodman and Blustein, "A New Pattern is Cut for Global Textile Trade" (see footnote 28 in this chapter).

45 The dynamics that led to the Doha Round's failure are covered extensively in my 2009 book *Misadventures of the Most Favored Nations* (see footnote 43 in this chapter). China drew a substantial amount of blame in the media, mainly because of clever spin by US officials, for the collapse of the July 2008 meeting — unfairly so, in my view. See chapter 13 of the book for a detailed account of that meeting.

that caused the China shock, the Chinese economy had suffered plenty of dislocation too. The restructuring of loss-making SOEs that had begun in the mid-1990s was continuing in the years after WTO accession, leading to joblessness on a scale that would have been unthinkable during the era of the iron rice bowl. Employment in SOEs and urban collectives shrank by about 70 million jobs between 1994 and 2006.[46] Although the official unemployment rate, as reported by the government, was barely above four percent, independent estimates put the figure much higher; one study calculated that joblessness in China averaged nearly 11 percent from 2002 to 2009.[47] Luckily for those laid off by SOEs, the private sector was generating a plethora of jobs. Private sector employment rose to 281 million in 2010, nearly four times the 1990 level.[48]

But hard work, investment, good infrastructure, leanness and meanness did not tell the whole story. China was giving itself a leg up in global markets that went beyond the normal rough and tumble of international capitalism.

46 World Bank, 2009, "China: From Poor Areas to Poor People," Report No. 47349- CN, March 5.

47 Shuaizhang Feng, Yingyao Hu and Robert Moffitt, 2015, "Long Run Trends in Unemployment and Labor Force Participation in China," NBER Working Paper No. 21460, August.

48 Nicholas R. Lardy, 2014, *Markets Over Mao: The Rise of Private Business in China*, Washington, DC: Peterson Institute for International Economics, September, chapter 1.

CHAPTER 5

CHEAP CURRENCY: IF ONLY THERE WERE RULES

In December 2001, just weeks after China's admission to the WTO, a veteran staffer at the IMF named Steven Dunaway became the Fund's mission chief for China. This meant that Dunaway, an American with a Ph.D. in economics from George Washington University, would head the team that the IMF sent each year to Beijing to conduct discussions with Chinese policy makers about economic and financial developments. Such discussions, which take place annually with most IMF member countries, are called "Article IV consultations" in the Fund's stodgy parlance (because they are required under Article IV of the Fund's articles of agreement). Following those discussions, Dunaway would also supervise the drafting of the IMF's annual Article IV report on China, assessing China's economic conditions and offering the Fund's recommendations on policy, which in turn would be submitted to the Fund's board, whose 24 members represent the 189 member countries.

The Article IV process is often bureaucratic and humdrum, but on occasion major issues are at stake and great controversy arises. For reasons that will be explained later in this chapter, a battle over one of China's Article IV reports would prove exceptionally consequential — the central bone of contention being the exchange rate of the Chinese currency, the renminbi (RMB).

Readers who wonder how Beijing kept its currency so cheap for so long will find the details revelatory. As we shall see, US efforts to muscle a change in China's currency policy produced some victories; however, they were short lived and hollow, and ended ignominiously in 2008 with the eruption of the financial crisis.[1]

Most of the world's major countries allowed their currencies to float in value on international markets, in accord with supply and demand, during the latter decades of the twentieth century. Not China, which used a different system that relied on strict controls over inflows and outflows of capital. Starting in 1994, Beijing pegged the RMB at 8.28 per US dollar, and for the first few years, this policy drew scant attention as the country's exports remained more or less in line with imports. But in the post-WTO accession period, China's exports not only soared but also outpaced imports by a wide margin, as noted in the previous chapter. Beijing's current account surplus — the broadest measure of the surfeit of exports over imports — amounted to more than seven percent of GDP in 2005, a higher percentage of its economy than either Japan or Germany had ever achieved.

Instead of allowing its currency to appreciate, which would normally happen in a country with a huge surplus, China held it down by intervening on a massive scale in currency markets to keep the RMB at the rate of 8.28 per dollar. Even when other currencies began rising substantially against the greenback in 2002 — including the euro, British pound, Japanese yen and the Canadian and Australian dollars — the RMB's exchange rate against the US dollar remained the same.

On the missions he led to Beijing, Dunaway argued that the RMB was significantly undervalued and that Chinese officials should loosen the exchange rate so that the currency could rise. He had a tough sell. His interlocutors liked to point out that during the Asian financial crisis, the IMF had been applauding them for doing exactly the opposite — keeping the RMB fixed against the dollar to help prevent currencies in the region from plunging out of control. The Chinese were also fond of citing a handful of prominent Western economists, including some Nobel Prize winners, who asserted that the RMB was appropriately valued. To these arguments, Dunaway and his team responded with a host of data showing unmistakable signs of undervaluation, and above all, they stressed that considerable benefits would accrue to China from a

---

1   Much of this chapter (although not all) is derived from a book I published in 2013, *Off Balance: The Travails of Institutions That Govern the Global Financial System*, Waterloo, ON: CIGI. That book was based heavily on confidential documents not available in the public record.

stronger RMB, including a stimulation of consumer spending (as imported goods became cheaper), which in turn would make the economy less dangerously dependent on exports and low-return business investment. In the IMF's Article IV report on China in 2005, the Fund publicly declared that evidence "points to increased undervaluation of the renminbi, adding to the urgency of making a move...greater exchange rate flexibility continues to be in China's best interest."[2]

IMF staffers could have added, of course, that China's currency policy was widely perceived as iniquitous in the United States. But there was no need for the Fund to belabour this point. A hue and cry was arising among American companies, labour unions and many economists, who saw the fixed-rate RMB as a classic manipulation of market forces to benefit Chinese workers at the expense of US workers (although American consumers enjoyed cheaper Chinese goods as a result).

Ranking high on the list of hard-hit US industries were manufacturers of automobile parts. American auto parts makers had expected to reap a bonanza from China's WTO accession, and for a while after 2001, the profits materialized pretty much as anticipated. Every month hundreds of thousands of Chinese were buying their first cars, many of which were full of US-made components, since the country's rapidly growing auto industry depended heavily on imported engines, transmissions, seating-control systems and the like. Moreover, China was cutting tariffs sharply on auto parts in accordance with its accession commitments.

But by 2005, the tables were turning. That year, for the first time, China exported more auto parts than it bought from abroad, with shipments to the US market leaping 39 percent to $5.4 billion.[3] The influx of Chinese parts exacerbated the woes of a US industry that was already struggling, as witnessed by the bankruptcy filing in October 2005 of Delphi Corp., the biggest US auto parts maker. While labour costs explained much about why Chinese firms had successfully penetrated sectors such as furniture and footwear, the exchange rate of the RMB was a major factor in the hyper-competitiveness of China's auto parts makers.

To show how the exchange rate affected his company, Larry Denton, the chairman and CEO of Dura Automotive Systems Inc., provided some

---

2   IMF, 2005, "People's Republic of China: 2005 Article IV Consultations — Staff Report," IMF Country Report No. 05/411, November, www.imf.org/external/pubs/ft/scr/2005/cr05411.pdf.

3   Peter S. Goodman and Paul Blustein, 2006, "China's Export Engine: Competitors Crying Foul Over Cheap Currency," *The Washington Post*, September 13.

persuasive arithmetic when I interviewed him in 2006 for a story I was writing. Headquartered in Rochester Hills, Michigan, Dura employed more than 6,000 Americans at 27 US factories and also had factories in China, so Denton had a good grasp of production costs in each country. He cited one of his products, parking brake cables, as a clear illustration of the exchange rate phenomenon.

Parking brake cables made at Dura's US factories sold for $4.50 apiece, with the company earning a profit of 35 cents on each cable, according to Denton. The sales price in the US market for comparable Chinese-made cables was $3.70, effectively less than the US cost of production, especially considering that 55 cents of that price reflected logistics (transportation across the Pacific and other importation costs). "If I were to balance the currency at the appropriate level" — that is, by raising the RMB as much as the euro, British pound and other currencies had risen against the US dollar in the past several years — "the Chinese sell price and the US sell price would be nearly identical, at $4.50," Denton told me. "We would compete in a level marketplace."[4]

A couple of months after I spoke with Denton, the company announced that its US and Canadian subsidiaries were filing for bankruptcy protection from creditors, and it soon thereafter embarked on a restructuring plan that included the closure of four plants in Indiana, Missouri, Pennsylvania and Ontario. The bankruptcy was attributable to a number of factors — rising raw material costs and production cuts by US automakers — but Chinese competition, aided by the cheap RMB, was also partly to blame.[5]

Here was the conundrum: nothing in China's WTO accession protocol required it to float the RMB or maintain any particular level for it against the dollar or any other currency. When the currency issue arose briefly during the accession negotiations, the powerful US Treasury had asserted its jurisdiction over the issue, telling Barshefsky and her fellow trade negotiators that exchange rates are a matter of international financial policy and are therefore in the bailiwick of finance ministries (i.e., the Treasury) and the IMF, not the WTO. And nothing in WTO rules expressly forbad China from cheapening its currency. The trade body's rules include broad provisions prohibiting countries from using "exchange action" to "frustrate the intent" of the agreements opening global markets,[6] or employing other subterfuge to "nullify or impair"

---

4   Ibid.

5   Reuters, 2006, "Dura Automotive files for bankruptcy," October 30; Reuters, 2007, "Dura Automotive to close 4 plants, sell 2 businesses," April 3.

6   Article XV of the GATT, "Exchange Arrangements."

the rights of other countries under the WTO treaty.[7] But these rules are murky, and have never been tested, and they clearly indicate that the WTO should defer to the IMF as the arbiter on exchange rate issues.

Indignant members of Congress introduced a variety of bills aimed at remedying this injustice. The most popular bill — it garnered 67 Senate supporters at one point — was one introduced by Senators Charles Schumer, a New York Democrat, and Lindsey Graham, a South Carolina Republican, which would impose 27.5 percent tariffs on Chinese goods, based on estimates by some analysts of the RMB's undervaluation.[8]

Noisy though such bombast may have been, US options were extremely limited. Slapping tariffs on Chinese goods unilaterally would be an egregious violation of WTO rules and would surely lead to economic warfare between Washington and Beijing — a nightmare scenario under almost any sensible estimation as far as the administration of George W. Bush was concerned. Interdependence bound the US and Chinese economies together in an embrace popularly dubbed "Chimerica,"[9] despite — or rather because of — their vast differences. By shipping tons of merchandise to American consumers, China was accumulating hundreds of billions of dollars annually, which it plowed into US securities of all kinds including US Treasury bonds and the bonds issued by US government-sponsored enterprises such as Fannie Mae and Freddie Mac. For its part, the United States, with its low savings rate, relied on that inflow of Chinese capital — and capital from other nations — to help keep interest rates down. Beijing got manufacturing jobs to lift its "floating population" out of poverty, while Americans got cheap electronic devices, clothing and other imported goods, together with bargain-rate mortgages. The two nations were linked in other ways, including the fact that many goods exported from China came from enterprises owned or partly owned by US firms. Furthermore, a web of supply chains extended throughout Asia where thousands of companies depended on selling components to China for assembly into finished products. A trade conflict that disrupted those supply chains and endangered the Chimerica arrangement would risk battering the entire regional economy — and probably the global economy as well, US officials believed.

---

7   Article XXIII of the GATT, "Nullification or Impairment."

8   Greg Robb, 2005, "China tariff bill gaining support-Schumer says," Marketwatch.com, June 8.

9   The term was popularized by British historian Niall Ferguson, who coined it together with German economist Moritz Schularick in 2006.

The US Treasury even shrank from naming China a "manipulator" of its currency in the semi-annual reports the department was required to issue regarding the foreign exchange policies of US trading partners. While privately acknowledging that the RMB was manipulated, Treasury officials feared that using such a politically explosive term would validate arguments for protectionist legislation and risk a trade war. They were able to avoid doing so thanks to a loophole in the law governing their reports. This law contained language targeting countries that manipulated exchange rates "to gain an unfair competitive advantage." It was impossible to prove that Chinese policy makers were motivated by a desire for competitive advantage, Treasury officials insisted. (Chinese officials often cited stability of the banking system to justify their policy — unconvincingly, as far as their US counterparts were concerned, but it was a different rationale than competitiveness.) The most effective approach, Treasury officials believed, would be diplomacy — the quieter the better because China would want to avoid even the appearance of giving in to US pressure. So off to Beijing went one of Washington's most seasoned financial diplomats.

"Mr. Kissinger says 10 percent. Is that your number?" Chinese Premier Wen Jiabao demanded.

It was May 25, 2005, and Wen was brandishing a copy of the *Financial Times*, which quoted former US Secretary of State Henry Kissinger stating that China needed to raise the RMB exchange rate by 10 percent. Wen's interlocutor was Olin Wethington, an attorney and former US economic official who had been dispatched as a special envoy of the Bush administration at the request of Treasury Secretary John Snow.

"Mr. Premier, I hadn't been aware of that, but with all due respect to Mr. Kissinger, that's not the American government's position," Wethington replied, according to his recollection in an interview. "OK, give me a number," Wen shot back, to which Wethington replied: "This is not about a number. We have too much respect for the market to give you a number. If your market was completely open, with the currency trading freely and without foreign exchange controls, we frankly don't know whether it would go up or down. This is about the quality of the exchange-rate mechanism and market-driven supply and demand."

That was the Bush administration's message on the RMB: flexibility, rather than a specific target for the exchange rate, was what mattered, and it would be in China's own economic interest to pursue such flexibility and market orientation for its currency and financial system in general. Wethington and others in the US government who engaged with the Chinese on this issue stuck with that argument, which they saw as the only approach likely to persuade Beijing because Chinese policy makers themselves were sharply divided.

The People's Bank of China (the central bank) and, in particular, its governor, Zhou Xiaochuan, were in favour of moving fairly rapidly toward letting the RMB rise and fall with market forces — that is natural for central bankers, who want to focus monetary policy on achieving price and financial stability rather than maintaining a fixed exchange rate. But many other centres of power in Beijing were adamantly opposed to tinkering with the RMB, including officials in economic planning agencies and the Ministry of Commerce. The opponents were coy about their reasoning in public, but feared that even a modest rise in the exchange rate might lead to large-scale unemployment in an export sector full of low-margin businesses — a huge worry for a regime whose legitimacy depended on its ability to generate jobs for millions of migrant workers. The opponents' attitude, as summed up by another former Beijing-based US Treasury official whom I interviewed, was, "We're growing at 10 percent a year with almost no inflation, and you're telling me there's a big problem with our exchange rate? You Americans are trying to contain our growth. You don't want a strong China."

Wethington operated as far under the radar as possible. His appointment was publicly announced[10] to show congressional hawks, such as Schumer and Graham, that the administration was working on the currency issue, but he cultivated allies in Beijing without fanfare and made sure to refrain from any hint of bullying or threatening, even in private, lest his mission backfire. Fearing leaks, he conveyed word to senior officials in Washington about his progress using the most secure modes of communication available. He requested a "window of silence" during which Schumer and Graham would keep their legislation in abeyance, so that the Chinese could change policy without feeling they had a gun to their head. At the same time, he asked his Chinese interlocutors for a confidential commitment that action would be forthcoming soon, as an inducement for Schumer and Graham to exercise restraint.

Wethington didn't know exactly when or how much China would move, but by mid-July 2005 he felt confident that the policy would change at least in a

---

10 US Department of the Treasury, 2005, "Treasury Secretary Snow Appoints Olin L. Wethington as Special Envoy on China," Press Release, May 19, www.treasury.gov/press-center/press-releases/Pages/js2459.aspx.

modest way, and he was right. On July 21, the central bank announced that it would increase the RMB exchange rate by 2.1 percent and would hence-forth allow the currency to fluctuate more widely than before. Widespread enthusiasm greeted this decision, which sounded as if it would soon lead to further RMB appreciation, but the Chinese currency rose painfully slowly in the months thereafter. Dissatisfaction remained strong in US industry circles and on Capitol Hill about the still grossly undervalued RMB.[11]

Given the limited upsides of bilateral diplomacy — and the downsides of unilateral US action — the idea of using multilateral institutions began to appeal more to the Bush administration. Robert Zoellick, who was US trade representative during Bush's first term, had ordered his staff to look closely at the option of bringing a complaint to a WTO tribunal. They concluded that the risks were unacceptably high because if the United States lost — as appeared likely — China would have gained even more validation for its currency practices. "The bottom line was, the WTO rules are thin, and rely on a finding by the IMF," said John Veroneau, who was the general counsel of the USTR at the time. "So in an environment where the IMF hasn't rendered a decision that country X is manipulating its currency, I thought we would have a very difficult time winning a WTO case."

Ah yes, the IMF.

———————————————

Like the GATT, the IMF was a postwar institution designed to ensure that the world would never again witness an epidemic of the "beggar-thy-neigh-bour" follies of the interwar period. These mutually deleterious policies, in addition to the erection of high tariff walls to protect domestic industries, had included the depreciation of exchange rates by a number of countries in desperate bids to spur exports and curb imports. Replacing that chaos with a rules-based cooperative institution was the vision of two men primarily responsible for shaping the Fund — John Maynard Keynes of the British Treasury and Harry Dexter White of the US Treasury. The institution that emerged, after a three-week international conference in Bretton Woods, New Hampshire in 1944, policed a system of fixed exchange rates during the first quarter century after World War II. When that system broke down in the early 1970s, the IMF's primary purpose became that of crisis preventer and manager. The Fund's articles and rules were changed to give member countries

---

11 Paul Blustein, 2005, "'Watershed' Yuan Revaluation Has Made Few Waves; China's Currency Has Barely Budged," *The Washington Post*, September 21.

wide latitude in choosing their exchange rate regimes — countries could allow exchange rates to float freely according to forces of supply and demand, or to be loosely pegged against other currencies, or to be rigidly fixed, or to be included in a currency union (such as the euro). But the institution was still responsible for "exercis[ing] firm surveillance over the exchange rate policies of members," which included a duty to prevent beggar-thy-neighbour policies. As the articles (from which the US Treasury's legal obligations were derived) stated: "Each member shall...avoid manipulating exchange rates or the international monetary system in order to...gain unfair competitive advantage over other members."

China's currency policy, in the view of a growing chorus of Western economists, was exactly what the founders of the IMF had in mind when they created an institution aimed at preventing countries from depreciating their currencies to enhance their industrial competitiveness. Dunaway may have been trying his darndest to convince the Chinese to revalue, but why wasn't the Fund doing more? In late September 2005, that argument got a forceful endorsement in a policy address that came to be known as the "asleep at the wheel speech," delivered by Timothy Adams, the newly installed US under secretary of the Treasury for international affairs.[12] A 43-year-old Kentuckian with an all-American demeanour, Adams issued a broadside at the Fund's handling of China's foreign exchange rate, although China was not mentioned by name. Adams wanted to see the IMF take up the cudgels; the language used in Fund reports was a far cry from a warning that the Chinese were playing fast and loose with the rules of the system.

As Adams noted in his speech, the IMF managing director was empowered to initiate "special consultations" with countries that were suspected of engaging in currency manipulation, with the implicit threat that the matter would be brought to the Fund's executive board where the alleged violator could be subject to further "naming and shaming." This authority, however, had only been invoked twice (both times in the 1980s), Adams pointed out, and in the absence of stern action by the Fund, aggrieved politicians — such as those in Congress — might resort to unilateral measures, with ruinous consequences. Hence his conclusion: "The perception that the IMF is asleep at the wheel on its most fundamental responsibility — exchange rate surveillance — is very unhealthy for the institution and the international monetary system."

---

12 Timothy Adams, 2005, "The U.S. View on IMF Reform," speech presented at the Conference on IMF Reform, Institute for International Economics, Washington, DC, September 23, www.iie.com/publications/papers/paper.cfm?ResearchID=564.

Adams's remarks landed with a thud in the IMF's executive suite where the initial reaction was to push back hard. "The influence of the Fund in the world comes almost entirely from its ability to persuade its members that they should follow its advice," declared Rodrigo de Rato, the IMF's managing director and Spain's former finance minister, in comments at the same conference where Adams had spoken. "If you're in a room with a friend you don't need to talk through a megaphone."[13] Along with many of his IMF colleagues, de Rato was irritated by what he saw as a US gambit to get the Fund to do Washington's dirty work.

Still, no IMF managing director can go too far in defying the United States, which is the Fund's biggest shareholder. And although the accusation of "asleep at the wheel" may have been aggravating, it rang true to a number of influential Fund policy makers, especially because the cheap RMB was contributing to a development that was stirring an increasing amount of head-scratching and hand-wringing around the world in the first few years of the twenty-first century.

Economic globalization was working in unexpected and arguably aberrant ways, commonly known as "global imbalances." Capital was flowing in unprecedented quantities from developing countries to advanced ones — Chimerica being only the biggest and catchiest example. Other emerging markets in addition to China (standouts included South Korea, Brazil and oil-exporting nations, such as Russia) were building up giant surpluses from their exports and investing the proceeds in US Treasury bonds and other similar assets. The unbalanced result was prominently reflected in the ever-widening US current account deficit, which by 2004 had surpassed $600 billion, or nearly six percent of GDP, and continued to swell thereafter. Although some analysts believed the imbalances could persist for decades, many feared that America's profligacy would lead sooner or later to a day of reckoning, most likely in the form of a crash in the dollar and a worldwide dumping of US securities. Since one key factor fuelling American purchases of Chinese goods was the low and government-managed RMB exchange rate, that was a legitimate source of concern for the IMF, not only because of the implications for Beijing and Washington but globally as well.

---

13 Rodrigo de Rato, 2006, "The IMF View on IMF Reform," in *Reforming the IMF for the 21st Century*, Edwin M. Truman (ed.), Special Report 19, Peterson Institute for International Economics, www.iie.com/publications/chapters_preview/3870/03iie3870.pdf.

The IMF therefore embarked on an initiative aimed at rectifying these problems, including China's currency policy.[14] This initiative was inspired to some degree by high-minded hopes for a breakthrough in the governance of the global economy, but it was destined to run up against cold, hard facts about the difficulties that often afflict international institutions' dealings with powerful member nations. And the outbreak of the global financial crisis would seal the initiative's doom. The result would be a debacle, one of the most embarrassing in the IMF's history.

What follows is a look back at this process, peering into the IMF's inner workings, based on interviews with scores of policy makers who were involved and thousands of pages of confidential documents — memos, emails, meeting notes and transcripts. The saga helps explain China's success in averting international action against its currency policy, and more broadly, it affords insight into the shifting global power dynamics by which China has been able to manage its economy in ways that grate on its trading partners' sense of fairness.

Among the 2,800 employees in the IMF's downtown Washington headquarters, many work in departments that oversee the regions of the world where the Fund's member countries are located — the Asia Pacific Department (on whose staff Dunaway served), the European Department, the African Department and so on. But one department, the Strategy, Policy and Review Department,[15] rides herd on the others, and is known sardonically as the "thought police," both because of its power and its role as enforcer of institutional orthodoxy. In 2006, the director of this department, an avuncular Englishman named Mark Allen, took charge of a small group of staffers to draft a revision of the IMF's rules regarding exchange rates. The reason for this project — here was another conundrum — was that the IMF's rules, like those of the WTO, failed to clearly prohibit China's policy of suppressing the RMB.

---

14 In addition to the initiative recounted in this book, known as the "2007 Decision on Bilateral Surveillance over Members' Policies," there was a second IMF initiative. Called the "Multilateral Consultations," it involved the Fund convening representatives of five major economies — the United States, China, the euro zone, Japan and Saudi Arabia — to discuss plans to shrink global imbalances. The story of the Multilateral Consultations is not particularly relevant to this book, but for details, and a more detailed account of the 2007 decision, see my book, *Off Balance* (see footnote 1 in this chapter), and a research paper, Paul Blustein, 2012, *A Flop and a Debacle: Inside the IMF's Global Rebalancing Acts*, CIGI Papers No. 4, June, Waterloo, ON: CIGI, www.cigionline.org/publications/flop-and-debacle-inside-imfs-global-rebalancing-acts.

15 The department's title at the time was Policy Development and Review, but for simplicity's sake the current name is being used.

The wording in the IMF's guidelines, focusing as it did on "manipulating exchange rates…to gain a competitive advantage," couldn't easily be used against Beijing because of the legal requirement to discern what motivated the manipulator. The guidelines had last undergone a major overhaul in 1977, and Fund staffers reasoned that if they were guilty of being "asleep at the wheel," the cause was not so much dereliction of duty as it was terribly outmoded and narrowly drafted rules. New rules were therefore in order, staffers concluded, and if the Fund pacified the US government by coming up with a better way of addressing the Chinese exchange rate issue, so much the better.

Allen's group soon coalesced around a new phrase — "fundamental misalignment" — as a more practical standard for determining whether a country's exchange rate policy was deserving of censure or possible sanctions. One big problem with this term was that it originated in a US Senate bill aimed at putting pressure on China. Critics, who included Dunaway and many of his colleagues in the Asia Pacific Department, scoffed that borrowing wording from US legislation would make the Fund look like America's patsy, and they also ridiculed and deemed impossible the crafting of rules that would reflect truly objective judgments about currency levels.

But with de Rato's encouragement, Allen and his lieutenants forged ahead, driven by an idealistic goal of making the IMF reflect the vision of its founders. The international monetary system needed better rules for identifying problematic exchange rate regimes, such as China's, Allen believed, and the Fund had a duty to engage in "ruthless truth-telling" (a favourite phrase of Keynes) when countries broke those rules — to that extent, he shared the US Treasury view. At the same time, Allen believed the guidelines needed updating to cover all kinds of situations in which one country's policies might affect others adversely. Doing so would be in accord with Keynes's cherished idea that the Fund's rules should apply symmetrically — that is, to curb both large surpluses and large deficits. In a memo to top IMF management dated June 19, 2006, Allen wrote that the new decision on exchange rate policy being drafted by his team could be used not only against China, but also "applies to the United States" because of Washington's budget deficits, which were an important contributing factor in global imbalances.[16]

Chinese officials smelled a rat. Based on the wording of the proposed rule, they had every reason to assume that the RMB was chief among the candidates for the labelling of fundamental misalignment. The indicators for

---

16 This memo is one of many confidential documents, not available in the public record, from which excerpts will be quoted in this chapter. Henceforth, such documents will be cited without footnotes.

making such a judgment — which included "unsustainable" or "excessive" current account surpluses or deficits and "protracted large-scale intervention in one direction in the exchange market" — applied to China in spades. Other countries, mostly in the developing world, were also leery about the new rule, which they feared might be used against them.

A long internal debate came to a head at an exceptionally dramatic meeting of the IMF's executive board on June 15, 2007, to consider the new decision on exchange rate policy. Meetings of the Fund's board are usually dull and stilted; by tradition the outcome is agreed by consensus, having been negotiated beforehand. But suspense permeated the boardroom on this occasion because a preliminary vote count showed that quite a few directors representing developing countries were opposed or at least reluctant to vote for approval. (Some directors represent constituencies of a number of countries; eight other directors represent single large countries, with each director's voting power based loosely on the size of the economy or economies being represented.)

A few hours before the start of the board meeting, the People's Bank of China summoned the Fund's Beijing representatives and handed them a letter, signed by Governor Zhou, addressed to IMF Managing Director de Rato, who received it by email. "The Chinese government expresses her deep concern over the Fund's intention to call the Board of Directors to vote," the letter said. "Such action will break the Fund tradition of passing major decisions based on broad consensus, and will also impair the cooperative relations between the Fund and its members." But de Rato was determined to push the proposal through that day, provided he could reduce the number of "no" votes to a small fraction of the total. He was under intense pressure from the US Treasury, which was eager to see rules promulgated that could lead to the designation of the RMB as fundamentally misaligned.

By late afternoon, after a three-hour lunch break for the drafting of hastily written compromise provisions, the board voted approval over the objections of the Chinese director, Ge Huayong, with only directors from Egypt and Iran joining Ge in opposition. The "2007 Decision on Bilateral Surveillance over Members' Policies," as it was officially known, was now IMF policy, and that evening, de Rato invited the staffers who had worked with him on the issue to his office for a champagne toast.

The cliché about prematurely uncorked champagne applies literally, and with force, in this case. The celebrants gathered in de Rato's office could scarcely imagine how muddled and feckless their institution would prove in the weeks and months ahead during the implementation phase of the new policy against fundamentally misaligned currencies. As for China, its trouncing in the boardroom that day would prove only a temporary setback.

Now that the IMF had its new exchange rate rule, which countries and currencies deserved to be labelled as offenders? That issue was the subject of a meeting of top IMF staffers who gathered in de Rato's office on June 22, 2007, one week after the board meeting. Agreement soon emerged that although the Chinese RMB should be high on the list, the designation of fundamental misalignment was also suitable for others, including the US dollar and Japanese yen. De Rato didn't flinch: "We need to apply the decision in as evenhanded a manner as possible," he said, according to notes of the meeting.

A series of reversals soon followed. De Rato announced on June 28 that for personal reasons he would step down as managing director, despite having two years left in his five-year term — depriving the new policy of its most powerful backer.[17] Meanwhile, China postponed any official judgment about whether its currency policy violated the new rules by insisting that it needed additional time to consult with the staff about its 2007 Article IV report.

Particularly cringeworthy in retrospect was the internal IMF debate in early July over labelling the US dollar as fundamentally misaligned. The idea wasn't as far-fetched as it might seem; all kinds of currency regimes, including floating ones, were supposed to be covered by the new rules. And with the US current account deficit hovering at a record six percent of GDP in 2006, the Fund's Research Department models estimated that that the dollar was somewhere between 10 and 30 percent overvalued — that is, a fall of that magnitude "would be required to eliminate the misalignment relative to medium-term macroeconomic fundamentals."[18] But one of the arguments in rebuttal, by staffers from the Western Hemisphere Department, was that the dollar's high exchange rate could be justified by the nation's financial efficiency; foreign investors were naturally eager to pour money into a country where banks and securities firms were using the world's most advanced and innovative techniques to invest capital. At the time, of course, the global financial crisis was still a year off and nobody could have imagined how stupefyingly off-base this argument was.

---

17 IMF, 2007, "IMF Managing Director Rodrigo de Rato to Leave Following the 2007 Annual Meetings," Press Release No. 07147, June 28, www.imf.org/external/np/sec/pr/2007/pr07147.htm.

18 IMF, 2007, "United States: Article IV Consultation—Staff Report," IMF Country Report 07/264, August, www.imf.org/external/pubs/ft/scr/2007/cr07264.pdf.

The greenback was spared, on the grounds that its misalignment was not "fundamental beyond reasonable doubt,"[19] and a similar ruling was applied to the Japanese yen as confusion and frustration mounted about the new rules. Another fiasco came on July 30, 2007, when the board met to consider the Article IV report for the Maldives, a tiny island nation in the Indian Ocean. Despite a staff report showing that the Maldives rufiyaa was fundamentally misaligned by pretty much any sensible interpretation of the 2007 decision, the board refused to endorse that finding.[20]

Just a month and a half had passed since the day of the champagne toast in de Rato's office, and it seemed clear that the IMF did not have the stomach to use its new rules for truth telling of the ruthless sort the drafters had originally intended. But might the fundamental misalignment label still be applied to China, whose foreign exchange policy had inspired the term?

Frustration among US Treasury officials over the IMF's impotence in dealing with China was reaching the boiling point in the spring of 2008. On April 25, Mark Sobel, a deputy assistant secretary in the US Treasury known for his blunt and acerbic advocacy of the US view, met with IMF staffers to convey the department's displeasure "with great conviction," according to a memo of the encounter by one of the Fund officials who attended. Sobel was quoted as asserting: "Getting the China Article IV done, with a [fundamental misalignment] finding, is crucial, and it needs to be done sooner rather than later, as the delay has already damaged credibility and may soon do so beyond repair."

The Treasury was then headed by Henry Paulson, the hard-charging former CEO of Goldman Sachs, who had extensive experience in China (more about him in the next chapter). Firm in his belief that bilateral threats by the United States on the currency issue were counterproductive, Paulson was keen for the IMF to call the RMB fundamentally misaligned, but ever since the rule change in June 2007, the Fund had been unable to finalize an Article IV staff report saying so, much less convene a board meeting to endorse such a conclusion. The Chinese had made sure that their economy would not be subjected to that type of affront, by asserting that they needed further discussions to make their case — and there was no easy way for the Fund to force the issue. To be sure, one of the obligations of IMF members is to

---

19 The decision was made by John Lipsky, the IMF's first deputy managing director, in a meeting that took place on July 10, recounted in detail in my book *Off Balance* (see footnote 1).

20 IMF, 2007, "IMF Executive Board Concludes 2007 Article IV Consultation with Maldives," Public Information Notice No. 07/100, August 9, www.imf.org/external/np/sec/pn/2007/pn07100. htm.

submit to regular Article IV surveillance; the managing director can technically put any country's review on the agenda for a board meeting, which can
be changed only if a board majority votes to do so. But in practice, given the
diplomatic niceties that govern board conduct, a single board member can
usually arrange a long postponement by claiming the need for time to hold
additional consultations.

Sobel's bluster at the April 2008 meeting was not just tough talk; the Americans
had even greater leverage than usual because the IMF wanted to sell some of
its gold stocks to shore up its finances, which required passage of congressional
legislation. According to the memo of the meeting, Sobel's "top level message was that the Fund needs to give clear signals when a country is offending
against the rules of the international monetary system, and that it is impossible
to defend the Fund before Congress if it does not do this." What was more, the
same table thumping was evidently occurring at much higher levels, between
Paulson and IMF Managing Director Dominique Strauss-Kahn, who had succeeded de Rato. As the memo put it, Sobel "was clearly very aware that his boss
was simultaneously giving a take-no-prisoners message to DSK."

IMF management and staff, therefore, began moving forward in the weeks
following with efforts to label the RMB as fundamentally misaligned, despite
warnings from Chinese officials that such an act would be "totally unaccept-
able" (a phrase cited repeatedly in IMF emails concerning conversations with
the Chinese). On May 16, the Fund threw down the gauntlet in the form
of a memo from Deputy Managing Director Takatoshi Kato to China's Ge,
spelling out how the process of labelling would work:

> As we discussed the other day [Kato's memo said], below is the lan-
> guage that reflects our current assessment of China's exchange rate
> and exchange rate policies in accordance with the 2007 surveillance
> decision....The language envisaged is as follows:

> Despite recent appreciation against the US dollar, the renminbi
> is judged by the staff to be substantially undervalued, indicating a
> fundamental misalignment in the exchange rate. Moreover, China's
> continued tight management of its exchange rate significantly con-
> tributes to external instability.

In support of this conclusion, Kato's memo cited the quadrupling of China's
current account surplus — it had swelled to 11 percent of GDP in 2007 —
and the quintupling of official reserves, to $1.7 trillion, over the previous five
years. Kato also expressed hope that a recently postponed IMF mission to

Beijing could be rescheduled promptly, with the aim of proceeding toward the finalization of the Article IV report.

A frosty retort was soon forthcoming from Ge. After noting that the RMB had appreciated 18 percent against the dollar, and 12 percent in real effective terms since July 2005, the Chinese executive director wrote back to Kato on May 27, 2008:

> In early 2008, South China was hit by a severe snowstorm and just two weeks ago, Sichuan province was struck by a devastating earthquake....Since the reform of the exchange rate regime, a large number of export enterprises experienced bankruptcy and loss of jobs. Even in this difficult situation, the Chinese authorities have continued to implement policy measures to correct the external imbalances, including exchange rate flexibility.

> We hope that the Fund will continue to carry out its duty as a trusted advisor to members....Rushed judgment before frank and comprehensive discussions should be avoided.

> Meanwhile, the Chinese authorities are preoccupied with earthquake relief and reconstruction, and it is extremely difficult to accommodate a consultation mission at this time.

Behind China's hard-nosed stance was more than just a desire to defend national dignity. Chinese officials were also concerned that if the IMF designated the RMB to be fundamentally misaligned, the result might be a WTO case that China would lose, which in turn might lead to economic sanctions against Chinese exports. Documents show that Ge and some colleagues from Beijing sought advice from the Fund's legal department about how vulnerable their country might be to a WTO case. In response, IMF General Counsel Sean Hagan wrote a memo to Ge that was somewhat comforting, although not entirely. The memo noted that under WTO rules, the trade body was bound to "accept the determination of the Fund," but the only basis for a WTO case would be a Fund ruling that China was violating its "obligations under the [IMF's] Articles,"[21] and a finding of fundamental misalignment wouldn't, by itself, imply a violation of obligations. Hagan added, however, that he couldn't guarantee how a WTO case would be resolved: "As an important qualification to this analysis, it should be emphasized that the above views may not necessarily be shared by the WTO Secretariat or a WTO dispute settlement panel."

---

21 Hagan cited Article XV of the GATT, referenced in footnote 6 in this chapter.

The Chinese needn't have gotten overly anxious. A number of forces were converging against those who would besmirch Beijing's foreign exchange policy.

A shift in opinion was under way among the IMF's member countries. No longer was China isolated on the IMF board; on the contrary, it had gained plenty of new allies amid growing resentment toward American treatment of the Fund. Particularly damaging to the US position was mounting evidence of the crisis that would soon erupt, the most salient manifestation being the downfall of the investment banking firm Bear Stearns in mid-March 2008. That disaster, and other signs of fragility in the US financial sector, showed all too clearly whose economy had eluded tough IMF surveillance.

Caught in the middle of all these irresistible forces and immovable objects was Strauss-Kahn, who knew that if he brought the Chinese Article IV review to the board, he would be unable to win a majority in favour of labelling the RMB as fundamentally misaligned. Yet the US Treasury was unrelenting, as revealed by notes of meetings the managing director held in mid-June 2008. In one tête-à-tête with Thomas Mirow, state secretary of the German Finance Ministry, Strauss-Kahn said: "The US wants to label the Chinese. Paulson says that if we don't use the 2007 decision, the Fund is dead...[It's] blackmail. If there is no solution [that suits] the US, it could endanger congressional votes," which the Fund badly needed for the sake of its own financial viability. Although Treasury officials understood that sentiment among executive directors was now heavily against labelling China, they still wanted Strauss-Kahn to bring the matter to the board, which would at least expose the Chinese foreign exchange regime to some public castigation.

The endgame for the IMF's verdict on the RMB was now at hand. A board meeting on China was scheduled for September 22, 2008 — at the time, no one knew it would come exactly one week after the most catastrophic financial episode in generations. The staff was putting the finishing touches on its 2008 Article IV report for China, which would have sharply rebuked Beijing, except that it would never see the light of day. Here is the crucial wording from the report's executive summary: "There are significant concerns that the exchange rate may be fundamentally misaligned and exchange rate policies could be a significant contributor to external instability....Accordingly, staff recommends that the executive board initiate an ad hoc consultation with China that would be expected to be concluded within about six months."

The September 22 board meeting was never held. The Article IV report was buried. Indeed, the US Treasury lost interest in prodding the IMF to label China. On September 15, Lehman Brothers went bankrupt; the following day the giant insurer AIG required an emergency $85 billion loan from the Fed to avoid Lehman's fate; even ostensibly healthy banks were frantically hoarding cash as panicked hedge funds pulled their money out. The staggeringly large financial gyrations that ensued for months thereafter shifted the balance of power again away from the United States and toward China — this time seismically, by several orders of magnitude greater than anything that had come earlier in the crisis.

Paulson's book, *On the Brink*, offers helpful insight regarding the reasons for that seismic shift. In his chapters about events immediately following the Lehman bankruptcy, the former Treasury secretary recounts numerous phone calls to Beijing in which he and other Treasury officials were essentially imploring Chinese leaders to see that it was in their own self-interest to help keep the rest of the US financial system afloat.[22] On the Saturday after Lehman collapsed, for example, Paulson called Wang Qishan, the vice premier responsible for economic and financial affairs, in the hope that a Chinese state-owned company would invest in the investment banking giant Morgan Stanley, which was in desperate need of a cash infusion. According to his book, the Treasury chief told Wang that Washington would "welcome" such an investment, adding that the US government "viewed Morgan Stanley as systemically important" — a virtual promise that American taxpayer dollars would be tapped, if necessary, to protect the Chinese against major losses. Wang's "unenthusiastic tone" convinced Paulson to back off. "China was already providing tremendous support to the US by buying and holding Treasuries and [other US] securities," Paulson writes.

According to the recollections of a senior US official who held major policy-making responsibilities:

> It was a terribly volatile time. The last thing we wanted in the middle of a crisis was a public row with China over its exchange rate policy. It was never explicit — it wasn't like the Chinese came back and said, "if you do this, we'll do that." It's just — of all the things that US policy makers had to deal with, was this the thing you wanted to make a priority at this point?

22 Henry M. Paulson, Jr., 2010, *On the Brink: Inside the Race to Stop the Collapse of the Global Financial System*, New York, NY: Business Plus.

Believe me, Hank Paulson thought it was in the best interests of China and the United States for China to move to a market-based exchange rate, but he didn't seriously consider labelling the Chinese as currency manipulators during the global financial crisis — and I don't think he should have. It wasn't a point-in-time decision. I think it was just the pragmatic evaluation that we were focusing on the most important things, and that moving down that path — particularly given that we were in the middle of a crisis — would have likely failed in influencing the Chinese to alter their policy and could easily have backfired and created greater risk at a very precarious time.

China not only emerged unscathed from the IMF's rule change against fundamentally misaligned currencies, it also turned the tables on Washington by taking pointed note of which country had, in the final analysis, proved most guilty of policies that harmed others. Yi Gang, deputy governor of the People's Bank of China, delivered a speech at the IMF-World Bank annual meetings on October 11, 2008, in which he asserted that the crisis "underscores the need for the Fund to maintain a sharp focus on risks in the major developed countries and their potential spillover effects." He accused the IMF of "mis-focused surveillance," and in a little-noticed but barbed rhetorical thrust, called on the Fund to "consider an ad hoc consultation with the United States."[23]

Humiliating retreat for the IMF came almost exactly two years after the board's approval of the 2007 rule change, when the Fund essentially vowed to abandon the term "fundamental misalignment."[24] Only then, in July 2009, did China allow the long-delayed completion of its Article IV report — and the report placed before directors contained much softer language on the RMB than the one that had been drafted in the fall of 2008.[25] This was emblematic of the elevated geopolitical status with which China emerged in the wake of the crisis.

Thus ends the story of the IMF's efforts to influence China's currency policy — with a whimper that, from Beijing's perspective, may have been a glorious bang. The RMB's exchange rate would not be subjected to multilateral condemnation, much less economic punishment. And a cheap RMB was not the only element of Chinese economic strategy that was evoking consternation in Washington and other foreign capitals.

23 Yi Gang, 2008, "Statement by Dr. Yi Gang, Deputy Governor of the People's Bank of China, at the Eighteenth Meeting of the International Monetary and Financial Committee," Washington, DC, October 11, www.imf.org/external/am/2008/imfc/statement/eng/chn.pdf.

24 IMF, 2009, "The 2007 Surveillance Decision: Revised Operational Guidance," June 22, www. imf.org/external/np/pp/eng/2009/062209.pdf.

25 IMF, 2009, "Public Information Notice: IMF Executive Board Concludes 2009 Article IV Consultation with the People's Republic of China," Public Information Notice No. 09/87, July 22, www.imf.org/en/News/Articles/2015/09/28/04/53/pn0987.

CHAPTER 6

NOT AN EXOTIC VERSION OF CANADA

When Hu Jintao became China's president on November 15, 2002, less than a year after the nation's WTO accession, Beijing insiders struggled to characterize the 59-year-old Hu as anything more than a bland, cautious enigma of strict loyalty to the Communist Party. Hu was not clearly identified with either the reformist or the conservative camp; his most salient trait was his disciplined discretion, especially in public. As Jiang's vice president, he had refrained from media interviews, and when giving speeches, he read verbatim from scripts that often included lengthy, statistics-laden passages about industrial or agricultural production. *Hao haizi*, or "good boy," was pretty much the snidest epithet his detractors aimed at him. One of the most revealing comments about the new president came from his 88-year-old great aunt, Liu Bingxia, who helped raise him after his mother died when he was young. Of her nephew, Liu said: "he never once interrupted his elders when they were speaking."[1]

Given Hu's careful, consensus-building approach, the odds appeared to favour continuity in policy by the new regime, including on economic matters, for which Hu delegated substantial responsibility to Premier Wen Jiabao.

---

1   Joseph Kahn, 2002, "Man in the News: Mystery Man at the Helm Hu Jintao," *The New York Times*, November 15.

In important respects, the Hu-Wen leadership duo did continue to pursue the market-opening path that had been blazed by Jiang and Zhu during China's entry into the WTO. Tariff cuts, quota eliminations and other policy measures promised in China's protocol of accession were implemented, as previously noted.

But in the early months of 2003, very soon after taking power, Hu and Wen laid the foundations for much greater economic intervention by Beijing than the United States and other WTO members had anticipated when they ushered China into the trade body. In particular, the Hu-Wen regime established three institutions that scholars would later identify as playing major roles in the "China Inc." system combining dynamic private enterprise with an all-powerful party-state. The importance of these institutions would be recognized in retrospect; their creation garnered little notice abroad at the time.

The first of these institutions, authorized at the 10th National People's Congress in March 2003, was the State-owned Assets Supervision and Administration Commission (SASAC), which took centralized control over the national government's shares of 196 of the biggest SOEs.[2] These companies were corporate behemoths, often with tens of billions of dollars in revenue — Petro China, China Mobile, Dongfeng Motors, Baosteel and Sinopec, for example — that competed fiercely in private markets, both domestically and internationally, and issued much of their stock to global investors. Some in SASAC's portfolio were even battling against other SASAC-owned firms, in industries such as petrochemicals, steel, airlines and telecommunications. But with the power to appoint (and remove) executives at many SOEs and a mandate to "maintain and improve the...competitive power of the State economy,"[3] SASAC was a completely novel instrument of economic management, even in a world where SOEs exist in many countries. As Mark Wu, a Harvard Law School professor, has written:

---

2   The number of SOEs in SASAC's portfolio has decreased by roughly half, but the assets under its control have dramatically increased, as shall be seen in chapter 8. Information about SASAC in this section comes from Li-Wen Lin and Curtis J. Milhaupt, 2013, "We are the (National) Champions: Understanding the Mechanisms of State Capitalism in China," *Stanford Law Review* 65 (4): May; Barry Naughton, 2003, "The State Asset Commission: A Powerful New Government Body," *China Leadership Monitor*, No. 8; Barry Naughton, 2005, "SASAC Rising," *China Leadership Monitor*, No. 14; and Mark Wu, 2016, "The China Inc. Challenge to Global Trade Governance," *Harvard International Law Journal* 57 (2): 261–324

3   Government of China, "Interim Regulations on Supervision and Management of State-owned Assets of Enterprises" ("SASAC regulation"), adopted at the Eighth Executive Meeting of the State Council, May 13, cited in European Commission, 2017, "On Significant Distortions in the Economy of the People's Republic of China for the Purposes of Trade Defence Investigations," Commission Staff Working Document, December 20.

Imagine if one U.S. government agency controlled General Electric, General Motors, Ford, Boeing, U.S. Steel, DuPont, AT&T, Verizon, Honeywell, and United Technologies. Furthermore, imagine this agency were not simply a passive shareholder, but also behaved as a private equity fund would with its holding companies. It could hire and fire management, deploy and transfer resources across holding companies, and generate synergies across its holdings.... In many ways, SASAC operates as other controlling shareholders do. It is happy to grant management operational autonomy so long as it delivers along the agreed-upon metric. The difference is that the metric is not pure profit, but rather the Chinese state's interest, broadly defined.[4]

Before SASAC, individual ministries and agencies held control of SOEs, a decentralized approach that fomented inefficiency and corruption. The "corporatization" of SOEs had afforded opportunities for well-placed executives to enrich themselves and their cronies, one method being to sell off assets and real estate at rigged prices with kickbacks distributed to parties in cahoots. Having seen what had happened in the former Soviet Union where oligarchs similarly took advantage of privatizations to become obscenely wealthy, China's Communist Party opted for a more closely regulated, public-spirited and transparent system with SASAC. Moreover, SASAC would enhance the Party's power, by ensuring control over the nation's largest enterprises and the patronage that came with appointments to plum jobs, as well as the pay the holders of those jobs received (since SASAC assumed responsibility for setting SOE executives' compensation packages). Further extending this power was the establishment of provincial and municipal SASACs that would act as controlling shareholders for enterprises owned by local governments.

Under its first chief, Li Rongrong, SASAC used its leverage to press SOEs for greater competitiveness and profitability. Li's mantra, similar to that of GE CEO Jack Welch, was that SOEs should stick to core businesses in which they could be number one, number two or number three in their market segments; any businesses that couldn't meet that standard should be discontinued. But maximizing the bottom line of individual companies was never the sole motivation for centralizing SOE control, as witnessed by the fact that Beijing sometimes arranged job switches among CEOs, including some involved in cutthroat competition with each other. At the behest of the Party, which shares hiring and firing power with SASAC, top executives at three of

---

4   Wu, "The China Inc. Challenge to Global Trade Governance" (see footnote 2 in this chapter). Reprinted here with permission.

the nation's biggest telecommunications companies were shuffled from one firm to another in 2004, to investors' stunned surprise. Wang Jianzhou, president of China Unicom, took over as general manager of China Mobile while Wang Xiaochu, deputy managing director of China Mobile, was transferred to work as managing director of China Telecom. A similar move would come in 2011 among top executives of state-owned oil companies.

One sector that was kept from SASAC control was banking, which came under the purview of Central Huijin Investment Ltd., another 2003 creation. Majority shareholdings in four giant banks that dominate China's financial industry — the Bank of China, the Industrial and Commercial Bank of China, the China Construction Bank and the Agricultural Bank of China — were obtained by Central Huijin, which also exercised various forms of control over a number of smaller financial institutions.[5] These banks were listed on major stock exchanges, operated branches worldwide, vied with one another for profitable lending business and were under pressure to generate high returns on their capital. But their control by Central Huijin provided the means for the state to direct their loans for national policy purposes when it chose to do so.

Although this arrangement was not nearly as *dirigiste* as the post-Mao period when banker-bureaucrats mindlessly shovelled subsidies to SOEs on orders from above, it was also a far cry from a pure free market. Government-set interest rates virtually guaranteed that the banks could earn comfortable spreads on their loans, and bankers knew that lending to government-backed SOEs or projects favoured by the Party was a relatively risk-free proposition. Top bank chieftains, like other SOE executives, owed their jobs to the Party and often held Party leadership positions, further cementing ties to the Beijing hierarchy. Underpinning the arrangement was the nation's banking law, which states: "Commercial banks shall conduct their business of lending in accordance with the needs of the national economic and social development and under the guidance of the industrial policies of the State."[6]

A third entity that arose in 2003 — morphing from predecessor institutions rather than springing anew — came to be known as a "super ministry" because

---

5   These were not just state holdings that already existed, but some new holdings created as a result of government-funded bailouts. Information about Central Huijin can be found in Wu, "The China Inc. Challenge to Global Trade Governance" (see footnote 2 in this chapter); Michael F. Martin, 2010, "China's Sovereign Wealth Fund: Developments and Policy Implications," Congressional Research Service, Report 7-5700, September 23; and European Commission, 2017, "On Significant Distortions in the Economy of the People's Republic of China for the Purposes of Trade Defence Investigations" (see footnote 3 in this chapter).

6   "Law of the People's Republic of China on Commercial Banks," available at: www.npc.gov.cn/englishnpc/Law/2007-12/12/content_1383716.htm

of its coordinating power over others. It was dubbed the National Development and Reform Commission (NDRC), and one of the main responsibilities assigned to its 30,000-strong bureaucracy was the design of China's five-year plan.[7] A number of countries, notably India, have planning ministries and multi-year national plans, as had China, starting in 1952 when Mao established a Soviet-style command-and-control authority called the State Planning Commission. The Chinese planners' clout had ebbed, and their agency had gone through several incarnations largely downgrading its influence, during the period of economic liberalization under Deng and Zhu. But with the NDRC, China was bulking up the planners' responsibilities, bestowing them with authority that imbued their goals with much greater force than mere guidelines. The prices of major commodities and inputs — in particular electricity, oil, gasoline, natural gas and water — would be set by the NDRC, which also allocated state investment funds and held power of approval over many large projects, such as infrastructure, factories and even amusement parks (the size of Shanghai Disneyland, for example, would come under the NDRC's jurisdiction).

Taken individually, the creation of each of these institutions might have signified only incremental accretions of state control; taken together, they gave Beijing a whole array of new levers for manipulating and influencing the actions of enterprises, both public and private, across the entire Chinese economy. And behind them — or more precisely, above them — loomed the ultimate authority in how those levers would be manipulated.

Of all the revelations in *The Party: The Secret World of China's Communist Rulers*, the most arresting may be the red phones that the book reports as sitting atop the desks of several hundred of the nation's most powerful individuals in government as well as the CEOs of the biggest SOEs. The phones, which have four-digit numbers and connect only to other similar phones in the same system, are called "red machines" because anyone calling on them is likely to rank high in the Party apparatus. "When the 'red machine' rings," a senior executive at a state bank told author Richard McGregor, "you had better make sure you answer it."[8]

---

7   Information about the NDRC can be found in Wu, "The China Inc. Challenge to Global Trade Governance" (see footnote 4 in this chapter) and Dexter Roberts, 2013, "China's Economic Policy Factory: The NDRC," *Bloomberg Businessweek*, June 21.

8   Richard McGregor, 2010, *The Party: The Secret World of China's Communist Rulers*, New York, NY: Harper Perennial, chapter 1.

The red phones are emblematic of the Party's reach, which extends not only to all levels, branches and agencies of national, provincial and local government but to industry, finance, the media and academia. Nearly every person holding ministerial or vice-ministerial rank at a government agency will be a Party member; the same goes for top executives at SOEs and banks as well as other institutions such as major universities, research institutes and news organizations. All such people will have received extensive training at Party schools and most will have been approved for their positions by the Party's Central Organization Department, a vast and hermetic bureaucracy whose criteria for evaluating candidates for hiring and promotion include "political reliability" (a euphemism for Party loyalty). In its role as a sort of gigantic human resources bureau, the department might transfer an individual from, say, an SOE vice chairmanship to jobs ranging from provincial deputy governor or municipal party secretary or institute director or newspaper editor. The heads of SASAC, Central Huijin and the NDRC are all Party-selected, and the Central Organization Department provides so much input to SASAC on the appointments of many SOE chieftains that such people are effectively Party choices. "A similar department in the US," McGregor writes, "would oversee the appointment of the entire US cabinet, state governors and their deputies, the mayors of major cities, the heads of all federal regulatory agencies, the chief executives" of about 50 big US companies, Supreme Court justices, the editors of major newspapers, TV network and cable station bosses, the presidents of top universities such as Yale and Harvard and the heads of think tanks such as the Brookings Institution.[9]

All this command and control — SASAC, Central Huijin, the NDRC and above all the Party — might have been used by China's leaders purely for political reasons, to entrench their rule and stifle dissent. If that had been the case, the implications for the trading system might have been minor. But about three years after assuming leadership, the Hu-Wen regime took major steps toward deploying the powers of the party-state to influence economic, industrial and corporate outcomes, a distinct course reversal from the market reforms of the Jiang-Zhu era.

In February 2006, the State Council issued a landmark document called the "National Medium- and Long-Term Plan for the Development of Science and Technology (2006-2020)," sometimes abbreviated as the "MLP." One phrase in its dense bureaucratese stuck in the craws of foreign business executives and trade officials: *zizhu chuangxin* or "indigenous innovation." That term implied that instead of importing goods from abroad or inducing foreign companies to

---

9   McGregor, *The Party* (see previous footnote), chapter 3.

invest and produce freely in China, the government was pivoting to a strategy of boosting Chinese enterprises, quite possibly to the detriment of foreign ones. As the plan took shape, with subsequent regulations and implementing policies, the suspicions of foreigners heightened.[10]

Partly inspiring the MLP lay a long-festering desire to close the gap with Western science and technology and hopefully overtake it, a natural and even admirable goal for a country that had paid so steep a price for falling behind the industrialized West and Japan in the nineteenth and twentieth centuries. The plan envisioned increasing China's gross spending on research and development from 1.3 percent of GDP in 2006 to 2.5 percent of GDP by 2020, when China would become a major centre of innovation, with the goal of becoming "a science and technology power by the middle of the 21st Century." Many of the areas targeted for scientific breakthroughs involved solving China's most pressing social and environmental problems, such as water shortages, food safety, air and water pollution and energy conservation.

So far, so benign — one of the noblest purposes of government, after all, is fostering scientific and technological research for society's benefit. But the plan was also redolent of industrial policy and import substitution schemes that use state power to nurture corporate national champions in sectors deemed strategically crucial to economic growth. As the plan stated:

> During the past two decades or so since we began to pursue the policy of reforms and opening to the outside world, our country has imported a huge amount of technologies and equipment, which played an important role in raising the overall technological level of our industries and promoting the country's economic development. However… [f]acts have proved that, in areas critical to the national economy and security, core technologies cannot be purchased. If our country wants to take the initiative in the fierce international competition, it has to enhance its indigenous innovation capability, master core technologies in some critical areas, own proprietary intellectual property rights, and build a number of internationally competitive enterprises.[11]

---

10 Information about the MLP in this section can be found in James McGregor, 2010, "China's Drive for 'Indigenous Innovation': A Web of Industrial Policies," US Chamber of Commerce, www.uschamber.com/sites/default/files/documents/files/100728china report_0_0.pdf; and Wayne M. Morrison, 2015, "China's Plan to Modernize the Economy and Promote Indigenous Innovation," Congressional Research Service, December 15.

11 State Council, The People's Republic of China, 2006, "The National Medium- and Long-Term Program for Science and Technology Development (2006-2020): An Outline," Section II, "Guiding Principles." www.itu.int/en/ITU-D/Cybersecurity/Documents/National_Strategies_Repository/China_2006.pdf.

The plan listed a number of "priority" sectors "that are both critical to economic and social development and national security and in dire need of [science and technology] support." These included high-speed rail, energy-efficient automobiles, "high performance, dependable computers," flat-panel displays, advanced medical equipment and renewable energy. Also specified were 16 "megaprojects" aimed at "assimilating and absorbing" technologies from abroad, by which China would "develop a range of major equipment and key products that possess proprietary intellectual property rights." The megaprojects included core electronic components, high-end chips and software; super large-scale integrated circuit manufacturing; next-generation broadband wireless telecommunication; advanced numeric-controlled machinery; large aircraft; nuclear reactors; pharmaceuticals; and genetically modified organisms. SOEs were directed to obtain know-how from foreign partners through "co-innovation and re-innovation based on the assimilation of imported technologies."

Innocuous as words such as "assimilation" and "co-innovation" might seem, they struck many foreigners as ominous. Intellectual property piracy of the old-fashioned sort (DVD copying, knockoffs of luxury-branded goods and so on) was on the decline, but there was a potentially more vexing concern — the pressure to hand over proprietary know-how that certain foreign companies were subjected to if they wanted to tap the Chinese market.

Although other countries, notably Japan, had employed similar strategies to their advantage in previous decades, official demands for technology transfer from foreign investors contravened the national treatment principle, and upon joining the WTO, Beijing had pledged to halt the practice, which it had once imposed explicitly. (The Protocol of Accession stated: "China shall ensure that… approval or importation, the right of importation or investment by national and sub-national authorities, is not conditioned on…performance requirements of any kind, such as local content, offsets, [or] the transfer of technology.") On the other hand, there was one big exception to this provision — namely cases in which Chinese government agencies were purchasers; China was still not among the 13 WTO members[12] that had signed the separate WTO agreement on government procurement. (At the time Beijing joined the WTO, Washington didn't insist on this point, as noted in chapter 3, partly because US officials didn't want to give China the reciprocal right of access to US government procurement.) Another obvious worry was the danger of secrets being misappropriated. In a report on indigenous innovation for the US Chamber

---

12 The 13 members that were signatories at the time included 25 member states of the European Union. A revised agreement has 18 members, including the European Union, as of late 2018.

of Commerce, Beijing-based analyst James McGregor (no relation to Richard McGregor), wrote: "the plan is considered by many international technology companies to be a blueprint for technology theft on a scale the world has never seen before."[13]

Further expanding the state's role in the economy — and its support for SOE national champions — was a directive issued by the State Council in December 2006 titled "Guiding Opinion on Promoting the Adjustment of State-Owned Capital and the Reconstruction of State-Owned Enterprises." It called on SASAC to "enhance the state-owned economy's controlling power" and "accelerate the formation of a batch of predominant enterprises with independent intellectual property rights, famous brands, and strong international competitiveness." In seven "strategic" industries — civil aviation, coal, defence, electric power and grid, oil and petrochemicals, shipping and telecommunications — state capital would play a leading role in every enterprise. In "pillar" industries, key enterprises were also to remain under state control; these included automotive, chemical, construction, equipment manufacturing, information technology, iron and steel, nonferrous metals, surveying and design.

What were the practical implications of these developments for foreign firms active in the Chinese market? The outcome in one "priority" sector is revealing.

Minutes after gliding out of Beijing South Station one afternoon in April 2017, the bullet train for Shanghai, which departs about 40 times a day, was smoothly accelerating to speeds of up to 380 km per hour, arriving at its destination in about five hours. Enjoying the view of the countryside whizzing by from the comfort of my coach-class seat, I marvelled at the contrast with train journeys I recall taking in China in the 1990s, when coaches were mobbed and rail travel between Beijing and Shanghai took around 16 hours. The Beijing-Shanghai route is just one of dozens connecting major cities in China; the country boasts a high-speed rail network that is roughly twice as long as the rest of the world's combined. The rapidity of this development is just as breathtaking as the trains — but not everyone who contributed is enraptured.

China first tried building a high-speed network in 2002, using a home-grown system developed by Chinese SOEs, but abandoned the effort within a couple

---

13 James McGregor, 2010, "China's Drive for Indigenous Innovation" (see footnote 10 in this chapter).

of years because the technology was insufficiently advanced. In 2004, the Railway Ministry decided that the nation's state-owned train manufacturers, China South Locomotive & Rolling Stock Corp. (CSR) and China North Locomotive & Rolling Stock Corp. (CNR), should look abroad. Four foreign firms signed contracts to sell equipment and teach their Chinese partners how to build high-speed trains. They were Alstom of France, Bombardier of Canada, Siemens of Germany and Kawasaki Industries of Japan, where high-speed rail was pioneered with the development of the legendary shinkansen (bullet train) in the 1960s. Eager to participate in what was shaping up as perhaps the biggest infrastructure-building project since the building of the American railroads in the nineteenth century, the companies agreed to the technology-transfer terms that the Chinese ministry demanded.[14]

Alstom and Kawasaki, which were the first to sign, exported their initial shipments of fully assembled trains, then set up factories in China, trained Chinese engineers and shared the technology required for building world-class engines, electricity transmission and signal control systems. Siemens and Bombardier followed suit. Although they were rewarded with juicy up-front payments, cause for regret emerged a few years thereafter.

The most aggrieved was Kawasaki, whose deal appeared promising at the start. For $1.5 billion, the Japanese firm exported nine sets of the iconic shinkansen called *Hayate* to CSR and then helped CSR manufacture about 50 more domestically with some of the most advanced components coming from Japan. Dozens of CSR engineers travelled to Japan for training before returning to China where they helped build CSR's factory in the port city of Qingdao. In a scene reminiscent of the shinkansen's inauguration coinciding with the 1964 Tokyo Summer Olympics, China's first high-speed train went into operation between Beijing and Tianjin in early August 2008, a week prior to the opening of the games in the Chinese capital.

By 2010, the Qingdao facility was churning out about 200 train sets a year. The market was exploding — Beijing was investing enormous sums in infrastructure as part of its efforts to keep the economy humming after the global financial crisis — but the market share of foreign suppliers was only 15 to 20 percent. That was partly because foreigners were facing requirements that

---

14 Information about China's development of high-speed rail can be found in Jamil Anderlini and Mure Dickie, 2010, "China: A future on track," *Financial Times,* September 24; Norihiko Shirouzu, 2010, "Train Makers Rail Against China's High-Speed Designs," *The Wall Street Journal,* November 17; Michelle Ker, 2017, "China's High-Speed Rail Diplomacy," U.S.-China Economic and Security Review Commission, Staff Research Report, February 21; Mure Dickie, 2010, "Japan Inc. shoots itself in foot on bullet train," *Financial Times,* July 9; and Clark Edward Barrett, 2014, "Chinese High Speed Rail Leapfrog Development," *China Brief* 14 (3), July 3.

all systems built for the Chinese market had to include 70 percent local componentry. Worse yet, the Chinese SOEs, contending that they had "digested" the foreign technology and had significantly improved it, were competing head-to-head with their former teachers for contracts around the world. High-speed rail projects in Turkey, Brazil, Russia, Saudi Arabia and California were either contracting with Chinese firms or considering doing so.

Unusually for Japanese businesses, which often shrink from criticizing China for fear of sparking anti-Japan ire, Kawasaki asserted that the Chinese trains were nearly identical to those produced by foreign partners, with the exception of some exterior tweaks and an enhanced propulsion system. "China says she owns exclusive rights to that intellectual property, but Kawasaki and other foreign companies feel otherwise," Kawasaki said in a 2010 statement. A senior executive at the company, speaking anonymously to *The Wall Street Journal*, went even further: "Claiming most of the recently developed bullet trains as China's own may be good for national pride...but it's nothing but deceitful propaganda."[15]

Officials in the Chinese government and SOEs bristled. Luo Bin, vice-chief engineer at CSR Sifang's Technology Development Centre, said of one of the company's new models, "This is an innovative design based on the technology we had already digested… This is completely the result of our autonomous design. It's got nothing to do with Bombardier or Siemens. It's got nothing at all to do with Shinkansen." He Huawu, chief engineer of the Railway Ministry, added: "China has made use of technology from around the world and through great innovation has made it Chinese."[16]

Other foreign companies were reluctant to complain publicly, according to news accounts at the time, for fear of losing the business they had. A Siemens spokesman said his company had "a trusting relationship" with its Chinese partners, and Bombardier China President Zhang Jiawei said "we have contracts and agreements, and both sides respect them." But the *Financial Times* quoted industry executives as privately estimating that about 90 percent of the high-speed technology used in China was "derived from partnerships or equipment developed by foreign companies." Kawasaki contemplated suing, but decided that challenging the Chinese government in court would be an exercise in futility.[17]

---

15 Shirouzu, "Train Makers Rail Against China's High-Speed Designs" (see footnote 14 in this chapter).

16 Anderlini and Dickie, "China: A future on track" (see footnote 14 in this chapter).

17 Ibid.

Whatever the merits of the allegations about technology copying, the foreigners miscalculated monumentally in perceiving how serious a competitive threat Chinese companies would pose in such a short period of time. By 2015, China was a technology leader, with the world's fastest trains and a national champion — a combined CNR and CSR, which merged in 2015 under the name China Railway Rolling Stock Corp. — that had revenue exceeding the combined total of its five top rivals.

High-speed rail may have been an extreme example, but it was by no means unique. The wind turbine industry offers another illustration of how government regulations, subsidies and other forms of support enabled Chinese companies to extract technological expertise from foreign investors and then, after capturing most of the domestic market, turn themselves into export powerhouses.[18]

Gamesa, a Spanish firm that was the world's number three wind turbine maker, began shipping large numbers of turbines to China around the turn of the century and became the leader with a 35 percent share of the Chinese market by 2005. But that year, the NDRC decreed that wind farms could buy only turbines containing more than 70 percent Chinese-made parts; "wind farms not meeting the requirement of equipment localization rate shall not be allowed to be built," the directive stated.[19] Gamesa responded by sending engineers to Tianjin, where they helped build an assembly plant and also trained Chinese suppliers to make components, such as steel forgings and electronic controls. Other multinational turbine makers took similar steps, and within five years, Chinese firms — backed by low-interest loans from state-owned banks and inexpensive land from municipal authorities — controlled 85 percent of the market; Gamesa's share had dwindled to three percent. The biggest Chinese turbine makers held nearly half of the global market in 2010 and were gearing up to grab more.

The imposition of local content requirements on wind turbines sold in China clearly violated WTO rules.[20] Even so, Gamesa was raising no fuss — the Chinese market had grown so large that even the company's shrunken share was amply profitable. "If you plan to go into a country, you really need to commit to a country," Jorge Calvet, Gamesa's CEO, told *The New York Times*

---

18 For a well-documented account of China's development of a domestic wind energy industry, see Keith Bradsher, 2010, "To Conquer Wind Power, China Writes the Rules," *The New York Times*, December 14.

19 NDRC, 2005, "Notice from the National Development and Reform Commission on the Relevant Requirements on the Administration of the Construction of Wind Farms," July 4.

20 The technology transfers demanded in the high-speed rail business were technically not violations because the buyer was the government, and as noted earlier, China was not a signatory of the WTO agreement on government procurement.

in 2010. As the paper reported, "the Chinese government bet correctly that Gamesa, as well as GE and other multinationals, would not dare risk losing a piece of China's booming wind farm business by complaining to trade officials in their home countries."[21]

Only in 2009 did the Obama administration, goaded by the United Steelworkers union, threaten China with a WTO complaint on wind turbines and Beijing quickly backed down, revoking the local-content requirement — but by then the Chinese industry's success no longer depended on that regulation. Worse yet, one of China's largest wind turbine manufacturers, Sinovel, was credibly accused of having pilfered key turbine-control software from its partner, American Superconductor, by bribing an Austria-based employee of American Superconductor, who confessed to the crime and served a prison sentence.[22]

Such tales raise the obvious question of what Washington had been doing while the Hu-Wen policies were going into effect.

Ask almost anyone who worked on China trade issues in the Bush administration during the first few years after China's WTO accession and they'll admit that their sanguine assumptions proved woefully off-base. Like the Clinton administration before it, the Bush administration was predominantly of the opinion that Beijing was progressing gradually but purposefully toward economic liberalization, thanks to the impetus of WTO membership. Although unhappy about China's foreign exchange policy, US officials were inclined more toward shrugging off rather than raising alarms about developments such as the formation of SASAC or approval of the MLP. Here is a representative sample of recollections from three people I interviewed who held high-ranking trade policy jobs during this period:

"The general view was that we're going to have bumps in the road with China, and they've just swallowed a huge elephant [i.e. WTO accession commitments], so we should be a little patient with them. Their policies will align with ours — not over months, but it's going to happen. There was great confidence in that. And if you're confident about the endpoint, it allows you to be more patient about missteps along the way."

"We really assumed that there was a natural physics, or natural gravity, to economic development, which would make sure the Party would stay relatively

21 Bradsher, "To Conquer Wind Power" (see footnote 18 in this chapter).

22 CBS News, 2016, "The Great Brain Robbery," *60 Minutes*, January 17.

out of the [economic policy-making] process. The notion was, we're creating a middle class that will want some sort of pluralism. China isn't necessarily going to 'look like us,' but this pluralism will limit their ability or interest in messing with the global system."

"In those days you still had this sense that they were on a reform trajectory. They were putting into place all these laws and regulations. People were very impressed with their commitment in joining the WTO, and the resources they were putting into making it work."

On many trade issues involving China, therefore, the US administration held its fire, especially during the period before 2006 when Beijing was scheduled to complete its WTO accession commitments. Nowhere was this forbearance toward China more consequential than in the matter of "pedestal actuators."

Pedestal actuators are mechanisms that adjust the height of seats on motorized scooters used by the physically disabled. In August 2002, a New Jersey maker of pedestal actuators that had lost a substantial amount of business to Chinese imports decided to strike back using the law. This was the first effort to use a special kind of safeguard that applied only to China.

As will be recalled from chapters 2 and 3, safeguards are supposed to provide temporary protection to a domestic industry that is threatened by a surge of imports, and during the course of its negotiations for entry to the WTO, Beijing had reluctantly agreed that its trading partners could resort to a "China product-specific" safeguard. Ordinary, plain-vanilla safeguards apply to imports from all countries, and temporary duties can be imposed only if imports are "causing or threaten to cause serious injury" to domestic makers. But under the terms of the US-China deal struck by Barshefsky, American manufacturers could get temporary duties or other protective measures levied on competing Chinese goods alone if the US International Trade Commission found that those imported goods were causing "market disruption" adversely affecting the US industry. Barshefsky prevailed upon Zhu to accept that these special rules would remain in effect for 12 years after China's accession and although the White House would have the power to waive the protective measures, the Clinton administration expected fairly robust use of this defensive tactic.[23]

---

23 At a congressional hearing in 2000, Barshefsky said: "We wanted to be sure we had strong anti-import surge mechanisms. China will become a much more forceful competitor in the future....This is a much different standard than [ordinary safeguards]. One, because we can take action just against China. Two, because a 'market disruption' standard is a very low legal threshold." US House of Representatives, 2000, "U.S.-China Bilateral Trade Agreement and the Accession of China to the WTO: Hearing Before the Committee on Ways and Means," February 16, www.gpo.gov/fdsys/pkg/CHRG-106hhrg67129/pdf/CHRG-106hhrg67129.pdf.

In the pedestal actuators case, a finding of market disruption was forthcoming on October 18, 2002, when the trade commission voted three to two in favour of imposing protective measures against Chinese imports. As is customary with this independent, quasi-judicial body, the vote came after hearings and the gathering of evidence by the commission staff. The "relief" recommended was quotas limiting the number of imported Chinese pedestal actuators for three years.[24]

But three months later, the White House announced that Bush was exercising his right to reject the commission's recommendation. That set a precedent followed in similar, subsequent cases: on April 25, 2003, the president refused to impose safeguard measures that the commission had recommended in a case involving imported Chinese wire hangers; he did it again in 2004, in a case involving imported Chinese "ductile iron waterworks fittings," which are used to join pipes and valves; and again in 2005 in a case involving steel pipe.[25] By consistently disallowing the measures favoured by the commission — even when the commissioners voted unanimously, as they did in the hangers and waterworks fittings cases — Bush sent the message that the China product-specific safeguard wouldn't be much use, at least while he was in office. US companies stopped filing such cases for the remainder of Bush's presidency, figuring that they would only waste time and money.

Explaining its decisions in these cases, the White House issued statements noting that under the law governing the China product-specific safeguard, the president is supposed to consider the overall impact on the US economy, not just the industry competing with Chinese imports. Restricting Chinese imports would lead to price hikes on users of those items, the White House statements pointed out; in the case of pedestal actuators, for example, "a quota would negatively affect the many disabled and elderly purchasers of mobility scooters and electric wheelchairs, the primary ultimate consumers of pedestal actuators," the presidential statement said.[26] Furthermore, even if the government blocked imports from China, similar products would soon come into the US market from elsewhere, rendering safeguards ineffective.

Omitted from these public statements were some of the deeper reasons for rejecting the use of the China safeguard. Bush's advisers, led by US Trade

24 United States International Trade Commission (USITC), 2002, "Pedestal Actuators from China," Investigation No. TA-421-1, Determination and Views of the Commission, USITC Publication No. 3557, November.

25 General Accountability Office, 2005, "U.S.-China Trade: The United States Has Not Restricted Imports under the China Safeguard," Report to Congressional Committees, GAO-05-1056, September.

26 Presidential document, 2003, "Presidential Determination on Pedestal Actuator Imports from the People's Republic of China," 68 Federal Register 3155, January 17.

Representative Robert Zoellick, worried that if one industry got protection under the safeguard, virtually every US manufacturer competing with Chinese imports would be clamouring for similar treatment. That would put the entire US-China trade relationship at risk, and US multinationals — which were reaping big profits in the Chinese market — lobbied heavily to avoid any major disruptions. Also tilting the scales was intensive lobbying by Chinese officials, who vehemently argued against US use of the discriminatory China safeguard. The White House had no choice but to listen, given foreign policy considerations such as securing Chinese support for the "global war on terror."

It wasn't that the Bush team adhered to ideological purity in its embrace of free trade. In March 2002, the president bowed to pressure from Rust Belt states by imposing tariffs ranging from eight to 30 percent on imported steel, including Chinese steel, using the general safeguard rules.[27] And following a pattern set during the Clinton administration, Bush's Commerce Department imposed anti-dumping duties against imports from China far more often, and far more punitively, than imports from any other trading partner. From 2002 to 2004, 19 Chinese products ranging from colour televisions to bedroom furniture to shrimp were found to be dumped in the US market, nearly half of all cases in which Washington issued such rulings. The duties that Commerce assessed on those Chinese imports averaged 148 percent, compared with 36 percent for other countries' imports that were penalized.[28] Moreover, in 2007, Commerce adopted a new policy allowing the imposition of both anti-dumping and countervailing duties on Chinese products — potentially penalizing them, in other words, for being unfairly subsidized as well as being priced below fair market value. Previously, Washington had entertained only anti-dumping cases against China on the grounds that it was legally classified as a non-market economy and stiff anti-dumping duties would therefore compensate for any subsidization.[29] (More about this in the next chapter.)

Bush resisted entreaties to come down harder on China — and he took considerable heat as a result. Even during the 2004 campaign, when he was getting pounded by Democratic candidate John Kerry for being soft on Beijing, the president forthrightly opposed demands by organized labour for sanctions

---

27 Paul Blustein, 2002, "Trade Partners Trading Threats: EU, Japan, Plan Retaliation for U.S. Tariffs," *The Washington Post*, April 27.

28 Chad P. Bown, 2007, China's WTO Entry, Antidumping, Safeguards, and Dispute Settlement," NBER Working Paper No. 13349, August, www.nber.org/papers/w13349.

29 The policy change came in the context of a case involving coated paper imports from China. Ibid.

against China's treatment of workers.[30] By remaining true to his convictions, Bush deserves credit for political courage. In hindsight, however, using the China safeguard — or just quietly threatening Beijing with its wide application — might have been effective at inducing a change in China's foreign exchange policy. That, in turn, might have blunted the impact of the China shock. Would such an approach have worked? That is an unanswerable question; in any event, the White House didn't try.

In Bush's second term, as troubling aspects of China's economic policies became more evident, top US officials began speaking more bluntly and acting more aggressively. "China has been more open than many developing countries, but there are increasing signs of mercantilism, with policies that seek to direct markets rather than opening them," warned Zoellick, who had been named deputy secretary of state, in a widely acclaimed address on September 21, 2005, which exhorted Beijing to become a "responsible stakeholder" in the international system. "The United States will not be able to sustain an open international economic system — or domestic US support for such a system — without greater cooperation from China, as a stakeholder that shares responsibility on international economic issues."[31]

Responding to intensified criticism in Congress, the new US trade representative, Rob Portman, vowed to undertake a "top-to-bottom review" of the administration's China trade policy. That review resulted in a February 2006 report citing, among other things, "continued Chinese barriers to some US exports; failure to protect intellectual property rights; failure to protect labor rights and enforce labor laws and standards; [and] unreported and extensive government subsidies and preferences for [China's] own industries."[32] The chief proposal, implemented soon thereafter, was a significant expansion of Washington's capacity for investigating Chinese trade practices and cracking down on infractions. The trade representative's office established a "China Enforcement Task Force," headed by a chief counsel for China trade enforcement. The new office was "charged specifically with pursuing...U.S. rights negotiated under trade agreements," including "the preparation and handling of potential WTO cases with China." Its first head was Claire Reade, senior international trade partner at the Washington law firm of Arnold & Porter.

30 Paul Blustein, 2004, "Government Rejects China Trade Sanctions," *The Washington Post*, April 29.

31 Robert B. Zoellick, 2005, "Whither China: From Membership to Responsibility?" Remarks to the National Committee on U.S.-China Relations, New York, September 21, https://2001-2009.state.gov/s/d/former/zoellick/rem/53682.htm.

32 US Trade Representative, 2006, "U.S.-China Trade Relations: Entering a New Phase of Greater Accountability and Enforcement, Top-to-Bottom Review," February, https://ustr.gov/sites/default/files/Top-to-Bottom%20Review%20FINAL.pdf.

A few months after the completion of that report, an even more powerful kingpin arrived in Washington to oversee US economic policies toward China. He knew the country well from years of interacting with Chinese government and business officials at the highest echelons. Unfortunately, he also stood at the nexus of the greatest vulnerability in the American economic system.

By the time he became Treasury secretary in July 2006, Hank Paulson had travelled to China about 70 times in his capacity as a top Goldman Sachs executive. Waxing nostalgic in his book *Dealing with China* about his first trip to Beijing in 1991, he recalls "landing at the old airport and driving to our hotel on a single-lane road jammed with horses and carts, wobbly bicycles, and speeding cars." The city was then filled with "swaths of hutongs, the characteristic Beijing neighborhoods centered on narrow lanes and residential houses built around courtyards.... On subsequent visits I watched the old neighborhoods being torn down as fast as you could blink, replaced by massive buildings housing government ministries and office, residential, and hotel complexes."[33] Paulson himself played no small part in this transformation, representing Goldman on deals including initial public offerings for Chinese companies, SOE restructurings and bankruptcy workouts for giant Guangdong investment groups. Blessed with an imposing physique — he starred as an offensive lineman for the Dartmouth College football team — Paulson became a familiar presence in the inner sancta of Chinese power; as early as 1997, he met Zhu Rongji, then a vice premier, at the Hall of Purple Light to discuss the offering of shares in China Telecom. Although not a speaker of Chinese, he had gleaned a keen sense of how the country's system worked and thanks to his work on projects such as improving management education at Tsinghua University and protecting the environment in the southwestern province of Yunnan, the leadership in Beijing viewed him as someone who genuinely cared about the welfare of the Chinese people. When Bush summoned him to the White House to offer the Treasury post, therefore, Paulson sought and obtained the president's approval for putting his experience to work on a new approach for US-China engagement.

Paulson's idea, which was named the "Strategic Economic Dialogue" (SED), was hatched over the summer of 2006 during brainstorming sessions with Deborah Lehr, who had served in the Clinton administration as a top China

---

33 Henry M. Paulson, Jr., 2015, *Dealing with China: An Insider Unmasks the New Economic Superpower*, New York, NY: Twelve, chapter 2.

trade negotiator and was married to Goldman's chief of staff. Tension over the foreign exchange issue was dominating the US-China economic relationship in an unhealthy way, Paulson believed. In the Senate, Schumer and Graham were pressing forward with their bill threatening Beijing with sanctions for its cheap-currency policy, which Paulson viewed as certain to boomerang, and although he acknowledged the importance of the issue, he argued that it was distracting attention from other, more systemic concerns regarding China's economic liberalization that could generate long-lasting benefits for both sides. Policy makers at senior levels should therefore convene twice a year for give-and-take on all manner of economic issues — not just hot-button trade, currency and investment topics but also financial market opening, energy, the environment, and food and product safety. Other Sino-US negotiating fora already existed (notably one initiated in 1983, called the Joint Commission on Commerce and Trade [JCCT]), but by choosing top economic priorities and putting maximum emphasis on them at the SED, the United States could convey more clearly to China what it wanted and what it was willing to give in return, Paulson contended. The Treasury chief wanted to include a large number of Chinese ministers and influential officials involved in economic matters, while also reserving time for brief engagement with the respective heads of state, Hu and Bush. That would be the most effective way of exploiting China's "top-down yet consensus-driven decision making," according to Paulson, who writes, "As I had long since learned: no one person could say yes, but many could say no. And you always wanted to get a blessing from the very top."[34]

A couple of months after taking office, Paulson took his first trip to China as Treasury secretary, obtaining the leadership's detailed assent to plans for holding SEDs, with the first scheduled for December 2006. And in an indication of the esteem in which he was held, he managed a brief tête-à-tête with Hu — just the two of them, plus an interpreter, an extraordinary courtesy since Paulson wasn't a head of state. During that chat, the Treasury chief made it clear that he couldn't ignore the foreign exchange problem completely in view of the pressure for action from Capitol Hill.

"In a way that could only be done in a truly 'private' meeting, I said something that I never divulged to members of the Congress or even to my fellow Cabinet members," Paulson writes in his book (adding that he did report the exchange to Bush.) "I gave him a number to work with. 'Mr. President,' I said, 'if your currency appreciated 3 percent against the dollar before the end of our

---

34 Ibid., chapter 11.

first SED session this December, the result would be good for China and it would help me convince Congress that the SED is working."' Hu's response — "I understand" — was enough to convince Paulson that Beijing would allow the RMB to appreciate more rapidly than before, and upon his return he called Schumer and Graham, who shelved their bill, at least for the time being.[35] The RMB did climb, although only by 1.3 percent in the last quarter of 2006, and 2.2 percent by the spring of 2007, at which time the IMF began assuming greater responsibility for the issue — with highly unsatisfactory results, as noted in the previous chapter.

As for the SED itself, the outcome can be described as incremental at best. The first session convened on December 14-15, 2006, in the Great Hall of the People, with the two delegations facing each other across long tables and video screens placed at intervals for viewing PowerPoint slides. Paulson was in a "super cabinet" position, leading a 28-person team that included six of his fellow cabinet members plus agency heads, notably Fed chairman Ben Bernanke. On the Chinese side, Iron Lady Wu Yi, now a vice premier, served as Paulson's counterpart, with 14 ministry-level officials in attendance along with high-ranking aides. Despite hopes for a spirited discussion on agenda items that included China's economic development strategy and specific energy and environmental issues, even Paulson had to admit that "speakers relied too frequently on set pieces or talking points."[36] Four more gatherings were held during the remainder of Bush's presidency — one in Washington, one in Annapolis, Maryland and two more in Beijing.

Some specific "deliverables" resulted, notably an agreement on air travel that more than doubled non-stop routes between the United States and China, a Chinese commitment on emissions trading and a tourism promotion accord.[37] But US trade officials who participated generally found the talks non-conducive to anything resembling breakthroughs on the issues that mattered to them. "It was interesting; there were these canned presentations, but absolutely nothing I could tell came out of it," Warren Maruyama, the USTR general counsel at that time, told me. "And things were going south in China — at USTR we knew we were in big trouble on the Hill. So the only thing we could do, to show we're being tough, was to file a bunch of WTO cases — which we promptly did." (The next chapter addresses China-related WTO litigation in detail.)

---

35 Ibid.

36 Ibid.

37 Mercy Kuo, 2016, "Assessing the US-China Strategic and Economic Dialogue: Insights from Daniel B. Wright," *The Diplomat*, July 20.

In any event, the SEDs were overtaken by other developments — in US financial markets.

The talks were supposed to be two-way, with China having reciprocal rights to air its concerns about US policies, and Chinese officials had a lot to talk about following the near-collapse of Bear Stearns in March 2008. Amid the steady debilitation of other Wall Street firms, Paulson was peppered with questions from the Chinese about the health of US banks, the adequacy of Washington's response and the safety of their country's holdings of US securities. At the SED in Annapolis in June 2008, Wang Qishan, who had known Paulson for 15 years and succeeded Wu Yi as the head of the Chinese delegation, pulled the Treasury secretary aside. "He wanted me to know that the financial crisis in the U.S. had affected the way he and others in the senior ranks of the Party saw us," recalled Paulson, who quotes Wang as saying: "You were my teacher, but now here I am in my teacher's domain, and look at your system, Hank. We aren't sure we should be learning from you anymore."[38]

The Lehman bankruptcy was yet to come, along with the even more humbling episodes for Paulson in which he had to beseech Wang and other Chinese officials to help avert a full-scale meltdown, as recounted in chapter 5. Here, ironically, was where the SED may have had its most significant impact. Crediting Beijing with "play[ing] a big role in helping the West survive and emerge from the worst of the crisis," Paulson concludes: "The relationships I had built in China, at Goldman and through the painstaking efforts of the SED, had paid off."[39]

The depths that America plumbed — and the crisis in Europe that followed — thoroughly discredited Western-style capitalism in the eyes of many Chinese. To the extent the US economy had been admired as a model that China should strive to emulate, the global financial crisis shattered such perceptions. Washington's bailouts of major banks and the auto industry further eroded America's moral standing as a paragon of market discipline. "Now our people are joking that we look at the U.S. and see 'socialism with American characteristics,'" chortled Gao Xiqing, the head of a firm that managed a hefty portion of the state's overseas investments, in an *Atlantic* magazine interview.[40]

The Chinese economy not only weathered the crisis, it grew so robustly as to emerge as the single most potent source of support for global recovery. When

---

38 Paulson, *Dealing with China* (see footnote 33 in this chapter), chapter 14.

39 Ibid.

40 James Fallows, 2008, "Be Nice to the Countries That Lend You Money," *The Atlantic*, December.

overseas demand shrivelled in the winter of 2008-2009, causing export orders to plunge and leaving millions of Chinese workers idle, Beijing responded with an emergency stimulus package that included spending of nearly $600 billion, or 12.5 percent of GDP, on priorities such as transportation, electrification, health care, education and low-income housing. The People's Bank of China, meanwhile, slashed interest rates and also used a policy tool available to few central banks elsewhere — it doubled the target for bank lending, to which major banks were obliged to obey with a splurge in credit for state-owned and private Chinese businesses. The payoff was that output expanded at a pace of 9.1 percent in 2009, almost matching the previous year's growth rate and far outstripping economies in the rest of the world.[41]

In China, reformers who favoured additional progress toward liberalizing markets and rolling back party-state control were thrown on the defensive. Statists were emboldened.[42] That presented the next US administration with even bigger problems.

Oval Office briefing sessions for Barack Obama almost invariably began with the president listening first to his advisers spelling out their analyses, then giving his perspective after contemplating what he had heard. But in late 2009, a briefing on China issues went differently because Obama had something on his mind. He opened the meeting by recounting a recent lunch he'd had with four CEOs "who had spent most of the time complaining about Chinese practices: violations of intellectual property rights, discriminatory actions by regulators, and favoritism for domestic companies," according to an account in a book by Jeffrey Bader, who was senior director for Asian affairs at the National Security Council. Bader's book continues: "The economic relationship with China was somewhat like a basketball game, [Obama] said. For years, we used to trounce them, so if they threw a few elbows around in the lane it didn't matter, we could ignore it. Now the game was much closer, and they were continuing to throw elbows around, but the referee wasn't calling any fouls. So he wondered if we didn't need to find a way to push back, to start throwing around a few elbows ourselves."[43]

41 For a detailed account of China's crisis response, see Adam Tooze, 2018, *Crashed: How a Decade of Financial Crises Changed the World*, New York, NY: Viking.

42 Charles W. Freeman III and Wen Jin Yuan, 2011, "China's New Leftists and the China Model Debate after the Financial Crisis," CSIS July, www.csis.org/analysis/chinas-new-leftists-and-the-china-model-debate-after-financial-crisis.

43 Republished with permission of Brookings Institution Press, from *Obama and China's Rise: An Insider's Account of America's Asia Strategy*, Jeffrey A. Bader, 2012; permission conveyed through Copyright Clearance Center, Inc.

The grievances expressed by Obama's lunch companions reflected an increasingly troublesome climate for multinationals operating in China. Among the chief sources of pique were demands for technology transfer, which were continuing, albeit in subtle and tacit ways, according to many in China's foreign business community. As a 2010 article in the *Harvard Business Review* put it, foreign CEOs were "in a terrible bind: They can either comply with the rules and share their technologies with would-be Chinese competitors or refuse and miss out on the world's fastest-growing market."[44]

No proof was offered to support claims that the Chinese government was coercing foreign companies or violating its WTO commitments regarding technology transfer. Beijing has routinely and repeatedly dismissed such allegations as baseless, insisting that any agreements to hand over intellectual property from abroad are strictly voluntary, resulting from private bargaining between foreign and domestic companies with no involvement by government officials. The evidence of forced transfers for market access can best be described as circumstantial. But it is not hard to see why such evidence strikes many foreigners in the business community — and some Chinese with whom I have spoken — as credible.

In some cases, Chinese officials have allegedly conveyed their demands without putting in writing anything that might be used in a WTO complaint. For example, according to confidential interviews conducted by attorneys at the law firm of Covington & Burling for a 2012 study commissioned by the US Chamber of Commerce, "Foreign automobile manufacturers have been told orally by NDRC officials that approval will not be granted for them to manufacture electric vehicles in China unless they assume a minority stake in a JV [joint venture] with a local company...transfer certain core technology to the JV, and agree to local branding for the vehicles."[45]

In other cases, the chain of causation has been even more roundabout. Before being allowed to invest or expand in China, foreign firms have to undergo an elaborate approval process involving various government agencies, in particular the NDRC. A lengthy document called the "Catalogue of Industries for Guiding Foreign Investment" divides industries and sub-industries into categories that are "encouraged," "restricted" or "prohibited" for multinational companies. Depending on which category a prospective investment was classified

---

44 Thomas Hout and Pankaj Ghemawat, 2010, "China vs. the World: Whose Technology Is It?" *Harvard Business Review*, December.

45 US Chamber of Commerce, 2012, "China's Approval Process for Inbound Foreign Direct Investment," www.uschamber.com/china%E2%80%99s-approval-process-inbound- foreign-direct-investment-impact-market-access-national-treatment.

in, scrutiny and application requirements can be tougher or looser; Chinese officials have considerable discretion in rendering judgment. For a number of industrial sectors — automotive being one of the main ones — China has required foreign investors to form joint ventures with domestic firms, and in such ventures, the Chinese partner handles the negotiations with the government. Oral instructions regarding technology transfer may therefore be conveyed indirectly via the Chinese partner — a maddeningly murky process.

Technically, foreign firms have the legal right to appeal such dictates, but based on the confidential interviews conducted for the Chamber of Commerce study, the authors concluded that the deck was stacked against protests of this nature. For one thing, the gathering of legally admissible evidence was nearly impossible. Equally important, "the reality [is] that potential investors are extremely reluctant to challenge the decisions of approval authorities, who have considerable power to affect the companies' business prospects in China," the study lamented. Foreign business executives see little prospect of success in court because "the decisions of approval authorities and the People's Courts are all subject to Party supervision and are expected to align with the same underlying policies of the Party." Similar difficulties "have also hindered the US Trade Representative's (USTR) ability to bring WTO cases against China," according to the study. "Even when hard evidence of WTO violations may exist, individual companies are reluctant to share such evidence with the USTR, because they fear negative repercussions if they are seen as supporting an action taken against the Chinese government."

Given foreign executives' aversion to lodging public complaints, one reasonably reliable source of evidence about what is happening is the confidential surveys that have been taken of their experiences. In a 2012 survey of member companies, the US-China Business Council — a group consisting of more than 200 large multinationals operating in China — found that 36 percent of respondents indicated that they had been asked in the previous three years to make a technology transfer as a requirement for getting an investment, project or market entry approval. Around the same time, a similar percentage (35 percent) answered positively when asked, by the American Chamber of Commerce in China, "Is de facto technology transfer as a requirement for market access in China a concern for you?"[46]

46 US-China Business Council, 2012, "USCBC 2012 China Business Environment Survey Results," www.uschina.org/sites/default/files/uscbc-2012-member-survey-results.pdf; and American Chamber of Commerce in China, 2013, "China Business Climate Survey Report," https://media.npr.org/documents/2013/may/AmChamSurvey.pdf.

In 2010, China's leaders unveiled the "Strategic Emerging Industries" (SEI) initiative, a refinement of the indigenous innovation policy. The concepts first adopted in 2005 and 2006 — "megaprojects," "pillar industries" and the like — were combined into seven categories and 37 subcategories of next-generation technologies into which hundreds of billions of dollars would be invested with the aim of fostering Chinese leadership. The seven SEIs included clean energy technology, next-generation IT, biotechnology, high-end equipment manufacturing, alternative energy, new materials and clean energy vehicles. The more specific subcategories included cloud computing, high-end servers, aerospace, solar and wind power, electric cars and many more.[47]

In part, the SEI was designed to defuse foreign complaints about indigenous innovation; it soft-pedalled requirements for technology transfer by foreign investors. But additional policy documents, and implementation of the new approach by Chinese authorities, strongly indicated that Beijing was continuing to forge a statist path of national-champion promotion with the access of many foreign companies contingent on their sharing of know-how with Chinese partners. The 12th Five Year Plan, adopted in March 2011, called for the government to "encourage leading enterprises in key industries... [to] accelerate the development of large scale enterprises with internationally renowned brands and core competitiveness." Highly specific targets were set for major industries — in autos, for example, planners said, "We shall vigorously promote the building of independent brands, encourage the merger and restructuring of enterprises, and form three to five large automobile enterprises groups with core competitiveness, and the industrial concentration of the top ten enterprises shall be up to 90 percent." A State Council document issued in April 2010 directed that "relevant departments...and the local people's governments at all levels are to...adhere to the guiding principles of active and effective utilization of foreign capital and selecting capital based on our own needs, and facilitating the combination of 'capital absorbing' with 'talent introducing' to constantly improve the utilization of foreign capital."[48]

Once a highly influential force for maintaining smooth relations between China and its trading partners, the US business community was becoming a voice of disgruntlement, even alarm. A letter from corporate groups to the White House dated January 26, 2010, warned of "systematic efforts by China

47 A detailed account of the SEI initiative can be found in James McGregor, 2012, *No Ancient Wisdom, No Followers: The Challenges of Chinese Authoritarian Capitalism*, Westport, CT: Prospecta Press, chapter 2.

48 These and other similar directives are cited in US Chamber of Commerce, 2012, "China's Approval Process for Inbound Foreign Direct Investment" (see footnote 45 in this chapter), Part VI.

to develop policies that build their domestic enterprises at the expense of U.S. firms," and asked the administration to give "urgent attention to policy developments in China that pose an immediate danger to U.S. companies." The signatories included the US Chamber, the Business Software Alliance and over a dozen associations representing hundreds of multinationals.[49]

Others drew more extreme conclusions from China's shift under Hu and Wen.

Robert Lighthizer, one of Washington's most redoutable trade hawks, was not an unbiased critic of the Chinese economic system. A deputy US trade representative during the Reagan administration, Lighthizer left government service in 1985 to become a partner at the law firm of Skadden, Arps, Slate, Meagher & Flom, where he spent the next three decades representing American steel companies and other US manufacturers in trade cases, often against Chinese competitors. But the denunciation he delivered on June 9, 2010, about China's overall direction since joining the WTO is noteworthy in view of the role he would later play in the Trump administration.

Looking back at the hopes that had been raised in the late 1990s and early 2000s regarding Beijing's entry into the trade body, Lighthizer punctured them, in particular, claims about the vast opportunities that would arise for American companies and workers. "U.S. businesses trying to enter the Chinese market continue to face an array of market distorting barriers," he said in testimony to a congressional commission. "These are not isolated problems, but part of a broader resistance within China to key WTO norms such as 'national treatment'…and 'transparency.'"[50]

"Why were so many experts — from across the political spectrum — so mistaken?" Lighthizer asked, and his answers were withering: "They failed to adequately account for many unique facts about China, including its political system, its commitment to mercantilism, and the potential size of its economy…. They suffered from hubris about the 'inevitable' triumph of democracy and capitalism…. [T]hey assumed that acceding to the WTO would cause China to become more and more Western in its behavior — almost as if it were merely a more exotic version of Canada."

49 Dexter Roberts, 2010, "China: Closing for Business?" *Bloomberg Businessweek*, March 26.

50 Robert E. Lighthizer, 2010, "Evaluating China's Role in the World Trade Organization over the Past Decade," Testimony before the U.S.-China Economic and Security Review Commission, June 10. As noted in chapter 3, footnote 2, Lighthizer opposed China's accession deal, although his public criticism at the time was based mainly on human rights and national security grounds.

Lighthizer's bottom line: "China presents a unique challenge to U.S. policymakers, and it may require a unique response," including "tariffs or quantitative limitations [on Chinese imports]," even if those "derogated" from WTO commitments. "The point is that an unthinking, simplistic and slavish dedication to the mantra of 'WTO consistency' — in the face of a trading relationship that is completely out of balance and that has grown increasingly divorced from any of the promises made when China joined the WTO — makes very little sense, and is plainly not dictated by our international obligations," he said.

The Obama administration was not standing idly by — far from it. Determined to show he would be tougher on Beijing than Bush, Obama used the China-specific safeguard that his predecessor had eschewed, approving 35 percent tariffs on imported Chinese automobile and light-truck tires in September 2009. The duties succeeded in sharply reducing the inflow of Chinese tires, and Obama would later proclaim that his action saved more than 1,000 American jobs. But the president's job-saving math was questionable; the hit to competition from China opened the door to more imported tires from Canada, South Korea, Thailand, Indonesia, Japan, Mexico and other countries.[51] Furthermore, Beijing struck back within a couple of days, slapping stiff anti-dumping duties on US products including chicken — specifically, chicken feet, which American poultry farmers were happily shipping to the Chinese market where they could get about 80 cents a pound for a chicken part that is consumed in China but almost nowhere else in the world. China's retaliatory move was based on blatantly twisted legal reasoning, and the United States eventually won a judgment to that effect at the WTO.[52] But the US poultry industry suffered significant lost revenue before the Geneva tribunal rendered its verdict. The episode afforded a sobering lesson in the risks of trade warfare with China — and the Obama administration did not resort to the China safeguard again.

During Obama's first term, his team stepped up WTO litigation against China, bringing cases (and winning) on Beijing's restrictions on foreign credit cards, imports of autos and sales of US high-tech steel, as well as its

---

51 Kenneth Rapoza, 2012, "Obama's Half-Truth on China Tire Tariffs," *Forbes*, January 25.

52 An illuminating account of this dispute can be found in Thomas J. Prusa and Edwin Vermulst, 2015, "China — Anti-Dumping and Countervailing Duty Measures on Broiler Products from the United States: How the chickens come home to roost," *World Trade Review* (14): 287–335, April 15.

restrictions on exports of raw materials and rare earth minerals.[53] At the insistence of Secretary of State Hillary Clinton, Obama put his own stamp on the SED by expanding it to include foreign policy and national security issues and renaming it the "Strategic and Economic Dialogue" (S&ED). On economic issues, much of the discussion revolved around the continued undervaluation of the RMB; China had halted upward movements in its currency at the time of the global financial crisis for fear of engendering instability in its own financial system. Treasury Secretary Timothy Geithner, like his Bush administration predecessors, strongly preferred quiet diplomatic methods to persuade Beijing that a stronger RMB was in China's own interest, as opposed to public threats or Schumer-Graham type legislation, and this approach arguably brought results, as the RMB would rise 16 percent against the US dollar in inflation-adjusted terms during Obama's first term.[54]

The S&ED also scored some success, at least on paper, on industrial policy. Several meetings of the S&ED and JCCT ended with the Chinese side reiterating vows to refrain from using technology transfer as a condition of market access. Chinese officials also agreed to rescind some aspects of indigenous innovation policy that had evoked howls of protest from foreign businesses, in particular, a requirement for government procurement to favour products using locally developed technology. But many foreign executives and trade policy makers remained skeptical that China, having introduced the concept of indigenous innovation and used informal methods to advance it, would change its policy in substance as well as form. Their wariness deepened when provincial and local governments continued to use catalogues of indigenous innovation products in making procurement decisions.[55]

Despite Obama's interest in "throwing elbows," his administration stopped well short of confronting China in the aggressive ways proposed by Lighthizer. The main economic policy heavyweights in the Obama White House — Geithner and National Economic Council Chairman Larry Summers — "were critical of the direction the Chinese economy had taken in recent years and were disturbed by the impact of its discriminatory practices on U.S. competitiveness," so they laid out a variety of options for the

---

53 Obama aides like to boast that they brought many more WTO cases against China than the George W. Bush administration did, but this is somewhat unfair, because the first term of Bush's presidency coincided with the transition period for most of China's WTO commitments, during which there was general agreement that Beijing should be given time to undertake the necessary reforms before complaints were lodged in Geneva.

54 Timothy F. Geithner, 2014, *Stress Test: Reflections on Financial Crises,* New York, NY: Crown Publishers, chapter 7.

55 Freeman and Yuan, "China's New Leftists" (see footnote 42 in this chapter).

president to consider "from relatively anodyne to draconian ones," according to Bader's book. "But at the end of each discussion or memorandum, they consistently concluded that the impact of China's practices on the U.S. economy was in fact quite small, and that even positive corrections would have considerably less impact in the United States than most people imagined. They also foresaw considerable risk of Chinese retaliation, mobilized by a state less bound by international rules and practices than the U.S. government was, that would cost us more than it would cost China. And they pointed out the potential reactions of markets to the appearance of protectionism by the administration."[56]

In assessing China's move toward statist policies during the Hu-Wen era, it is important to recognize that private enterprise and freely functioning markets were continuing to propel much of the nation's economic dynamism. Nearly six million private firms were registered in 2011, compared with just 443,000 in 1996, and private urban employment totalled 253 million — which was nearly three times the number of people employed in China's public sector, including SOEs. Although total public sector employment was still huge in absolute terms, at 87.4 million, it was only 11 percent of China's economically active population, a smaller fraction than the comparable figures for the United States, France and Germany, as Nicholas Lardy has pointed out.[57] Private sector firms were earning significantly higher returns on assets than SOEs, Lardy's research shows, and the favouritism that SOEs received from the government often failed to achieve the desired result because SOEs were disincentivized to become competitive on their own. The auto sector was a perfect example of this phenomenon; domestic model cars were much less popular in the Chinese market than foreign brands such as General Motors and Volkswagen (which were produced by China-based joint ventures), and no Chinese-brand car was penetrating overseas markets with any success.

Still, the party-state's influence over economic decisions at the micro level was clearly on a steep rise since 2001. Not that this was easy to demonstrate by citing chapter and verse — quite the contrary, because the influence was typically exercised via channels to which outsiders lacked access. That gave Chinese officials plausible deniability; when confronted with accusations that they were, say, forcing foreign companies to transfer technology or bestowing preferences on domestic firms or manipulating markets in other ways

---

56 Bader, *Obama and China's Rise* (see footnote 43 in this chapter), chapter 11.

57 Nicholas R. Lardy, 2014, *Markets Over Mao: The Rise of Private Business in China*, Washington, DC: Peterson Institute for International Economics, chapter 4.

inimical to WTO principles, they could insist that all players were simply acting voluntarily. Beijing veterans who have tangled frequently with the party-state, however, know that its power is much more than a figment of their imaginations.

One such veteran is Tim Stratford, a former USTR official who has spent much of his adult life in China as a diplomat and private attorney. "There's an ambiguity that China's government delights in fostering — they like to have it both ways," Stratford told me, and he offers the following example:

> I was the lead negotiator on the tires case, the China specific safe-guard [ultimately approved by Obama]. The Chinese said, "OK, we get it, the US thinks we're shipping too many tires, so let's just address the problem. Tell us how many tires you want, and we'll impose a quota." I said, "Thank you for trying to work with us, but quotas are illegal under the WTO." And they said, "How about if we talk to the industry association, and persuade them to exercise some self-discipline so they don't exceed the limit?" I said, "Thank you for thinking creatively, but our Justice Department would say that would be an illegal cartel."

> The point is, they have a fluidity in terms of how they characterize things. If they want it to be state action, they can have that, and if they want it to be private action, they can characterize it as that too.

Can a system like that be amenable to WTO litigation? That is the subject of the next chapter.

CHAPTER 7

CHINA IN THE WTO DOCK

Anyone who has been a stranger at a social gathering can relate to the experience of the Chinese delegation members who filed into one of the large meeting rooms at the WTO headquarters, the Centre William Rappard, on April 11, 2002. According to Yang Guohua, who was attending in his capacity as a trade ministry official, awkwardness engulfed them as they surveyed the scene.

Attendees from other WTO member countries "greeted each other. They shook hands," while those in the Chinese delegation "looked around the room and found very few familiar faces," Yang later wrote of the episode. Even more embarrassing, "The tables of the people from all the other eight members were covered with documents and materials, while only a few pieces of paper, including the name lists of different delegations, were in front of my Chinese colleagues."[1]

The occasion was the opening session of a WTO dispute regarding the United States' imposition of safeguard duties on steel. China had attained membership in the trade body only four months earlier and was not expecting

---

1   Yang Guohua, 2015, "China in the WTO Dispute Settlement: A Memoir," *Journal of World Trade* 49 (1): 1–18.

to become involved in a dispute so soon, but the US action affected steel from China as well as other nations, so Beijing joined the others as a complainant.[2] As a novice in such proceedings, however, "we could not contribute much to this case," Yang wrote. "We could not even understand what [the others] were talking about!"

This was China's initiation to the WTO's dispute settlement system. For a country where litigation was still a foreign concept, China's discomfort with the system was understandable, but that would prove only temporary. China would eventually become a frequent — and frequently victorious — disputant.

In the mantra of WTO enthusiasts, dispute settlement is the trade body's "crown jewel." Just as governments have courts to resolve conflicts and interpret laws passed by their legislatures, the WTO's tribunals render judgment as to whether one nation or another is violating basic tenets, such as the MFN principle, or is failing to adhere to commitments in WTO agreements. These judgments have teeth: as previously noted, a country found guilty of violations can exercise its sovereign right to refuse alterations in its laws, but it may face economic punishment, usually in the form of tariffs levied on its products by the winner. The WTO can therefore claim "clearly the most powerful dispute settlement system at the international level that we have today or perhaps ever in the history of the world," as John Jackson, the law professor who first proposed the trade body's creation, once put it.[3]

The system's importance extends far beyond the rulings handed down in individual cases, because its very existence helps to defuse tensions that inevitably arise in commerce among nations. When a country's politicians and citizens are up in arms over another country's trade practices, bringing a case to the WTO can help lower the political temperature. Instead of lashing out by unilaterally imposing sanctions, which might well provoke retaliation and counter-retaliation, a country's trade minister can call a news conference and righteously announce plans to pursue litigation in Geneva with the intention of bringing the offender to justice. Aggrieved parties can take comfort in knowing that their case has been turned over to an impartial body for adjudication, and that the body has robust methods of enforcing its decisions.

---

2   The case was first brought by the European Union, which was soon joined by Japan, South Korea, Switzerland and others including China.

3   Merit E. Janow, Victoria Donaldson and Alan Yanovich, eds., 2008, *The WTO: Governance, Dispute Settlement and Developing Countries,* Huntington, NY: Juris Publishing, 388.

Under the GATT, the system tended to be "diplomacy oriented," with a chief aim of reaching a negotiated settlement between the disputants — a rather flimsy method of dispensing justice that, given its lack of enforceability, ultimately proved inadequate to containing trade tensions. With the creation of the WTO came a much more "rules-oriented" and "sanctions-based" system. It was based on the theory that countries ought to be encouraged to settle their differences, and to be given plenty of time to do so, but if they can't, a decision will be rendered as to who's right and who's wrong, backed by the threat of punishment against non-compliers. All this sets the WTO apart from other international institutions.

For all the system's virtues, however, its effectiveness with regard to Chinese trade practices was a source of deepening misgivings as Beijing neared the end of its first decade in the WTO. Countries had brought complaints against China to the trade body's tribunals and gotten satisfaction; the WTO was by no means impotent. But China's policies were bedevilling the trade body in ways that were unforeseen at the time the country joined and were becoming increasingly glaring given the immensity of the Chinese economy. That was giving rise to a view trenchantly articulated by Lighthizer in his June 2010 testimony cited in the previous chapter: "The WTO dispute settlement system is simply not designed to deal with a legal and political system so at odds with the basic premises on which the WTO was founded."[4]

To elucidate this subject, this chapter will examine two WTO disputes involving China in detail.[5] The first case involves allegations that Beijing took unfair competitive advantage of its control over rare earths, the minerals that played an important part in the Sino-Japanese conflict concerning the ship collision recounted in chapter 1. The second case involves a clash between China and the United States over whether Beijing was subsidizing certain products, such as tires for tractors and construction vehicles, that Chinese companies were exporting to the US market. This case is considered a landmark because WTO jurists confronted a central question about the Chinese economy: where is the line between private enterprise and the party-state?

Case number one was a Chinese defeat; case number two was a Chinese victory. The purpose of chronicling them is not to belabour the obvious point that "you

---

4   Robert E. Lighthizer, 2010, "Evaluating China's Role in the World Trade Organization Over the Past Decade," Testimony Before the U.S.-China Economic and Security Review Commission, June 10.

5   Sources for this chapter include scores of people interviewed in Beijing, Brussels, Geneva, Tokyo and Washington, as well as a review of thousands of pages of documents in the public record. As with other chapters, nearly all interviews were conducted on a "deep background" basis, the purpose being to elicit the maximum amount of candour. To the extent sources of information can be identified, footnotes are provided, but full attribution would be impossible without compromising interviewees' confidentiality.

win some, you lose some" at the WTO, just as in tribunals elsewhere. Rather, it is to show how the system functions, and where its strengths and weaknesses lie, especially with regard to China.

During its first five years of WTO membership, China was a reticent, almost timorous player in disputes. When other countries brought cases against Beijing or even threatened to — an example being a 2004 complaint by the United States, European Union and other WTO members alleging discriminatory Chinese rebates of semiconductor taxes — Chinese officials negotiated settlements as quickly as possible for fear of becoming embroiled in litigation or, worse, suffering humiliating defeat. The filing of a case against China was often taken in Beijing as an affront; so furious was Iron Lady Wu Yi upon hearing that the United States was proceeding with a complaint that she stopped speaking to Susan Schwab, the US trade representative, according to the recollections of people who were involved. Meanwhile, Chinese government trade lawyers were educating themselves about the system's ins and outs, attending countless hearings during 2003–2006 involving other countries. (The public is usually barred from legal sessions in WTO disputes, but member countries can send delegations as "third parties" with interests in the case.)

Once China's WTO commitments were fully phased in, it began to accept that dispute settlement was a normal aspect of membership — and it had little choice, because complaints were flying. From 2006 to 2010, China was the defendant in 20 WTO cases, nearly 24 percent of the total filed, with the United States and the European Union the main complainants;[6] subsequent years brought a similar amount of litigation. Beijing itself lodged a number of complaints, mostly against Washington and Brussels. When China has lost, or backed down — as it has fairly often, in cases involving issues such as imports of auto parts, financial information services and export restraints on raw materials — its compliance has been commendable on the whole. (One oft-cited exception: a case involving the access of foreign credit card companies to the Chinese market, where China has dragged its feet.[7]) Being keenly sensitive to

---

6   Scott Kennedy, 2016, "The WTO in Wonderland: China's Awkward 15th Anniversary," CSIS, December 11, www.csis.org/analysis/wto-wonderland-chinas-awkward-15th-anniversary.

7   This case is often depicted in the media as if China disregarded a firm commitment at the time of WTO accession to open its market to foreign credit cards, then decisively lost a WTO panel ruling in 2012, and then ignored the ruling, but the facts are nowhere near as straightforward as that. The panel actually ruled in China's favour, and against the United States, on a number of issues, and the decision was regarded by a number of experts as mixed. For a detailed account of the case and its origins, see Bernard M. Hoekman and Niall Meagher, 2014, "China — Electronic Payment Services: Discrimination, Economic Development and the GATS," *World Trade Review* 13 (2): 409–42. The panel did rule that some of China's regulations were discriminatory and unfairly disadvantaged foreign credit card companies, so China altered those regulations. But foreign credit card issuers, such as Visa and Mastercard, complained that the regulators still effectively prevented them from making major headway in the Chinese market until Chinese competitors had attained dominant positions.

its international reputation, Beijing can take satisfaction that its record of obeying WTO tribunal rulings has been superior to that of the United States, which has ignored or skirted negative decisions in several cases.[8]

But whether those outcomes provide adequate remedies for the challenge China poses to the trading system is a legitimate matter of debate. The problem is not that the WTO is designed to accommodate only purely capitalist countries; even in the days of the GATT, rules were agreed to cover economies with heavy elements of statism, including those transitioning from socialism, such as Poland, Hungary and the Czech Republic. Obviously, the negotiations concerning China's accession added more rules, including some specific to Beijing, with the aim of addressing "socialism with Chinese characteristics." But all that came before the developments in China that created a unique economic structure not envisioned by the rule-drafters.

Informing this debate is the reason for this chapter's detailed perusal of two disputes. As with all such cases, a fair amount of dry technicalities infuse the arguments. But to a greater extent than usual, these cases lend themselves to being presented as tales about conflicts involving real-life people, businesses, government officials, lawyers and judges.

Case number two involves exactly the kind of Chinese practices that are difficult for WTO rules to cover. Partly because of its legal importance, this case shall be chronicled at greater length than the rare earths case. The tale of case two also illuminates controversies about the WTO's dispute settlement system and US actions that threaten to undermine it — another profoundly worrisome problem facing the trade body.

Accusations of WTO unfairness have often emanated from Washington. A number of US trade policy makers and members of the American trade community — Lighthizer prime among them — decry what they perceive as bias on the seven-member Appellate Body, the WTO's version of the Supreme Court, which weighs appeals of decisions that have been rendered by three-member panels. In this view, the Appellate Body has gone overboard in interpreting the rules to suit its predilections, showing excessive distaste for trade remedy laws heavily used by the United States. Washington has been throwing its weight around to correct this perceived bias for some time, as

---

8   The most notorious example was a 2004 loss to Brazil in which a panel found US cotton subsidies to be in violation of America's WTO obligations. Even after the Appellate Body affirmed the panel's decision, and other panels repeatedly ruled that the United States was out of compliance, Washington refused to change its cotton subsidy program meaningfully. Only in 2014, when Brazil was threatening to slap tariffs on a number of American products, did the US government settle the dispute by paying $300 million to the Brazilian Cotton Institute.

we shall see, and US assertiveness is on a sharp rise in the Trump era, to the point of casting doubt on the dispute settlement system's ability to continue functioning.

To what extent is the WTO effective in addressing the challenge posed by China's economic system, and to what extent is it deficient? How well-deserved is the sobriquet "crown jewel" for the dispute settlement system? Are the trade body's flaws fatal? Are they fixable? Enhanced understanding of these issues can be derived from the recounting of the two WTO cases below.

In capacious rooms at the Centre William Rappard, like the one where Yang Guohua and his colleagues first attended WTO dispute proceedings, a crowd of about 100 people gathered for three days in late February 2013 as a tribunal began considering a case dubbed *China — Rare Earths*.[9] For anyone prone to sentimentality about the glories of international governance, the scene afforded ample validation.

Speakers stuck to the merits of their arguments; the ineffectiveness of shouting or theatrics was well understood by all. Sitting on a raised dais were three judges — or panellists, as the WTO prefers to call them — from countries that were not parties to the dispute. The panel chairman, Nacer Benjelloun-Touimi, was a former Moroccan ambassador and WTO official; his colleagues were from Uruguay and Zambia. On one side of the panel sat legal teams from the complainants — the United States, European Union and Japan — and also present, sitting behind the panel, were a number of legal specialists from the WTO Secretariat assisting the panellists. On the second day, representatives also attended from 13 third-party countries that took an interest in the issues at stake.

The largest group by far, 35 people, was sitting on the defendants' side — that is, China's. It is typical for China to send much bigger delegations than any other WTO member to these proceedings, which some of the Americans find off-putting, especially since Chinese participants are often seen carrying shopping bags from fancy Geneva boutiques and get ferried to and from their hotels in a fleet of luxury sedans. (The US mission in Geneva uses a minibus

---

9   The full official name of the case is *China — Measures Related to the Exportation of Rare Earths, Tungsten, and Molybdenum* (WTO case numbers DS431, DS432 and DS433). Information about many of the episodes and arguments that were made comes from interviews, but the specific quotations cited herein from written briefs and oral presentations can be found in the panel report and Appellate Body reports on the WTO website, www.wto.org/english/tratop_e/dispu_e/cases_e/ds431_e.htm; and in the archive pages of the USTR website, https://ustr.gov/archive/WTO/Section_Index.html.

to transport the trade lawyers sent from Washington and other US personnel.) Moreover, nearly all of the Chinese attendees stay silent, leaving most of the talking on their country's behalf to high-priced attorneys from foreign firms that Beijing routinely hires for representation in Geneva — in the rare earths case, these lawyers came from Sidley Austin, a Chicago-based firm that has the world's biggest practice in WTO litigation.[10] But the size of China's presence serves a noble purpose, namely, to show officials from the affected ministries and industries how fairly and thoroughly Beijing's arguments are being heard by WTO arbiters. Officials from the Ministry of Commerce, the boosters-in-chief of the WTO in Beijing, want to ensure that these other Chinese stakeholders will honour the decision and, more generally, appreciate the importance of abiding by WTO rules.

International interest in the case was high because of the public attention rare earths had seized during the 2010 faceoff between China and Japan. That episode did not bear directly on the WTO dispute, but it cast a spotlight on the fact that China was virtually the only country producing these strategic minerals, and afterwards, world prices of rare earths skyrocketed. The main reason for this was Beijing's policy of restricting exports (to all foreign buyers, not just the Japanese), by imposing duties on rare earths shipped abroad as well as quotas limiting the amounts.

The closer trade officials from the United States and other countries looked at what was happening, the more clearly they perceived a pattern that, they concluded, reflected a strategy formulated by Chinese economic planners to benefit favoured industries on a discriminatory basis. China-based manufacturers buying rare earths could enjoy a significant cost advantage over foreign manufacturers, because the domestic firms were not subject to the export restrictions. The United States and the European Union had won a case against China involving a similar export policy on raw materials such as bauxite and zinc,[11] so they decided to haul Beijing before the WTO again, this time enlisting the help of Japan, which was still smarting from the ship collision.

In written and oral arguments to the panel, the Sidley lawyers representing China defended Beijing's rare earths policy as necessitated by horrific pollution problems. Rare earth production requires floating powder from crude ores on water, to which chemicals are added, a process leading to the concentration of toxic and radioactive substances in large ponds — all of which

---

10 Also providing legal counsel to China in this case were attorneys from a Chinese firm, AllBright.

11 The full name of this case is *China — Measures Related to the Exportation of Various Raw Materials* (WTO case number DS394).

"constitute a major environmental health risk," the Chinese side asserted, adding that exposure increases the likelihood of maladies including lung lesions, skin diseases and problems of the central nervous system. "While many countries benefit from China's resources, China stands almost alone in bearing the burden of this production," so Beijing was entitled to limit the amount sold abroad, according to the country's legal briefs.[12]

The Chinese legal team acknowledged that by imposing restrictions on rare earths exports — these included duties of up to 25 percent, as well as the quotas — China had technically abrogated certain WTO obligations. (The duties violated specific terms of China's Protocol of Accession; the quotas violated general provisions of international trade law.) But one of the WTO's cardinal principles is that member countries can exercise their sovereign rights to override trade rules when there are legitimate grounds for attaching priority to other socially important goals. And one of the most important of those goals is "protection and preservation of the environment," China's attorneys noted, citing the preamble to the 1994 agreement that established the WTO. Such rights are also clearly spelled out in provisions of international trade rules known to experts as "Article XX exceptions," which exempt countries from their trade obligations when human health, resource conservation or other such objectives may be adversely affected.

In rebuttal, the Americans and their co-complainants contended that China's policies were masquerading as environmental when the true intent was industrial. Beijing's rare earth restrictions, in other words, were not aimed at addressing environmental concerns but were rather a clever scheme to distort markets in favour of Chinese competitors. Without disputing the desirability of reducing pollution caused by rare earths mining, lawyers from Washington, Brussels and Tokyo derided export restrictions as a poor method of solving the problem — indeed, a perversely ineffective one, since large amounts were still being mined for the benefit of Chinese firms that were enjoying low prices.

"The average 2012 Chinese export price for yttrium was 250 percent higher than the average Chinese domestic price," one of the US attorneys said in an oral statement. "The export prices for europium and terbium were more than

---

12 WTO, 2014, *China — Measures Related to the Exportation of Rare Earths, Tungsten, and Molybdenum,* Reports of the Panel, March 26. https://docs.wto.org/dol2fe/Pages/FE_Search/ FE_S_S006.aspx?Query=(@Symbol=%20wt/ ds431/r*%20not%20rw*)&Language=ENGLISH& Context=FomerScriptedSearch&language UIChanged=true#, pages 75–77.

double the corresponding domestic price."[13] The conclusion, which was especially compelling because a similar argument had been used successfully in the raw materials case, was that "China's measures undermine core principles of the multilateral trading system — they discriminate against foreign users of these materials and provide substantial and unfair advantages to Chinese users when they compete with foreign industries and workers."[14]

Then China's foes went even further, advancing a point of law that infuriated the Chinese delegation. According to attorneys from the United States, the European Union and Japan, the environmental justification Beijing had used for its export restrictions was not only specious, it was beyond China's legal right to invoke. They cited precise wording from China's Accession Protocol, noting that Beijing never insisted upon inserting the right to impose export duties even though other WTO members could. As EU lawyers put it, the terms were "carefully negotiated and crafted," and if China was supposed to enjoy the same rights as other WTO members regarding this issue, "the drafters... would have stated it specifically."[15]

This line of reasoning elicited an emotional reaction from Zhao Hong, an attorney who worked at China's WTO mission. According to people who witnessed the incident, Zhao slammed the table as she spoke, reflecting her indignation that her country, where sensitivity over past subjugation runs deep, was being relegated anew to second-class status. She was regarded by many Geneva insiders as one of Beijing's most strident advocates, and few could have imagined that she would be selected as an Appellate Body member in January 2017. But her reaction concerning the narrow issue that arose in the 2013 hearing was understandable. Suppose, after all, that China had a valid rationale — environmental, social or otherwise — for invoking the Article XX exceptions in situations such as the rare earths case. Should it be prohibited from doing what other countries are allowed to do simply because of a legalistic textual analysis? Such an outcome would be "repugnant," China's lawyers asserted in their briefs.[16]

The verdict came in October 2013. Eagerly awaited though it may have been, the process bore no resemblance to the climactic scenes from courtroom dramas such as *Perry Mason* or *Law and Order*.

13 USTR, 2013, "China — Measures Related to the Exportation of Rare Earths, Tungsten and Molybdenum (DS431), Opening Oral Statement of the United States at the First Substantive Meeting of the Panel with the Parties," February 26, 19.

14 Ibid., 2.

15 WTO, *China — Measures Related to the Exportation of Rare Earths, Tungsten, and Molybdenum* (see footnote 12 in this chapter), B-25.

16 Ibid., 63.

When WTO panels render decisions, they do not summon the parties to tension-filled chambers for solemn pronouncements of guilt or innocence. Rather, they send the parties an "interim report" about their conclusions, which is supposed to remain confidential, with the purpose of receiving feedback that might prompt some modifications in case panellists recognize the need. Sometimes the results are leaked; they were in *China — Rare Earths*, although the final report was not issued until March 26, 2014.

The outcome was rightly hailed as a victory by USTR Michael Froman[17] — indeed, it constituted a near-demolition of China's defence. All three panellists agreed that Brussels, Tokyo and Washington had made a convincing case that Beijing's export restrictions on rare earths were designed to promote domestic industry rather than protect the environment or conserve natural resources. "We do not consider that China has rebutted this evidence," the panel stated.[18] Furthermore, two of the three panellists ruled in the complainants' favour on the technical issue that had riled Zhao.[19] An effort by China to overturn the ruling failed when the Appellate Body upheld the panel's decision in August 2014.

To this day, Chinese lawyers and officials seethe over the decision. But Beijing obediently implemented the order (or "request," in WTO parlance, since sovereign nations are involved) to bring its rare earths policies into compliance with the trade body's rules, by rescinding the export restrictions. International trade rules, and the pursuit of litigation to enforce them, had disrupted a patently unfair aspect of Chinese industrial policy — a triumph for global governance.

Or so it might seem — the reality was more complex. For one thing, the proceedings had taken so long that, in the interim, Beijing had achieved some of its industrial policy goals, in particular inducing foreign companies to move or expand operations to China for the sake of ensuring reliable and inexpensive

---

17 USTR, 2014, "United States Wins Victory in Rare Earths Dispute with China," Press Release, March, https://ustr.gov/about-us/policy-offices/press- office/press- releases/2014/March/ US-wins-victory- in-rare-earths-dispute-with-China.

18 WTO, *China — Measures Related to the Exportation of Rare Earths, Tungsten, and Molybdenum* (see footnote 12 in this chapter), 79.

19 On the technical issue, the majority acknowledged that it would be "manifestly absurd and unreasonable" for any WTO member to be "legally prevented from taking measures that are necessary to protect the environment or human, animal, or plant life or health." Ibid., 65. But they contended, emphasizing "how limited the implications of this finding are" that China could not use export duties for such a purpose as other WTO members could. A third panellist — whose identity was undisclosed, in keeping with WTO custom — dissented on the technical issue but concurred on the broader question of whether China's rare earths policies violated WTO rules.

rare earth supplies. Examples included a Japanese optical device maker, Hoya Corp., which established a subsidiary in China's Shandong Province to produce digital camera lenses, and a Japanese chemicals firm, Showa Denko KK, which increased production at its Chinese plant of an alloy used in hybrid car motors.[20]

Therein lies a big defect in WTO dispute settlement — the lack of retroactivity. As long as China changed its policies to comply with the ruling, it would not suffer any punishment or pay compensation for harm it had caused in the past. And China is hardly the only country that has taken advantage of this weakness in the system. The safeguard duties that George W. Bush imposed on imported steel blatantly violated WTO rules, giving American steelmakers a couple of years of protection from foreign competition until WTO judges could issue decrees against the US measures.

In the rare earths case, the economic benefits for the victors were limited for another reason as well — namely, the laws of supply and demand. Prices for rare earths had plummeted by the time the WTO issued its ruling, because production expanded outside of China (in Australia and Malaysia, for example) and firms found substitutes for some of the minerals.[21]

Still, *China — Rare Earths* showed the WTO working pretty much as might be hoped, without undue difficulties concerning China's unique economic structure. The same cannot be said of *US — Anti-Dumping and Countervailing Duties (China)*, also known as *US — AD/CVD*,[22] the case that will be scrutinized next.

Save heartland America companies and workers! Cheap Chinese imports are killing our business! That was the message delivered on July 8, 2008, in Washington, DC, by a group of executives from tire companies with plants in towns such as Freeport, Illinois; Des Moines, Iowa; Bryan, Ohio; and Unicoi, Tennessee.[23]

---

20 Keiko Yoshioka, Akihiro Nishiyama and Tetsuo Kogure, 2011, "WTO Report on Unfair Trade Infuriates China," *Asahi Shimbun* (English edition), July 7.

21 Alan Beattie, 2015, "Rare Earths and China's Self-Correcting Folly," *beyondbrics* (blog), January 8, www.ft.com/content/17085d7c-78b1-3ddc-9ba0-4bcde804da39?mhq5j=e5.

22 The full official name of the case is: *United States — Definitive Anti-Dumping and Countervailing Duties on Certain Products from China* (WTO case number DS379), www.wto.org/english/tratop_e/dispu_e/cases_e/ds379_e.htm.

23 US International Trade Commission, 2008, "In the Matter of Certain Off-the-Road Tires from China," Hearing Transcript, July 8-9.

The product line that concerned the executives was "off-the-road" tires, the heavy-tread kind used on tractors, earth movers and other agricultural and construction vehicles. In testimony to the US International Trade Commission, the executives complained that imports of such tires, mainly from China, had surged from 19 percent of the US market in 2004 to 37 percent in 2007, because the Chinese tires were priced well below comparable domestically made tires thanks to subsidies the Chinese producers received. The profits of US tire makers were shrinking, and workers were being laid off — employment in the industry had declined by more than five percent between 2005 and 2007, according to union representatives at the hearing, despite the rising incomes of farmers and strong demand for agricultural equipment.

"Imports of dumped and subsidized tires are destroying the market," Don Mateer III, president of Specialty Tire of America, told the commissioners. "On average, Chinese tires undersell our prices by 30 percent." Speaking in support of the US tire makers were several members of Congress, among them Rep. Leonard Boswell, whose southwestern Iowa district included two large tire plants. "An entire domestic industry is threatened, not by healthy competition, but by the unfair trade practices supported by a foreign government," Boswell declared.[24]

The tire makers were seeking the imposition of high duties on imported Chinese off-the-road tires, using trade remedies. In this case, the remedies demanded included anti-dumping (AD) and countervailing duties (CVD) because Chinese tires were allegedly being sold at less than fair value in the US market in addition to being subsidized.

Trade remedies are the single biggest bone of contention in WTO litigation. Although the amount of goods affected by trade remedies is a small fraction of global commerce, disputes over them account for close to half of the cases on which WTO tribunals have ruled. And China is the single biggest target of trade remedies, which is predictable given the size of its export machine but also because of the myriad and often mysterious ways in which Chinese companies receive support — sometimes directly from the government, sometimes in more subtle forms via SOEs or Party directives.

This is why *US — AD/CVD* is a landmark case: a method of assessment was needed for claims that Beijing's invisible hands were at work. Playing one of the starring roles in this dispute was the US off-the-road tire industry,

---

24 Ibid.

although the executives who testified at the July 2008 hearing could not have known it at the time.

Here is also where the stormiest clash has arisen over the Appellate Body's alleged bias. In a number of cases, rulings by the WTO's top judges have sharply curbed the legal flexibility US officials believed they had to use trade remedies. The Appellate Body's decrees on safeguard rulings, for example, have made that type of trade remedy very hard for countries to use. In other cases, a method the United States favours for calculating anti-dumping duties, called "zeroing," has been found in violation of WTO rules.

This "all-out assault on trade remedy measures" was the result of "rogue WTO panel and Appellate Body decisions," according to a blast levelled in 2007 by Lighthizer, whose steel industry clients had suffered some of the worst set-backs.[25] His assertion that WTO jurists were "overreaching" and "inventing" law was shared by some legal experts, notably trade officials in the Bush and Obama administrations. But embitterment in Washington over these rulings is dismissed in other quarters as little more than the arrogance of sore losers, especially since the United States has a better-than-average record of winning WTO disputes.[26]

Whether US acrimony is merited or not, the *US — AD/ CVD* case has stoked it further, because of the confounding implications regarding China.

At its core, *US — AD/CVD* is a case about whether China Inc. really exists or is a sort of phantasm in the minds of China's trading partners. To understand why the case incites passions in Washington, it is instructive to look at how the US government concluded that China was subsidizing off-the-road

25 US Senate Finance Committee, 2007, "Hearing on Trade Enforcement for a 21st Century Economy," Testimony of Robert E. Lighthizer, June 12. Lighthizer and his allies were particularly aggrieved (and remain so today) over the rulings against zeroing, a practice that was used by the Commerce Department in deciding the extent to which foreign goods were sold at unfairly low prices in the US market. When calculating how high the duties ought to be, Commerce officials "zeroed" out sales that were made at high prices (i.e., above the level deemed "fair"), while counting sales that were made at low prices. Critics assailed this practice as biasing the department's calculations so that dumping could be found where none was occurring, or setting anti-dumping duties higher than they otherwise would be. The Appellate Body ruled the practice illegal on the grounds that it violated requirements in the WTO's anti-dumping rules for "fair comparison" to be made between products' export prices and their "normal value." In his testimony, Lighthizer countered that "there is no explicit or, for that matter, implicit prohibition of zeroing in the relevant WTO agreements." He also argued that zeroing was "essential to combat the problem of masked dumping," by which he meant that foreign companies "often dump on certain sales to secure accounts in the United States and then sell at higher prices on other sales so as to mask their dumping." Without zeroing, he said, "companies will be able to dump with impunity."

26 Andrew Mayeda, 2017, "America Often Wins With Trade Referee That Trump Wants to Avoid," Bloomberg News, March 27.

tires and imposed duties to "countervail" the subsidies. From an American perspective, this process exposed a classic example of China Inc.'s stealthy machinations to benefit Chinese industry, and the efforts by US officials to thwart those machinations should therefore be lauded. From Beijing's perspective, the process was an unwarranted and abusive infringement on legitimate Chinese business.

In the summer of 2007, law firms representing US tire companies and unions filed thousands of pages of documents with the Commerce Department enumerating a wide array of Chinese practices that allegedly bestowed unfair advantages on China's tire producers.[27] Some of these practices involved relatively straightforward grants and tax exemptions by governments at the national and provincial level. Others involved less direct forms of aid, notably cheap land, electric power and low-interest loans from China's giant state-owned banks, even to tire companies that were struggling financially and would presumably be deemed uncreditworthy in pure market economies.

In addition, other practices involved such opacity that the conferral of benefits was impossible to detect with precision, but grounds for suspicion appeared ample. According to the documents, when rubber prices shot up around 2003, the Chinese government established a program to help tire companies cope by stabilizing the domestic rubber market, with SOEs providing the obvious mechanism for accomplishing this aim. Natural rubber, "designated a strategic commodity and industrial raw material," came from state-owned Sinochem International Corp., Yunnan Natural Rubber Industrial Co. and Hainan Natural Rubber Group Co., which had received hundreds of millions of dollars in loans from state-owned banks; "these subsidies to rubber producers are passed through to tire producers in the form of low prices for natural rubber," the documents asserted. A similar process for synthetic rubber was spelled out in the documents, which identified state-owned China Petroleum & Chemical Corp. (Sinopec), the country's largest petrochemical firm, as a major supplier of a key component in synthetic rubber called butadiene. Both synthetic rubber and butadiene were designated as "encouraged" by China's industrial planners, the ultimate result being that Chinese off-the-road tire producers "pay at least $63 per metric ton less [for synthetic rubber] than the market would demand," according to the documents.

---

27 From case no. C-570-913, on file at the US Department of Commerce Central Records Unit: Law firm of Stewart and Stewart, "Petitions for the Imposition of Antidumping and Countervailing Duties on Certain Off the Road Tires from The People's Republic of China," vol. 3, June 18, 2007; Law firm of King & Spalding, "Countervailing Duty Investigation on New Pneumatic Off-Road Tires From the People's Republic of China: Bridgestone's New Subsidy Allegations," September 5, 2007; and King & Spalding, "Countervailing Duty Investigation of New Pneumatic Off-The-Road Tires From the People's Republic of China: Additional Clarifying Information For Bridgestone's New Subsidy Allegations," September 19, 2007.

Having received those allegations, Commerce Department officials were obliged to seek China's response. On August 17, 2007, the department sent a lengthy questionnaire to the Chinese government and three major off-the-road tire producers — Heibei Starbright Tire Co., Guizhou Tyre Co. and Tianjin United Tire & Rubber International Co.[28] The questionnaire demanded that the companies submit massive amounts of information, including audited financial statements and tax returns translated into English, plus detailed data about their sales and exports of off-the-road tires, payments for land and electricity, interest costs on bank loans and purchases of rubber.

In some cases, the burden of answering so many queries leads foreign companies to throw up their hands in disgust, even when they know that by failing to respond, they are consigning themselves to the imposition of very high duties that may doom their fortunes in the US market. The questionnaire about Chinese off-the-road tires did elicit a response, albeit a chilly one, two months later.

On almost every point, China denied that its markets were rigged in the ways that the US industry claimed. Regarding the alleged provision of cheap loans for industrial policy purposes, for example, Chinese officials maintained that no such phenomena existed. "Commercial banks in China determine, based on their own independent criteria, whether to provide a loan to an applicant, what interest rate should be charged, and the appropriate term of the loan," stated a letter submitted to the Commerce Department by a Washington law firm representing Beijing, adding that market forces likewise determined other costs — land, electricity and so on — that exporters incurred.[29]

China's protestations of innocence fell on deaf ears at the Commerce Department, where officials received more evidence and conducted analyses they considered strongly indicative of Chinese government intervention in support of its off-the-road tire industry. For example, once month-by-month data was available about the prices Chinese tire exporters had paid to SOEs and other suppliers for various types of rubber, officials found numerous instances indicating "less than adequate remuneration" — bureaucratese for fishy discounts.[30]

Predictably, Washington soon erected protective walls against Chinese imports in the US off-the-road market. Preliminary duties levied in December

28 Letter (with attached questionnaire) from Barbara E. Tillman, director of AD/CVD Operations 6, to Dai Yunlou, minister counselor, Embassy of the People's Republic of China, April 17, 2007.

29 Letter from Hogan & Hartson to Carlos M. Gutierrez, Secretary of Commerce, October 15, 2007.

30 USTR, 2009, "United States-Definitive Anti-Dumping and Countervailing Duties on Certain Products from China: First Written Submission of the United States," May 27, 100-101.

2007 sharply reduced sales of Chinese tires,[31] and in July 2008, Commerce officials announced the final conclusions of their investigation. Heibei Starbright was hit hardest, with a dumping "margin" of 19.15 percent (meaning it was found to be selling tires at roughly that percentage below fair value) and a subsidy rate of 14 percent.[32] The fact that both anti-dumping and countervailing duties were assessed irritated Beijing all the more because it represented a newly aggressive policy by Washington, which Chinese officials argued would result in "double counting," i.e., duties being piled on top of duties for the same alleged economic distortion.

Raising dudgeon in Beijing even higher, the US off-the-road tire industry was only one of several in heartland America getting this kind of protection from Chinese competition. Around the same time as the off-the-road tires case, Washington imposed stiff duties — well over 300 percent in some instances — on other Chinese imports based on principles similar to the ones used for off-the-road tires. They included laminated woven sacks (the heavy bags used to hold cement and large quantities of rice), circular welded steel tubes and light-walled rectangular steel pipes and tubes. In each case, China was found to be subsidizing its manufacturers of these products in various ways, notably via the provision of inputs by SOEs for "less than adequate remuneration." Just as Chinese off-the-road tire producers were getting natural and synthetic rubber from SOEs at a discount, so were Chinese sack makers getting cheap petrochemicals, and steel tube and pipe makers getting cheap hot-rolled steel, according to the Commerce Department.[33]

The Americans cannot treat us like this, Chinese officials thought — at least, not under WTO rules. Before long, *US — AD/CVD* was under way in Geneva, with opening arguments being presented on July 7, 2009.[34]

---

31   US International Trade Commission, "In the Matter of Certain Off-the-Road Tires from China" (see footnote 23 in this chapter).

32   US Department of Commerce, 2008, "Fact Sheet: Commerce Finds Unfair Dumping and Subsidization of New Pneumatic Off-The-Road Tires from the People's Republic of China," July 8.

33   Federal Register, 2008, "Circular Welded Carbon Quality Steel Pipe from the People's Republic of China: Notice of Amended Final Affirmative Countervailing Duty Determination and Notice of Countervailing Duty Order." 73 Federal Register 42545, July 22; "Light-Walled Rectangular Pipe and Tube from the People's Republic of China: Notice of Countervailing Duty Order." 73 Federal Register 45405, August 5; and "Laminated Woven Sacks From the People's Republic of China: Countervailing Duty Order." 73 Federal Register 45955, August 7.

34   As in the account of arguments made in oral and written presentations in the rare earths case, specific quotations from arguments in *US — AD/CVD* come from the panel report (see WTO, 2010, *United States — Definitive Anti-Dumping and Countervailing Duties on Certain Products from China*, Report of the Panel, July 23, www.wto.org/english/ tratop_e/dispu_e/cases_e/ds379_e.htm) and the Appellate Body report (WTO, 2011, *United States — Definitive Anti-Dumping and Countervailing Duties on Certain Products from China*, Report of the Appellate Body, March 11, www.wto.org/english/tratop_e/dispu_e/cases_e/ds379_e.htm; as well as the archive pages of the USTR website, https://ustr.gov/archive/WTO/Section_Index.html.

Now it was up to a panel chaired by David Walker, New Zealand's ambassador to the WTO, whose fellow panellists were a South African and a Jamaican, to decide: Had China really subsidized its exports of tires and other products? Were the US duties consistent with WTO rules?

The Chinese complaint in *US — AD/CVD* was based on a number of arguments. But the most important and contentious element of China's case (and the one that this chapter focuses on) concerned the definition of the term "public bodies." Adjudication on this issue was crucial to determining where, for legal purposes, China's truly private sector leaves off and China Inc. begins.

Spearheading China's legal team this time were attorneys from the Washington-based firm of Steptoe & Johnson. They contended that Beijing had been unjustifiably accused of channelling loans and other subsidies for the production of off-the-road tires and the other products on which countervailing duties had been imposed. Under WTO rules, a subsidy can only be provided by "a government or any public body" — and according to the Steptoe lawyers, that description fit none of the SOEs that had provided inputs such as rubber, steel and chemicals to exporters of the products in question. Rather, those inputs had come from "corporate entities with separate legal personalities," providing goods and services based on their own self-interested judgment.[35]

Sure, those enterprises may have been majority owned by the Chinese government, but that was an absurdly broad criterion by which the US Commerce Department had deemed them to be public bodies, the Steptoe lawyers argued. To be a public body, they continued, an SOE would have to be "exercis[ing] powers and authority vested in it by the State for the purpose of performing governmental functions" — that was a definition enshrined in international law. And to be providing a subsidy, the enterprise would have to be "entrusted or directed" by the state to do so.[36] Commerce officials had not even tried to ascertain such facts; therefore, US subsidy allegations were unfounded, according to the Steptoe legal briefs.

The US defence, in a nutshell, went as follows: do not let China Inc. get away with this.

---

35 WTO, 2010, *United States — Definitive Anti-Dumping and Countervailing Duties on Certain Products from China*, Report of the Panel, July 23, www.wto.org/english/ tratop_e/dispu_e/cases_e/ds379_e.htm, A-2.

36 Ibid., A-2, A-3.

"The term 'public body' should be interpreted so that subsidizing governments cannot use SOEs to avoid the reach" of rules on subsidies, US lawyers asserted.[37] In Washington's view, majority ownership by the state was a perfectly valid criterion, because "a majority owner can control that which it owns. The majority owner of a firm normally can appoint a majority of the firm's board of directors, who in turn can select the firm's managers. Even if the owner does not interfere in day-to-day operations, the managers of the firm ultimately are accountable to the owner."[38]

It was not necessary, either legally or in common-sense terms, to require evidence such as "entrustment and direction" to show that a Chinese SOE was acting on behalf of the government, US lawyers argued. That position drew support from Canada, one of the third parties in the dispute, whose brief stated: "China's interpretation of the term 'public body' would render such term *inutile*."[39]

The United States won — at the panel level — on that key point. "We find no legal error, in analyzing whether an entity is a public body, in giving primacy to evidence of majority government-ownership," Walker and his two colleagues stated in their decision officially issued on July 23, 2010.[40] Although it was conceivable that a government-owned entity might be "completely insulated" from state influence over its operations, no such unusual circumstances were present in this case, so Washington was within its rights to levy countervailing duties on Chinese off-the-road tires and the other imports, the panel ruled.[41]

But the panel did not have the final word. China appealed, and during the week of January 17, 2011, the Appellate Body met in Geneva to discuss the arguments. By coincidence, on one of the very days that this momentous case was coming before the WTO's top judges, their institution would come under an unprecedented assault.

---

37 Ibid., A-12.

38 USTR, 2009, "United States — Definitive Anti-Dumping and Countervailing Duties on Certain Products from China: Responses of the United States to the Panel's First Set of Questions to the Parties," July 28, 12.

39 WTO, *United States — Definitive Anti-Dumping and Countervailing Duties* (see footnote 35 in this chapter), B-18.

40 Ibid., 62.

41 The panel's ruling (see ibid.) did require some modifications in the US duties for reasons unrelated to the definition of "public bodies."

Among the attendees at the January 2011 meeting was Jennifer Hillman, an American, who was then serving her fourth year on the Appellate Body. She was hoping to serve a second four-year term, but as she was about to learn, Washingtonians in high places had other ideas.[42]

When I first interviewed Hillman in her office in 2008 for a book I was writing, she proudly noted the artwork by her two school-aged sons on the walls and the photos of her family on her desk. Her point was that she was displaying only personal mementos rather than any that might reflect national loyalty, such as an American flag or the photo she had of herself with Bill Clinton, in whose administration she served as a high-ranking trade policy maker in the mid-1990s. In my book, I quoted her saying: "The idea is to have objective judges. I try to make sure that the appearance matches the fact that I'm not in any way, shape, or form advocating for, or on the side of, the United States."[43]

Hillman's office decor was a small part of the WTO's elaborate effort to enhance the dispute settlement system's authority and credibility by keeping its jurists free from any taint of partiality or bias. Each Appellate Body member is nominated by their own country, and certain economic powers (the United States and European Union prominent among them) are virtually guaranteed to get one member by unwritten tradition. But a special committee of senior ambassadors from WTO countries makes the final selections, which must be approved by consensus of the entire membership. Then, following selection, an Appellate Body member undergoes a sort of indoctrination process, often including a retreat with colleagues — perhaps at a Swiss or French resort — the purpose being to instill a strong ethos of fidelity to the WTO and the international community without regard to citizenship. Members are adjured to rule "unflinchingly," even if that means issuing decisions against their own countries. Collegiality and consensus are also heavily stressed; the Appellate Body prides itself on deciding most cases without dissenting opinions, which sometimes requires intensive back-and-forth among members, but helps reinforce the institution's legitimacy.

In *US — AD/CVD*, Hillman's influence was limited. When the Appellate Body reviews a case, only three of its seven members — called a "division"

---

42 This section and the one that follows are based on interviews with numerous sources who requested confidentiality, but whose perspectives and recollections of events sometimes conflicted. To the extent facts were in dispute and could not be confirmed by more than one interviewee, they have been omitted. Otherwise, the narrative of events is a composite of interviewees' accounts based on careful cross-checking and follow-up interviews.

43 Paul Blustein, 2009, *Misadventures of the Most Favored Nations*, New York, NY: Public Affairs, chapter 13.

— make the actual ruling, with the division for each case chosen using a random selection system. The reason is to spread the heavy workload facing the Appellate Body among its members; the job is not full time. The division for *US-AD/CVD* consisted of Ricardo Ramírez-Hernández of Mexico, Peter Van den Bossche of Belgium and Lilia Bautista of the Philippines, so they alone had the authority and responsibility for deciding whether the panel was correct on issues such as the definition of public bodies. But the other four members get a chance to offer input at an "exchange of views" with the division, and the main purpose of the January 2011 meeting was to exchange views on *US — AD/CVD*.

During the meeting, Hillman excused herself because she had an appointment that she could not miss, with Michael Punke, the US ambassador to the WTO. A few weeks earlier, Punke had conveyed a jarring message to Hillman: the US government would not support her reappointment to a second four-year term. This news had taken Hillman by surprise. With her combination of practical policy experience and academic expertise, she was generally held in high esteem as one of the Appellate Body's most knowledgeable and influential members. She knew that a number of trade hawks in Washington were angry about Appellate Body rulings on trade remedies — in fact, an American who preceded her had quietly bowed to pressure for departure after a single term. But Hillman herself had never served on a division that had ruled against the United States, except for one case involving a complaint that Washington had failed to properly comply with an earlier ruling on trade remedies. So she was perplexed by Punke's message.

In addition to wanting to understand the reasons for US dissatisfaction with her, Hillman wanted to know how far US officials would go. She knew she could gain a second four-year term even without the United States affirmatively offering its endorsement; in most instances, Appellate Body members who wanted a second term had gotten their wish almost as a matter of course. But if Washington was going to actively block her reappointment, the lack of a consensus among WTO member countries would automatically preclude her from serving again.

Now, in January 2011, the time had come for Hillman to receive more definitive word about her future. She and Punke met in a public lounge near the WTO's main entrance, to avoid any appearance that the US government was privately seeking to twist her arm regarding any Appellate Body decisions. Punke confirmed her worst fears, telling her that the United States would exercise its power to withhold consensus for any slate of judges that included her name. Answers to her queries about the rationale left her no less confounded than before. As a lifelong Democrat, she expressed willingness to step down if President Obama preferred someone to replace her, but Punke said the administration had no particular nominee in mind, and he assured her that her professional qualifications were not at issue. Rather, he said, the administration wanted to put its own stamp on the Appellate Body, and Hillman did not align with the administration's plans for the institution.

Hillman warned that a decision to block her reappointment was bound to become public sooner or later, and it would adversely affect both the WTO's credibility and Washington's reputation for supporting multilateralism. Moreover, any American appointed to replace her would be obliged to overcome suspicions about being a tool of the US government.

Hillman agreed there were problems with the Appellate Body; however, there was someone else whose removal Washington ought to prioritize.

Werner Zdouc is arguably the most powerful international civil servant that nobody has ever heard of. An Austrian who heads the Appellate Body Secretariat, Zdouc regularly works from early in the morning to late at night and on weekends and holidays. He has devoted much of his career to the WTO, and having accumulated encyclopedic knowledge on the issues he is confronting — his colleagues joke that he sleeps with the WTO texts under his pillow — he asserts his opinions forcefully, often with the intended effect.

A time-honoured description of the WTO is "member-driven institution," meaning that its Secretariat of 634 people lacks bureaucratic clout, and power resides almost exclusively with the governments of its members (in contrast to, say, the IMF, whose management and staff wield considerable influence). But Zdouc stands out in the generally weak WTO Secretariat for the ways in which he exerts control over important decisions affecting trade policy. Appellate Body members are much too busy to read all the lengthy briefs and voluminous documents filed in the cases they review, and most lack native-level fluency in English. So, to a large extent, they depend on the lawyers in the Appellate Body Secretariat, just as judges elsewhere depend on clerks, to make sure they are informed about the crucial issues in a case, and also to draft opinions. Zdouc not only oversees these Secretariat staffers, he reviews virtually every document they submit to the Appellate Body members, often revising their work — in other words, he effectively "holds the pen" in the drafting process for many decisions. Moreover, he participates in virtually every important discussion members have about cases, and he is so relentless in debate that, according to numerous people who have worked with him, those who resist his arguments sometimes give up from sheer exhaustion. Some in Washington and Geneva who consider the Appellate Body too hostile toward trade remedies put much of the blame on Zdouc.

Zdouc's defenders contend that his power and efforts to exert it are often overstated. By all accounts, Appellate Body members who are reasonably up to speed on their cases have little difficulty ignoring his advice if they disagree with it. To the extent he holds sway over some of the less diligent Appellate Body members, his arguments are generally perceived as stemming from a passion to safeguard institutional respectability — in particular, ensuring that new rulings follow principles set forth in prior cases — rather than pursuing some political agenda. His overriding goal, in other words, is that the Appellate Body should be consistent.

But his zeal, critics contend, surpasses the limits that should constrain an ostensible technician and reflects a stubborn refusal to allow the Appellate Body, which is not legally bound by precedent, to admit and rectify past mistakes. That was the view held by Hillman, whose former WTO colleagues recall her saying that Zdouc, for all his good intentions, had utterly lost perspective. She was often at loggerheads with him during her tenure and grew increasingly confident in telling him to stop intervening. When she found her reappointment threatened, she entreated Punke and other US officials to realize that unseating her would probably mean losing a chance of moving Zdouc out of his job.

Hillman's argumentation was in vain. As she learned in the weeks and months after the meeting with Punke, control over the decision to replace her lay firmly in the hands of Timothy Reif, the general counsel of the Office of the USTR, who made no secret of his displeasure with the Appellate Body. Reif was convinced that the body's previous rulings on trade remedies had grossly twisted the wording in agreements that US officials had painstakingly negotiated at the WTO's inception — an example being the one division on which Hillman participated that ruled against the United States. He and a handful of colleagues in the trade representative's office, including Punke, wanted US judges to have an impact on the direction the Appellate Body took on trade remedies, perhaps by actively dissenting in cases, and disrupting the body's treasured collegiality, even if they were not on the divisions making the rulings. Hillman had shown no inclination to go that far; Reif was adamant that she must go.

The six other members of the Appellate Body were continuing their exchange of views on *US — AD/CVD* while Hillman was meeting with Punke, and upon her return they were indignant to hear that the US government was blocking her reappointment. A discussion ensued about the possibility of recruiting officials from other countries to confront the Obama administration over the matter. But at the end of the day, there was agreement that no matter how upset other countries' officials might be, they would not be able to influence the course of events. Hillman would have to raise the issue with other policy makers in Washington, the risk being that the news media would catch wind of what was going on (which did in fact happen).[44]

Discussion then resumed on *US — AD/CVD*, with Hillman voicing strong opposition to China's stance on "public bodies." Although she did not endorse the US position that an enterprise majority-owned by a government was automatically a public body, she rejected the definition favoured by China — "vested with governmental function or authority" — as far too extreme and difficult to prove.

The exchange of views ended without a clear indication of how the division would decide that matter. But when the ruling was issued two months later, on March 11, 2011, Hillman was appalled, because the three members of the division had reached conclusions far different from what she had expressed or expected. She registered emphatic disappointment, some of her colleagues recall, and she could not help wondering whether the impending end of her term had diminished her influence.

Appellate Body decisions are long — one reason being to assure all parties that their arguments have been carefully considered — and *US — AD/CVD* was no exception. Following an introduction, the decision devoted 42 pages to reciting China's arguments, 34 pages to US arguments, 18 pages to third-party arguments and 124 pages to analysis and conclusions. But stripping away the legal mumbo-jumbo and laying bare the essence, here was the main take-away from the Appellate Body's ruling: a country that imposes duties on Chinese imports because of alleged subsidies must have very strong evidence that Beijing is truly subsidizing. Simply showing that an enterprise is owned by the Chinese government will not suffice to demonstrate state involvement.

---

44 *Inside US Trade*, 2011, "USTR Blocks Hillman's Bid for Second WTO Appellate Body Term," April 29.

That, of course, was a reversal of the panel's decision. It meant that the United States had lost on the most important issue — how to discern intervention by China Inc. — and was therefore violating WTO rules by levying such heavy duties on Chinese off-the-road tires and other products.

The Appellate Body agreed with Beijing: "A public body...must be an entity that possesses, exercises or is vested with governmental authority," the ruling stated, and overturning the panel on a number of points, it continued: "the mere fact that a government is the majority shareholder of an entity does not demonstrate that the government exercises meaningful control over the conduct of that entity, much less that the government has bestowed it with governmental authority."[45]

The decision was not a total Chinese victory. The Appellate Body ruled that China's giant state-owned banks were public bodies because their legal charters clearly vested them with the authority to function for purposes specified by Beijing; therefore, their loans, if found to be artificially cheap, might be subject to countervailing duties.

But critics assailed the ruling as effectively giving China carte blanche to subsidize its industries and manipulate its markets in other ways, considering the impracticality of showing conclusively that the Chinese authorities had induced a state-owned company to take a particular action. "The conditions required by the [Appellate Body] for a determination that an SOE is a public body...constitute an excessively burdensome test," wrote three former trade officials (none of them American) in a leading journal. "Interpretation of [WTO] rules must... avoid awkward and incoherent results that do not reflect realities of international trade."[46] The authors had all been heavily involved in negotiating the terms of WTO rules on subsidies, which lent extra credence to their complaint that the Appellate Body had failed to interpret the rules as the drafters had intended.

The United States did not take this defeat lying down. On May 18, 2012, the Department of Commerce issued a memorandum setting forth how it would comply with the Appellate Body decision — and it was essentially a plan to make it easier than ever to impose countervailing duties on imports of Chinese products, in ways that would drive Beijing crazy.[47]

---

45 WTO, *United States — Definitive Anti-Dumping and Countervailing Duties on Certain Products from China*, Report of the Appellate Body, March 11 (see footnote 34 in this chapter).

46 Michel Cartland, Gérard Depayre and Jan Woznowski, 2012, "Is Something Going Wrong in the WTO Dispute Settlement?" *Journal of World Trade* 46 (5): 979–1016.

47 Memorandum to Paul Piquado, assistant secretary for import administration, "Section 129 Determination of the Countervailing Duty Investigation of Circular Welded Carbon Quality Steel Pipe; Light-Walled Rectangular Pipe and Tube; Laminated Woven Sacks; and Off-the-Road Tires from the People's Republic of China: An Analysis of Public Bodies in the People's Republic of China in Accordance with the WTO Appellate Body's Findings in DS379," May 18, 2012.

The WTO's top judges had made it clear, the memo noted, that a high standard of evidence was required for identifying a Chinese public body — specifically, "a proper evaluation of the core features of the entity concerned, and its relationship with the government." So in future subsidy investigations, Commerce officials would submit questionnaires to China demanding all kinds of new information from Chinese enterprises that might be conduits for subsidies, including the roles played by Communist Party members in their management and boards of directors. Indeed, the memo showed that the Commerce Department was prepared to be more aggressive than before in identifying public bodies, which might even include private firms with Communist Party managers and directors. And, of course, if China refused to supply the requested information, Commerce officials would be legally allowed to assume whatever facts would result in the highest duties.

The upshot is that Washington's loss in *US — AD/ CVD* has had no impact so far on the US economy or economies elsewhere; the floodgates have not opened wider to imports of subsidized Chinese goods. But the reasoning in *US — AD/CVD* may have broader implications than the area of trade remedies. If it is necessary for those complaining about China's system to show definitively that Chinese authorities are quietly intervening in all manner of decisions — say, concerning demands for the transfer of technology — challenging Beijing in the WTO will become much more daunting.

Two WTO cases: one shows that the tribunals in Geneva can readily handle China Inc.; the other raises disconcerting questions about whether the trade body's rules apply to the most problematic aspects of the Chinese system as it has evolved in the years since WTO entry. Taken together, they illustrate that the WTO is far from perfect regarding the quandaries posed by China's rise, and in need of improvements on other issues as well, but well-suited in many respects to fulfilling a mission that is essential to global stability. Regarding the term "crown jewel," I trust that its aptness has been amply justified.

Developments in the years subsequent to these two cases have exacerbated the woes afflicting the WTO's dispute settlement system. Even before Trump's election, American deprecation of the Appellate Body reached new levels of intensity, evoking heightened alarm that US browbeating would erode faith in the impartiality of WTO jurists.

In 2016, the United States publicly blocked the consensus for the reappointment of another member, Seung Wha Chang of South Korea, charging that some of his decisions egregiously deviated from acceptable boundaries of jurisprudence. Washington plowed ahead despite scant evidence that it had reaped much benefit from removing Hillman; the American who replaced her, Thomas Graham, has been well regarded in Geneva, but he dashed the hopes of Washington trade hawks for an aggressive advocate.

Chang was an easy target in certain respects. A cerebral legal scholar, he had a penchant at oral hearings for asking attorneys questions on topics that seemed only tangentially related to the cases at hand and insisting upon getting answers, which made him unpopular. US officials maintained that he was likewise prone to inserting rules into opinions that were either extraneous to the issue in dispute or exceeding the bounds of negotiated agreements — or both. But Washington was totally isolated in its anti-Chang campaign. In an extraordinarily heated meeting of WTO member countries' representatives on May 23, 2016,[48] Punke laid out the US justification for denying him a second term — to which a host of his counterparts responded with condemnations of the systemic dangers the US action posed. They included representatives from Canada, Brazil, the European Union, India, Japan, Egypt, Indonesia, Switzerland, Thailand and Vietnam; one of the angriest statements, predictably, was South Korea's.[49] A letter of protest, publicly released by the other members of the Appellate Body, declared: "The dispute settlement system depends upon WTO members trusting the independence and impartiality of Appellate Body Members. Linking the reappointment of a Member to specific cases could affect that trust." In a like vein, all 13 living former members signed a letter warning, "There must be no opening whatsoever to the prospect of political interference in what must remain impartial legal judgments in the WTO's rule-based system of adjudication."[50]

Complaints about the Appellate Body are not wholly misplaced, as this chapter has shown. Any court makes mistakes, and the WTO's top judges need to squarely face theirs. If they can't because of loss of perspective by an

---

48 WTO, 2016, "WTO members debate appointment/reappointment of Appellate Body members," May 23, www.wto.org/english/news_e/news16_e/dsb_23may16_e.htm.

49 "This opposition is, to put it bluntly, an attempt to use reappointment as a tool to rein in Appellate Body Members for decisions they may make on the bench," the South Korean statement said. "Its message is loud and clear: 'If AB members make decisions that do not conform to U.S. perspectives, they are not going to be reappointed.'" Punke stoutly denied any linkage to losses the United States had suffered. "There can always be legitimate disagreement over the results," his statement said, contending that the reason for the US veto of Chang's reappointment was "We do not think his service reflects the role assigned to the Appellate Body by WTO Members in the WTO agreements." United States, 2016, "Statement by the United States at the Meeting of the WTO Dispute Settlement Body," Geneva, May 23.

50 Both letters were reprinted in WTO, 2017, "Appellate Body Annual Report for 2016," Annex 3, www.wto.org/english/tratop_e/dispu_e/ab_an_rep_e.htm.

influential Secretariat member like Werner Zdouc, they should find different sorts of experts to help guide them.[51] However, it would be the ultimate loss of perspective — indeed, the ultimate throwing out of the baby with the bathwater — if the United States were to wreck the WTO out of pique over Appellate Body rulings on issues such as trade remedies. The possibility that Trump administration actions may lead to just such an outcome will be discussed further in chapter 10.

Whatever the Appellate Body's fate, thorny and consequential questions remain about whether the WTO can survive the continued rise of China Inc. For all its flaws, the WTO constrains Chinese policy within certain bounds — recall the respect for WTO rules that impels large delegations from Beijing to attend dispute settlement hearings in Geneva. Is this degree of constraint sufficient? Making the affirmative case has become increasingly difficult because of the direction China has taken under Xi Jinping, the subject to which this book turns next.

---

51 I do not mean to suggest in the least that Zdouc has acted dishonorouably — he has not. But the concerns I heard from a number of people about his loss of perspective struck me as highly persuasive.

CHAPTER 8

PARTY LIKE IT'S 2025

Mystery continues to this day over the disappearance of Xi Jinping shortly before his installation in the fall of 2012 as China's paramount leader. For two weeks in September of that year, the 59-year-old Xi simply ceased appearing in public, issuing statements or even receiving mention in official state media, and meetings he was supposed to have attended with visiting dignitaries, including US Secretary of State Hillary Clinton, were cancelled without explanation.[1] Beijing was abuzz with rumours that Xi had suffered a heart attack, or been injured in an auto accident, or was stricken with crippling back pain, or had been the target of an assassination attempt; according to one report, attributed to a supposedly knowledgeable insider, he had been hit by a flying chair during a rancorous gathering of Communist Party princelings. For a regime that took enormous care to ensure orderly leadership successions — Xi had been clearly designated as Hu Jintao's presumptive heir in 2007 and was scheduled to take the reins as the Party's general secretary in November 2012 — this episode was well out of the ordinary, if not downright alarming. It was also uncharacteristic of Xi,

1 Information on Xi's disappearance can be found in Ian Johnson, 2012, "Communist Leader's Absence Sets Off Rumor Mills in China," *The New York Times,* September 10; Mark Kitto, 2012, "What really happened to Xi Jinping," *Prospect Magazine,* October 31; and Malcolm Moore, 2012, "Xi Jinping, China's next leader, ends 14 day-long vanishing act with visit to farm school," *The Telegraph,* September 15.

who spent his teenage years during the Cultural Revolution exiled to a poor village in western China following his father's purge from leadership ranks but later described his experience of "eating bitterness" as having reinforced his loyalty to the Party. When Xi resurfaced on September 15, 2012, to give remarks at an agricultural university in Beijing, photos were distributed to the media, as if to confirm his good health, although no account was provided of his whereabouts or activities for the previous 14 days. Nor was such information forthcoming when he assumed the general secretaryship a couple of months later and the state presidency in March 2013.

Nobody outside a tight inner circle knows the truth about Xi's vanishing act, but with the passage of time a version has surfaced that has a ring of plausibility. By this account, Xi went with a few close aides to Zhejiang Province, where he had been Party secretary, to ponder his vision for the nation, which would involve a renewed assault on SOEs and revival of Zhu-style economic reform. Zhejiang, a coastal province south of Shanghai, was a hotbed of entrepreneurialism, having benefited from low barriers to private industry; its most famous magnate was Jack Ma, who was, at the time, well along in building his Alibaba empire.[2]

At the time, the likelihood of China progressing further toward free-market capitalism appeared promising. One of the most auspicious signs was a report published jointly by the World Bank and a top Chinese government think tank, the Development Research Center (DRC) of the State Council, in early 2013. The World Bank-DRC report recommended that China pursue a much less interventionist approach in the future, and although it wasn't formally endorsed by the government, the think tank's imprimatur was a striking indication of opinion among many in Beijing's highest echelons.[3]

Despite its fantastic growth of the previous three decades, China was at risk of getting stuck in the "middle-income trap," the report's authors warned, referring to the typical pattern that had befallen many countries in Latin America and the Middle East of becoming competitive in labour-intensive, low-cost products but failing to make the leap into the ranks of more technologically advanced, high-income economies. "As an economy approaches

---

2   Lingling Wei, 2017, "China's Xi Approaches a New Term With a Souring Taste for Markets," *The Wall Street Journal*, October 16.

3   World Bank and the Development Research Center of the State Council, People's Republic of China, 2013, *China 2030: Building a Modern, Harmonious, and Creative Society*, Washington, DC. The report "was written and produced by a joint team from DRC and the World Bank who worked together as equal partners," the introductory section explained, although it added the caveat that the conclusions "are those of the authors and do not necessarily reflect the views of nor imply an official endorsement by The World Bank…or the Government of China."

the technology frontier and exhausts the potential for acquiring technology from abroad, the role of the government needs to change fundamentally," the report stated. "Direct government intervention may actually retard growth, not help it. Instead, the policy emphasis needs to shift even more toward private sector development, ensuring that markets are mature enough to allocate resources efficiently and that firms are strong and innovative enough to compete internationally in technologically advanced sectors...Innovation is not something that can be achieved through government planning." In China's case, the authors continued, "SOEs consume a large proportion of capital, raw materials, and intermediate inputs to produce relatively small shares of gross output and value added," and the barriers to private firms in the sectors dominated by SOEs "tend to inhibit private sector growth and development, dampen innovation and creativity, and slow productivity growth." Beijing should therefore "withdraw [SOEs] gradually from contestable markets" and confine them to sectors involving "the provision of public goods and services" such as defence, infrastructure, and basic research and development. Instead of a powerful SASAC, "the government could consider establishing several state asset management companies (SAMCs) that would represent the government as shareholder and would professionally manage and trade these assets in financial markets where feasible."

In the first major policy document of the Xi era, the Chinese leadership manifested a strong inclination to adopt something akin to the World Bank-DRC prescriptions. "We must ensure that the market has a decisive role in the allocation of resources," stated the Third Plenum of the 18th Party Congress in November 2013. "We must substantially reduce the direct allocation of resources by the government." The words "decisive role" marked a significant step forward from previous Party documents, which had suggested that market forces would "supplement" or play roughly equal roles with state planning in guiding the economy.[4]

For key elements of China Inc., survival — or at least continued bureaucratic power — was at stake. A proposal was circulating among Xi's advisers to reconfigure SASAC into an institution like Temasek, the Singaporean fund that managed the city-state's sovereign wealth. Since Temasek delegated the running of Singapore's state-owned companies to professional executives, this idea would amount to a severe clipping of SASAC's wings.[5]

---

4   Nicholas R. Lardy, 2017, "State Resurgence in China," in Adam Posen and Jiming Ha (eds.), *US-China Cooperation in a Changing Global Economy*, chapter 13, Peterson Institute for International Economics, June, https://piie.com/publications/piie-briefings/us-china-cooperation-changing- global-economy.

5   Wei, "China's Xi Approaches a New Term With a Souring Taste for Markets" (see footnote 2 in this chapter).

Also under siege, and scrambling to defend itself, was the NDRC. Its army of planners had been riding high in the years immediately following the global financial crisis, when the agency was charged by the Hu-Wen regime with approving and coordinating many of the investment projects in the government's stimulus package. But the 2013 National Party Congress pledge to give market forces a "decisive" role in resource allocation sent a rude jolt coursing through the NDRC's corridors. Worse yet, from the agency's perspective, was a vow by Li Keqiang, the new premier, who in a press conference following the Party Congress announced his intention to cut one-third of the 1,700-odd administrative approval procedures that were a major source of the NDRC's leverage. Media outlets began reporting on how low the mighty "super ministry" had fallen, noting, for example, a drastic decline in the number of projects it was approving and the numbers of cars with non-Beijing licence plates parked outside its offices — supposedly an indication of provincial officials' sense of obligation to visit.[6]

This flowering of free-market sentiment did not last long. Within a couple of years after Xi's rise to power, it was clear that he was more of a fair-weather liberalizer than a philosophically committed one. Under his leadership China has embarked on strenuous efforts to surmount the middle-income trap, elevate its technological capacity and shed its dependence on low-wage labour — but using an approach that is as disparate from those recommended in the World Bank-DRC report as can be imagined. Industrial policy has been intensified, with far more ambitious goals and the use of many more government levers than before, all presided over by a leader who has accumulated much more power than his predecessors.

One reason for Xi's apparent change of course may be a worrisome bout of instability that afflicted China's financial markets starting in June 2015. The nation's stock exchanges tumbled after enjoying an extraordinary run to giddy heights; then, in the fall, the RMB, which had been allowed to float more freely, came under pressure from speculators who were reacting to a flow of capital out of the country that swelled to a rate of hundreds of billions of dollars per month. That forced the central bank to step in and prop up the RMB, and the financial authorities clamped down on capital flight. The turmoil was redolent of America's 2008 crisis — an especially embarrassing setback for a leader who had promised to preside over a "great rejuvenation" of the Chinese people that would bury past humiliations — and it

---

gave Xi and his colleagues an eye-opening lesson in the dangers of leaving markets to their own devices.[7]

Those financial perturbations, however, provide only a partial explanation for the path China has followed since Xi's ascendancy. He is a fervent believer in the Communist Party's responsibility for China's success and the need for the Party to maintain a firm grip over all major aspects of the nation's development. To explain why Xi sometimes veers toward market-opening policies and other times toward heavy-handed *dirigisme*, Chinese scholars have told me that Xi holds both Deng and Mao in high esteem — that is, he appreciates the economic progress that stemmed from Deng's reform and opening up, but he also attaches tremendous value to the unity and sense of national purpose that was the hallmark of the Mao era. Furthermore, he is convinced that there is no fundamental contradiction between the two; both leaders' approaches can, with some deft management, work in tandem.

In one important respect, China turned away from mercantilism under Xi: instead of relying so heavily on exports, the Chinese economy has grown in a much more balanced manner, thanks to strong domestic demand fuelled by the nation's increasingly prosperous and confident consumers. The trade surplus in goods and services, which had swollen to a grossly exorbitant 8.7 percent of GDP in 2007, shrank to 2.2 percent of GDP in 2016 and would continue to decline in years thereafter. The RMB had appreciated by more than 45 percent over that period[8] (as noted above, the central bank was actively propping it up in 2015), which further spurred imports and tempered export growth.

Still, developments on a host of other fronts reflected the increasing tendency since 2013 for Beijing to assume control over the inner workings of the economy, with ever-greater clout accruing to the Party and Xi personally, due in part to an anti-corruption campaign he spearheaded that resulted in the punishment of hundreds of thousands of officials. An overarching theme, echoed ruefully by proponents of market-oriented reform, would be *guo jin min tui* — "the state advances, the private sector retreats." Although that phrase had circulated years earlier in describing Hu-Wen policies, it applied in spades to Xi's, and nowhere was the phenomenon more manifest than in the initiative dubbed "Made in China 2025."

---

7   Wei, "China's Xi Approaches a New Term With a Souring Taste for Markets" (see footnote 2 in this chapter).

8   The Bank for International Settlements real effective exchange rate index (2010=100 rose from 83.5 in June 2007 to 122.9 in December 2016, a cumulative appreciation of 47 percent. See www.bis.org/statistics/eer.htm.

In 2013 and 2014, "Industrie 4.0" was all the rage among Germany's business, academic and policy establishment. It envisioned revolutionary innovations in manufacturing by advancing to a new stage in which "smart factories" would use digitized automation and new internet-based technologies to dramatically improve quality and increase efficiency. When the government of Chancellor Angela Merkel decided to make Industrie 4.0 a central plank of Germany's economic strategy and provided funds for research, Chinese policy makers were intrigued and were soon incorporating elements of the German plan into a blueprint of their own for the coming decade. Unveiled in May 2015, Made in China 2025[9] was often described in the media as having been cribbed from Industrie 4.0,[10] but the Chinese masterplan, with the principal goal of turning the country into a "manufacturing superpower," was far grander in scale and funding, and much more hands-on.

By commonly accepted definitions, China was already a manufacturing superpower in 2015. In categories such as computers, colour TV sets, mobile phones and air conditioners, Chinese factories accounted for dominant shares (ranging from 60 to 90 percent) of global production; China also manufactured about half the world's steel and more than one-quarter of its autos.[11] But much of China's manufacturing base still consisted of low-value-added assembly and heavily polluting, energy-intensive facilities; the nation's leaders wanted to leapfrog past that stage of development and simultaneously decrease dependence on foreign technology. Thus, Made in China 2025 aimed for a decade of unprecedented progress by Chinese firms in 10 sectors — advanced information technology, aerospace and aeronautics, automated machines and robotics, new energy vehicles and equipment, rail transportation, power equipment, pharmaceuticals and advanced medical devices, agricultural machinery and new materials. Several of these had been included in previous industrial policy schemes, but not with the level of subsidization, specificity and breadth of targets and pressure for domestic production that Made in China 2025 would involve. To many foreign firms, the objective — or at least the likely outcome — was that steroid-fed national champions would swamp them in unfair competition, both in China and abroad.

---

9   State Council, 2015, "Notice on Issuing Made in China 2025," May 8 (hereafter "Made in China 2025"). The literal translation is "China Manufacturing 2025," but "Made in China 2025" has become the commonly accepted term in English.

10 Jane Perlez, Paul Mozur and Jonathan Ansfield, 2017, "China's Technology Ambitions Could Upset the Global Trade Order," *The New York Times*, November 7.

11 European Union Chamber of Commerce in China, 2017, "China Manufacturing 2025: Putting Industrial Policy Ahead of Market Forces," http://docs.dpaq.de/12007-european_chamber_cm2025-en.pdf.

The sums mobilized to finance Made in China 2025 have been estimated in the hundreds of billions of dollars; although precise figures are impossible to calculate, the total dwarfed the $250 million that the German government allocated for Industrie 4.0. "Investment funds" endowed with government outlays, contributions from SOEs, and private money proliferated around the time Made in China 2025 was released, many with the aim of pouring financial resources into sectors prioritized in Made in China 2025 and other government initiatives. In 2015 alone, almost 300 funds holding more than $200 billion were established, and in November of that year the Finance Ministry issued a notice stating that such funds should be used to "invest in priority sectors for social and economic development."[12] Separately, directives issued by government ministries called upon the banking industry to support Made in China 2025-related projects and enterprises.[13]

China had the right under WTO rules to provide such subsidies,[14] just as other countries' governments were free to impose countervailing duties if they believed that their industries were being harmed by subsidized Chinese imports. But taking such defensive action takes time, and identifying the degree of subsidization in a system like China's is difficult for reasons explained in previous chapters. An even more nettlesome problem for the trading system posed by Made in China 2025 was the use of government power to favour local production and domestic firms in the Chinese market, as evinced by the market share targets.

The term "self-sufficiency" permeated the plan, with the overall goal of China becoming 40 percent "self-sufficient" by 2020 and 70 percent "self-sufficient" by 2025 in core components and materials in many of the targeted industries. Economic actors were exhorted to "rely still more on domestic equipment [and] rely on domestic brands."[15] A "Made in China 2025 Key Area Technology Roadmap" compiled by academics and other experts under the guidance of the Chinese Academy of Engineering, released in October 2015, spelled out concrete market share targets for Chinese producers to achieve,

---

12 Ministry of Finance, 2015, "Notice regarding Publication of the Provisional Measures for the Administration of Government Investment Funds," November 12, cited in European Commission, 2017, "On Significant Distortions in the Economy of the People's Republic of China for the Purpose of Trade Defence Investigations," Commission Staff Working Document, December 20, chapter 6.

13 Ministry of Industry and Information Technology, 2016, "Action Plan to Improve Information Sharing and Promoting Industry and Finance Cooperation," March 3, cited in European Union Chamber, "China Manufacturing 2025" (see footnote 11 in this chapter).

14 Certain types of subsidies are illegal or restricted under WTO rules, notably subsidies contingent on promoting exports, but not general subsidies.

15 Made in China 2025, section 1.3, cited in European Commission, "On Significant Distortions," chapter 4 (see footnote 12 in this chapter).

not only in the Chinese market but also globally, in numerous sectors. Indigenous new energy vehicles were slated to capture 80 percent of domestic sales by 2025, for example, with 10 percent of such vehicles going for export; moreover, two of the top 10 international brands should be indigenous. In the energy equipment industry, a 90 percent share of the Chinese market was envisioned for domestically produced equipment, and exports were to account for 30 percent of production. For industrial robots and advanced medical devices, the target for made-in-China products was 50 percent of the domestic market by 2020 and 70 percent by 2025.[16]

Chinese officials maintained that the targets in the "roadmap" were merely the visions of academics and industry experts, rather than government-mandated figures, which might violate WTO rules against local content requirements. That explanation struck foreign companies and governments as a clever ploy designed to disguise the degree of state involvement and deflect accusations of WTO-illegality. A vice premier, Ma Kai, endorsed the roadmap, and the Chinese Academy of Engineering was a think tank with ministerial-level status; the document clearly signalled the government's objectives.[17]

Much hype has been generated about Made in China 2025, some of which is vastly overblown, in particular, claims that it is a plot for world economic domination.[18] If anything, Made in China 2025 can be seen as motivated by determination to ensure that no technological gap of the sort that reduced China to inferiority in the nineteenth and twentieth centuries will ever materialize again.[19] A related motivation is to reduce the risk that, in the event of military conflict, China's adversaries could cut off supplies of essential goods, using economic extortion to force Beijing into submission. As chauvinistic and predatory as the intentions of Made in China 2025 may appear, it stemmed in large part from a deep-rooted sense of national insecurity. And its success was open to doubt.

Semiconductors are an illuminating example. To provide the logic and memory that run the computers, mobile phones and other high-tech devices

---

16 China Academy of Engineering, 2015, "China Manufacturing 2025 Key Area Technology Roadmap," October, cited in European Union Chamber of Commerce in China, "China Manufacturing 2025" (see footnote 11 in this chapter), section 4.

17 US Chamber of Commerce, 2017, "Made in China 2025: Global Ambitions Built on Local Protections," section 1.

18 Senator Marco Rubio of Florida, in a tweet on June 15, 2018, said that with Made in China 2025, China "aims to not just invest billions, but also cheat & steal their way into becoming the dominant industrial & high-tech country in the world." Marco Rubio, Twitter post, June 15, 2018, 3:30 p.m., https://twitter.com/marcorubio/status/1007752169502670850?lang=en.

19 Zheng Yongnian, 2018, "China and the U.S.: A clash of techno-nationalists," *The Washington Post*, May 14.

churned out by Chinese factories, China "consumes" integrated circuits in voluminous quantities — in 2015, its industry bought 58 percent of the $354 billion worth of chips sold worldwide.[20] But nearly 90 percent of those chips were either imported into China or made by foreign companies there because firms such as Intel, Micron and Qualcomm maintain enormous technological leads, especially in the most advanced microprocessor segments where their engineers have accumulated know-how that comes only with decades of experience in developing new generations of products. Indeed, the Chinese economy depends on foreign chipmakers even more than foreign petroleum; the nation's bill for semiconductor imports surpassed its bill for imported crude oil in 2012, and the gap continued to widen in years thereafter.[21]

Going back as far as 1991, Beijing's five-year plans have flagged development of a domestic semiconductor industry as a national priority,[22] only to see foreign chipmakers sprint further ahead with next-generation innovations. In June 2014, the nation's program went into high gear with the issuance of "Guidelines for the Development and Promotion of the Integrated Circuit Industry," backed by serious money in the form of a "National Integrated Circuit Fund," with capital of about $21 billion from official and private sources aimed at upgrading the industry's design and manufacturing capacity. Made in China 2025 further elaborated that initiative, envisioning expansions of the fund's scope and the addition of more funds, along with self-sufficiency targets — 35 percent for mobile phone chips by 2020.[23]

Could this latest iteration of China's industrial policy for semiconductors fare any better than previous ones? It is easy to exaggerate the threat that economic plans such as these — conceived by bureaucrats from on high — pose to the more nimble, market-driven system of entrepreneurial capitalism prevalent in Western countries. Consider another illustrative industry.

20 PricewaterhouseCoopers LLP, 2017, "China's impact on the semiconductor industry, 2016 update," January, www.pwc.com/gx/en/technology/chinas-impact-on-semiconductor-industry/assets/china-impact-of-the-semiconductor-industry-2016-update.pdf.

21 Bob Davis and Eva Dou, 2017, "China's Next Target: U.S. Microchip Hegemony," *The Wall Street Journal*, July 27.

22 USTR, 2018, "Findings of the Investigation into China's Acts, Policies, and Practices Related to Technology Transfer, Intellectual Property, and Innovation Under Section 301 of the Trade Act of 1974," March 22 (hereafter "USTR Section 301 technology transfer report"), section IV.

23 Jost Wübbeke, Mirjam Meissner, Max J. Zenglein, Jacqueline Ives and Björn Conrad, 2016, "Made in China 2025: The making of a high-tech superpower and consequences for industrial countries," Mercator Institute for China Studies (MERICS), MERICS Papers on China No. 2, December, chapter 2, www.merics.org/sites/default/files/2017- 09/MPOC_No.2_MadeinChina2025.pdf.

On May 5, 2017, a passenger jet with a green-and-blue striped tail taxied into takeoff position, barrelled down a Shanghai runway and ascended into the sky, spending about an hour in the air before landing safely as a throng of government officials and aerospace industry executives watched and applauded.[24] This was the maiden test flight for the C919, a plane that China hopes will become a significant entrant in the world's commercial aircraft market. The milestone was duly noted at Boeing and Airbus, the giants of global aerospace, as an indicator of China's progress in the industry they dominate.

China's aspirations to build commercially competitive aircraft have long worried trade hawks in Washington, who see it as a canonical case of how Beijing exploits its rapidly expanding market to nurture domestic manufacturers at foreigners' expense. A 2005 report of the US-China Economic and Security Review Commission, a body created by Congress to monitor and investigate Sino-American economic relations, warned of China's adroitness at dangling the prospect of large purchase orders to extract valuable concessions. "By playing Airbus and Boeing off one another, China elicits agreements from each to shift new production and technology" to Chinese facilities, the report's authors wrote. "Over the long term, these dynamics undermine U.S. global leadership in aircraft manufacturing."[25]

There is no doubt that in their pursuit of an indigenous aviation industry, China's state planners have used every tool in their industrial policy kit.[26] In 2008, they ramped up their efforts with the establishment of a national champion, the Commercial Aircraft Company of China (COMAC), as a spinoff from the SOE that is responsible for producing military jets. State aid for developing the C919 soon followed after the NDRC approved the project, which is aimed at producing a single-aisle airliner similar to the Boeing 737 and the Airbus A320. The central government provided COMAC with $2.8 billion in paid-in capital, and many billions more came in the form of investments from other state agencies and SOEs, plus loans from state-owned banks. Work also proceeded apace on a smaller plane, the ARJ21,

---

24 Keith Bradsher, 2017, "China's New Jetliner, the Comac C919, Takes Flight for the First Time," *The New York Times,* May 5.

25 U.S.-China Economic and Security Review Commission, 2005, "2005 Report to Congress," November, chapter 1, www.uscc.gov/sites/default/files/annual_reports/2005-Report-to-Congress.pdf.

26 Information on China's aviation policies can be found in Keith Crane, Jill E. Luoto, Scott Warren Harold, David Yang, Samuel K. Berkowitz and Xiao Wang, 2014, "The Effectiveness of China's Industrial Policies in Commercial Aviation Manufacturing," RAND Corporation, www.rand.org/content/dam/rand/pubs/research_reports/RR200/RR2 45/RAND_RR245.pdf; James Fallows, 2012, *China Airborne,* New York, NY: Random House; and CSIS, 2018, "China's Turbulent Aircraft Sector: Challenges, Opportunities and Prospects," October 11, www.csis.org/events/chinas-turbulent-aircraft-sector- challenges-opportunities-and-prospects.

which is intended to compete with the "regional jets" produced by Canada's Bombardier and Brazil's Embraer.

Nor is there any question that foreign aerospace companies have won more sales if they are perceived as "friends of China" — meaning they set up joint ventures with SOEs for final assembly of their own airplanes and components, or participate in the C919 project or furnish technological expertise in some other manner. Before 2005, Boeing was the number one supplier to Chinese airlines by far, but that year Airbus agreed to establish an assembly line in Tianjin — its first outside of Europe — to assemble most of the Airbuses sold in China, and over the following decade, Airbus more or less split the Chinese market with Boeing. With similar motivations in mind, GE reached an agreement with COMAC in 2011 to share some of its technology for building jet engines. Foreign firms are well aware that China's three major airlines — AirChina, China Eastern and China Southern — are all state-owned, with CEOs appointed by SASAC along with the Party's Central Organization Department. The fleets of those airlines, already the world's fastest-growing, are poised to expand even more exponentially in coming years; China's aviation market will reach 1.3 billion passengers in 2035, surpassing the US market, according to the International Air Transport Association.[27] Beijing's airport has become the world's second-busiest, behind Atlanta's, and the Chinese government has built scores of new airports throughout the country in recent years.

In view of the above factors, the goals set in Made in China 2025 for the nation's aviation industry — more than five percent of the domestic aircraft market by 2020 and more than 10 percent by 2025 — might seem readily achievable, with COMAC threatening to eventually overtake Boeing and Airbus. But many industry experts regard China's ambitions in this sector with deep skepticism. An extensive study by the RAND Corporation concluded in 2014: "COMAC has yet to show that it will be able to produce commercially viable aircraft, much less show that it can become commercially competitive"[28] — an assessment that appears just as valid as this book goes to press. Delivery of the first C919s, originally scheduled for 2015, is at least six years behind schedule. Chinese authorities haven't yet submitted the plane for certification by the US Federal Aviation Administration, whose rigorous and unyielding scrutiny of every aspect of aircraft manufacture and maintenance make it the de facto global arbiter for whether planes

---

27 International Air Transport Association, 2016, "IATA Forecasts Passenger Demand to Double Over 20 Years," Press Release, October 18.

28 Crane et al., "The Effectiveness of China's Industrial Policies," (see footnote 26 in this chapter), xiii.

are safe to carry passengers. Although orders for the C919 (almost all by Chinese state-owned airlines) are officially put in the hundreds, evidence is scant that those orders are backed by actual deposits of money.[29]

Making a $100 million plane (the approximate price for a 737 or A320) that airlines will willingly buy is far more daunting than other manufacturing challenges that China has surmounted. It is no coincidence that only a handful of companies dominate the production of major components — in particular, engines (GE, Pratt & Whitney, Rolls-Royce) and avionics (Honeywell, Rockwell Collins). Even when the C919 comes to market, most of its value will consist of such parts, with much of the profit going to the foreign suppliers. Beyond those high-value parts, immense difficulties are involved in the fabrication of lightweight aluminum airframes and aerodynamic wings and tails and, above all, the "systems integration" required to pull all these elements together so that the aircraft is optimized for safety, fuel efficiency, expense of operation, passenger comfort and so forth. So far, COMAC-made planes shape up as significantly heavier, more costly to fly and dated in design compared with next-generation foreign competitors, according to the RAND study and other authoritative sources. That may limit their sales even in China, where airline executives are obliged to keep their fleets operating safely and profitably.

The possibility that China will someday become a commercial plane-making powerhouse cannot be dismissed out of hand, to be sure, given all the sectors in which Chinese manufacturing prowess has taken the world by surprise. But in his entertaining book about Chinese aviation, *China Airborne*, writer James Fallows lists good reasons to believe that, under its current system at least, Beijing will come up short:

> Modern China is the world's great success story at the "hard" elements of [industrial development]: creating infrastructure, lowering production costs, doing any- and everything at a great scale. But it has yet to show comparable sophistication with the "soft" ingredients necessary for a fully functioning, world-leading aerospace establishment. These include standards that apply consistently across the country, rather than depending on the whim and favor of local potentates. Or smooth, quick coordination among civil, military, and commercial organizations. Or sustaining the conditions — intellectual-property protection, reliable contract enforcement and rule

---

29 For an up-to-date assessment, see CSIS, "China's Turbulent Aircraft Sector" (see footnote 26 in this chapter). See also Richard Aboulafia, 2017, "A Reality Check on China's C919 Jetliner," *Forbes*, May 8.

of law, freedom of inquiry and expression — that allow first-rate research-and-development institutions to thrive and to attract talent from around the world.[30]

Do China's travails in industries such as semiconductors and aviation mean that the West should shrug off Made in China 2025? Not at all; the approach taken in Made in China 2025 has put non-Chinese companies on the back foot, both in China's domestic market and worldwide. In aircraft, for example, even if COMAC's jets never match those of its foreign rivals in quality, it is conceivable that Chinese state-owned airlines would be pressured to buy enough C919s to put a major dent in the export sales of Boeing and Airbus. As a study by the Berlin-based MERICS astutely observed:

> Made in China 2025 will probably fail in its endeavour to catalyse a comprehensive, broad-scale technological upgrading across the Chinese economy. The strategy's effectiveness is limited by the mismatch between political priorities and industry needs, the fixation on quantitative targets, inefficient allocation of funding and campaign-style overspending by local governments. The lack of bottom-up initiative and investment is a pronounced weakness of Made in China 2025.

But the study's authors continued:

> Even with mixed success, China's technology policy will create tremendous challenges for international corporations and entire economies of industrial countries. The economic advancement of China is principally positive and can create mutually beneficial opportunities for China and its economic partners. It would be unproductive to perceive China's technological rise as a zero-sum game in which increased Chinese strength directly weakens other industrial countries. However, it is a valid concern that the active industrial policy by the Chinese state results in an uneven playing field in which foreign competitors are at a disadvantage.[31]

Whatever comes of Made in China 2025, it is only the most salient and widely publicized facet of the statism and associated problems for China's trading partners that have materialized during Xi's tenure as Beijing's top

---

30 Excerpt(s) from CHINA AIRBORNE by James Fallows, copyright © 2012 by James Fallows. Used by permission of Pantheon Books, an imprint of the Knopf Doubleday Publishing Group, a division of Penguin Random House LLC. All rights reserved.

31 Wübbeke et al., "Made in China 2025" (see footnote 23 in this chapter), chapter 1. Reprinted here with permission.

ler. There are many more such facets, which have enlarged the schism sep-
ating the Chinese economic model from others. The following are the most
important.

Multi-level Micromanagement: The 13th Five-Year Plan

China's five-year plans are no longer the Soviet-style, command and control
documents that Party cadres piously strove to fulfill to the letter during the
Maoist era. They are, however, authoritative directives that the leadership provides to guide economic and social policy at the national, provincial and local
levels and at SOEs. Thousands of officials and outside experts are involved
in the drafting and consultation process, which spans more than two and a
half years, with the NDRC acting as the nerve centre while the State Council,
key Party committees and top leaders all weigh in before the final product is
approved by the National People's Congress. Although not all of the goals and
targets are "mandatory" (some are merely "predictive"), the degree to which
they are achieved may affect careers positively or negatively. The 13th Five-Year
Plan, approved in March 2016 to cover the years 2016–2020, gave Xi his first
opportunity to put his paramount-leader stamp on such a comprehensive set of
priorities and prescriptions, and he took an avid interest. Nobody reading the
13th Five-Year Plan could conclude that private sector forces were supplanting
the NDRC or other power centres in Beijing in determining which sectors and
sub-sectors would flourish.

Overall, the 13th Five-Year Plan aimed to shift the economy away from heavy
industry and investment to high tech and services, while cleaning up the environment and strengthening the social safety net. A major theme, fostering
innovation, was incorporated into a list of technologies and sectors that were
targeted for advancement. Such lists could be found in previous five-year plans,
but as noted in an analysis by CSIS in Washington, "compared to earlier plans,
the 13th is incredibly ambitious." Not only the Made in China initiative, but
altogether 75 priority technologies were highlighted, more than the 57 in the
12th Five-Year Plan. "Moreover, each of these 75 technology areas actually
includes a range of more specific technologies and products," the CSIS study
observed. "For example, there are six [strategic emerging industries]…and at
least 50 specific technologies that fall within these categories. The detailing of
such specific technologies is the most important signal that the Chinese state is
still not a passive observer focused solely on providing public goods."[32] Premier
Li Keqiang had already announced that the government was budgeting about

---

32 Scott Kennedy and Christopher K. Johnson, 2016, "Perfecting China, Inc.: China's 13th Five-Year Plan,"
Washington, DC: CSIS, www.csis.org/analysis/perfecting-china-inc.

$75 billion on 13th Five-Year Plan projects in 2016,[33] and more was sure to come from state-controlled banks and investment funds.

Beyond the national plan were hundreds of five-year plans for individual sectors, provinces, counties and municipalities, each of which provided much greater specificity than the goals and targets of the national plan. For example, the National Mineral Resources plan spelled out tonnage amounts to be produced for resources including natural gas, copper and lithium energy metal materials. The Robotic Industry Development Plan called for 100,000 industrial robots to be produced annually by 2020. To ensure that lending officers at state-owned banks understood the importance of this goal, a State Council website stated: "Special funds from the central budget will be earmarked to support robotics research and development, and financial institutions are encouraged to finance robotic projects."[34]

For insight into how the 13th Five-Year Plan worked at the provincial level, consider the one for Hebei Province. It called for "ensur[ing] that strategic emerging industries represent at least 20 percent of the large-scale industry's added value [in the province]," and "ensur[ing] that by 2020 the number of large size industrial enterprises...reaches 20,000 with an added value of RMB 1.5 trillion." The 2020 target for science and technology small and medium-sized enterprises (SMEs) in Hebei Province was 80,000 and for high-tech enterprises, 3,500. Provincial planners earmarked numerous projects for support from the provincial government, in three categories: 120 "projects aiming at planning and start of operations"; 100 "projects aiming and continuing construction and getting fully operational"; and 120 "pre-projects." Each category included dozens of projects in "strategic emerging industries," and the individual recipient companies were named.[35]

The guiding principles of the 13th Five-Year Plan reiterated the 2013 language about the market playing "the decisive role in resource allocation." But the emptiness of those words was starkly apparent in the plan's interventionist substance and level of detail.

---

33 State Council, 2016, "Report on the Work of the Government, Delivered at the Fourth Session of the 12th National People's Congress of the People's Republic of China," March 5, cited in European Commission, 2017, "On Significant Distortions in the Economy of the People's Republic of China for the Purposes of Trade Defence Investigations," Commission Staff Working Document, December 20, chapter 4.

34 European Commission, "On Significant Distortions," chapter 4 (see footnote 12 in this chapter).

35 Ibid.

An Antitrust Crackdown

Dawn raids at corporate offices, verbal browbeating by officials, forced apologies and banning of lawyers during interrogations: so it went at foreign companies subjected to a rash of enforcement actions by the Chinese agencies responsible for administering the country's anti-monopoly law. At one session in which a foreign technology firm was undergoing investigation, the government official in charge snarled at his interpreter, "I want you to translate my curses."[36]

China's anti-monopoly law, enacted in 2008 after years of consultation with authorities abroad, was a much-needed measure to punish avaricious and rapacious business practices — just as the Sherman Antitrust Act of 1890 had been in the United States. At first, the statute stayed on the books with few probes or penalties assessed, but shortly after Xi took power, the regulators went into overdrive, increasing their enforcement activity several-fold in 2013 and 2014. Among the companies accused of wrongdoing were six Korean and Taiwanese LCD panel makers, which allegedly formed a price cartel; five foreign eyewear manufacturers, including Johnson & Johnson and Nikon, for price manipulation; and auto and auto-parts makers, including Audi, Chrysler, Mercedez-Benz plus a number of Japanese competitors for a variety of monopolistic practices. The biggest case was lodged against Qualcomm, the San Diego-based world leader in semiconductors and other equipment for wireless telecommunications systems. In February 2015, Qualcomm, which derived about half of its revenue from sales in the Chinese market, agreed to change its pricing and pay a fine of nearly $1 billion for allegedly exploiting its dominant market position to overcharge Chinese customers.

Groups representing multinational corporations in China cried foul. It was no coincidence, they asserted, that most of the mergers and acquisitions rejected by regulators involved foreign investors, while the vast majority of Chinese-only business deals were approved. Similarly, actions against companies such as Qualcomm were obviously designed to enhance the competitiveness of domestic firms, which could buy Qualcomm's chips at significantly lower cost. "It has become increasingly clear that the Chinese government has seized on using the [anti-monopoly law] to promote Chinese producer welfare and to advance industrial policies that nurture Chinese enterprises, rather than the

---

36 Information on the controversy over accusations of anti-monopoly violations, including the conduct of Chinese officials, can be found in Michael Martina and Matthew Miller, 2014, "'Mr. Confession' and his boss drive China's antitrust crusade," Reuters, September 15; Jamil Anderlini, 2014, "Multinationals fret as China's antimonopoly probes intensify," *Financial Times*, August 6; Laurie Burkitt and Colum Murphy, 2014, "China Using Antimonopoly Law to Pressure Foreign Businesses," *The Wall Street Journal*, August 4; *The Economist*, 2014, "Unequal before the law?" August 23; Samson Yuen, 2014, "Taming the 'Foreign Tigers': China's anti-trust crusade against multinational companies," *China Perspectives* 2014 (4): 53–59; and Paul Mozur and Quentin Hardy, 2015, "China Hits Qualcomm With Fine," *The New York Times*, February 9.

internationally accepted norm of using competition law to protect consumer welfare and competition," the US Chamber of Commerce wrote in a letter to top Obama administration officials,[37] and the European Union Chamber of Commerce in China agreed that "foreign companies are being disproportionately targeted."[38]

Officials from the three Chinese agencies responsible retorted that their integrity was being outrageously impugned by foreigners seeking to deflect blame for their own market abuses.[39] The NDRC, which policed pricing offences under the law, pointed out that foreign firms comprised only 10 percent of the 335 enterprises it had investigated for monopolistic conduct. "Everyone is equal before the law," Li Pumin, the NDRC's secretary-general, declared,[40] and another NDRC official asserted that its cases were selected based on information from whistle-blowers and consumers. As for Qualcomm, it had faced antitrust scrutiny in other countries; the same was true of Microsoft, another of Beijing's targets.

The number of cases dropped sharply after 2015, and foreign firms have stopped listing the issue as one of their main concerns about doing business in China. But the arbitrary and non-transparent manner in which the law was enforced continues to exert a chilling effect, according to some in the foreign business community, who say that the fear of antitrust investigations makes them more susceptible to pressure from Chinese interlocutors.[41]

Worries about capricious regulators would matter less in a country where businesses and individuals had recourse to an independent judiciary that put the law above all other considerations. But Xi's China was no such country.

"Retreat" from Rule of Law
Nicknamed "the stone-cold [faced] judge," Qin Lingmei was lionized in the state media during the late 1990s when China was preparing for WTO entry and rule of law was taking hold. She enjoyed a reputation for impassiveness

---

37 Matthew Miller, 2014, "China's latest anti-trust probes revive protectionism concerns," Reuters, August 7.

38 European Chamber of Commerce in China, 2014, "European Chamber releases statement on China AML-related investigations," Press Release, August 13, www.europeanchamber.com.cn/en/press-releases/2132/european_chamber_releases_statement_on_china_aml_related_investigations.

39 Michael Gu and Yu Shuitan, 2014, "Chinese Competition Authorities Hold Joint Press Conference in Response to Criticism from E.U. and U.S. Trade Groups," *China Law Vision*, September 19, www.chinalawvision.com/2014/09/competition-law-anti-monopoly- law/chinese-competition-authorities-hold-joint-press-conference-in-response- to-criticism-from-eu-and-us-trade-groups/.

40 *The Economist*, "Unequal before the law?" (see footnote 36 in this chapter).

41 For an example involving a 2017 investigation of DuPont Co., see Lingling Wei and Bob Davis, 2018, "How China Systematically Pries Technology From U.S. Companies," *The Wall Street Journal*, September 26.

and strict neutrality, regardless of the parties whose cases she heard, and she made a habit of avoiding contact with disputants after hearings. Among Judge Qin's quirks that the media celebrated was her eschewing of glasses while working despite being nearsighted — a symbol of her readiness to administer blind justice.[42]

But half a decade or so after WTO accession, legal and judicial theory in China was starting to head in a different direction. The Hu-Wen regime stoked a "socialist rule of law" campaign, which emphasized Communist Party doctrine and subordination of written law to the interest of social stability. In March 2008, the Supreme People's Court got a new president, Wang Shengjun, a Party functionary who had no formal legal training. The "model judges" hailed in the media tended to be those who worked hard at mediating agreements among disputants and promoting the Party's goal of a "harmonious society" rather than those who, like Qin, issued rulings after listening dispassionately to the arguments and strictly applying the law.[43] In a 2010 speech, Jiang Ping, the former president of China University of Politics and Law — who helped draft many civil and administrative codes during the reform era — lamented, "China's rule of law is in full retreat."[44]

The retreat turned out to be less of a full rout than a combination of forward and backward steps. After Xi assumed leadership, Beijing took measures to depoliticize the judiciary at the provincial and local levels by depriving local officials of some control over courts — a key element in Xi's anticorruption campaign and important improvement in the right to seek legal redress. Moreover, standards and professionalism of judicial personnel have been enhanced.[45] But as for the central government, any hopes for a significant judicial check were dashed by a 2015 statement on the official website of the Supreme People's Court under the name of Zhou Qiang, who succeeded Wang as China's chief justice. "All courts shall use the spirit of Xi Jinping's series of major speeches to arm their minds, guide their practice, [and] foster their work," the statement said, adding that courts should "foster the creation of teams that are loyal to the Party, loyal to the State, loyal to the People, loyal to the Law," and "shall earnestly fulfill the historical mission of People's Courts...to ensure the country is ruled in accordance with the law, [and]

---

42 Carl Minzner, 2011, "China's Turn Against Law," *American Journal of Comparative Law*, http://ir.lawnet.fordham.edu/faculty_scholarship/4.

43 Ibid.

44 Jiang Ping, 2010, "China's Rule of Law is in Full Retreat," February 21, cited in Minzner, 2011, "China's Turn Against Law (see footnote 42 in this chapter), translation available at: http://lawprofessors.typepad. com/china_law_prof_blog/2010/ 03/jiang-ping-chinas-rule-of-law-is-in-full-retreat.html.

45 Rebecca Liao, 2017, "Judicial Reform in China," *Foreign Affairs*, February 2.

ensure strictly the Party's rule everywhere."[46] Even blunter was Zhou's 2017 statement, in a speech to jurists in Beijing, that "China's courts must firmly resist the Western idea of judicial independence and other ideologies that threaten the [Party's] leadership," including the separation of powers.[47] Xi himself made similar comments in a 2018 speech.[48]

In addition to the judiciary, the Party's clutch was tightening in other areas of the Chinese economy and society.

The Party's Growing Reach in Business

At the Beijing unit of Bosch Rexroth, a German engineering firm, Party members study Xi speeches on Saturdays. The Chinese joint venture of Renault, the French automaker, has organized lectures for new foreign employees on the Party's role. Walt Disney Co.'s Shanghai theme park has about 300 Party members among its staff, who attend Party lectures during business hours at a special Party centre featuring Mickey Mouse decorations. At Cummins Engine, plans to appoint a new manager for one of the company's China businesses were scotched when Party representatives nixed the choice.[49]

Doing business in China has long required some sort of Party involvement, but until recently, most Party cells were more symbolic than active. Under Xi, as the anecdotes above illustrate, even foreign companies and their joint ventures are expected to afford the Party, which has about 89 million members, greater prominence and influence.

For SOEs, the Party has become particularly assertive — one key piece of evidence being notifications to stock exchanges by publicly traded SOE units that they are changing their articles of incorporation to increase the power of internal Party committees in corporate governance. More than 30 SOEs listed on the Hong Kong exchange injected such phrases into their articles in 2017; in many cases, these clauses obliged boards of directors to consult Party cells before finalizing major decisions. The articles of association for China Railway Group, for example, were altered to state that "when the board of directors decides on material issues, it shall first listen to the opinions of the

46 Zhou Qiang, 2015, "Fostering Courts that are loyal to the Party, loyal to the State, loyal to the People and loyal to the Law," www.court.gov.cn/zixun-xiangqing-13285.html (in Chinese), cited in European Commission, "On Significant Distortions," chapter 3 (see footnote 12 in this chapter).

47 Reuters, 2017, "China's top judge warns courts on judicial independence," January 15.

48 Charlotte Gao, 2019, "Xi: China Must Never Adopt Constitutionalism, Separation of Powers, or Judicial Independence," *The Diplomat*, February 19.

49 Information about the Party's role in foreign companies can be found in Chun Han Wong and Eva Dou, 2017, "Foreign Companies in China Get a New Partner: The Communist Party," *The Wall Street Journal*, October 29; and Alexandra Stevenson, 2018, "China's Communists Rewrite the Rules for Foreign Businesses," *The New York Times*, April 13.

party committee of the company." Among other SOEs that have changed their bylaws in such ways during the Xi era (or whose major units have) are Sinopec, China National Materials Group, Industrial and Commercial Bank of China, No. 1 Auto Plant and China Pacific Insurance.[50]

Xi's personal interest in this trend is evident in comments and directives he has issued. "Party leadership and building the role of the Party are the root and soul for state-owned enterprises," he was quoted as saying at an October 2016 meeting with senior government officials and SOE executives. "The Party's leadership in state-owned enterprises is a major political principle, and that principle must be insisted on....The weakening, facing, blurring or marginalization of Party leadership in state firms will no longer be tolerated."[51]

SASAC Redux and SOEs, Too

By October 2017, the number of SOEs in SASAC's portfolio had declined by half, to 98, from the 196 that the agency had at its inception in 2003. But SASAC was not in danger of being downgraded to a Temasek-style, profit-seeking investor that passively administered the assets of national patrimony as its officials had feared around the time Xi took office. On the contrary, SASAC's power had grown significantly.

The assets under SASAC control had multiplied seven-fold to more than $7.5 trillion during its decade and a half of existence.[52] SOEs were fattening up on bank loans, which were going increasingly to the state sector at the expense of the private sector. The share of loans going to state firms rose from 28 percent in 2011 to 69 percent in 2015 — a reversal of the trend in earlier years of China's WTO membership, when privately owned companies received the lion's share of credit. And that was despite SOEs' deteriorating financial performance; ordinary market incentives were being overridden. In industrial sectors, SOEs were earning much lower returns than private companies (more than three times lower in 2016), and during the decade from 2007 to 2016, roughly half of SOEs failed to earn enough to cover all of the interest and principal payments due on their borrowings.[53]

---

50 Information about the Party's growing role in SOEs can be found in Bloomberg News, 2016, "Xi Boosts Party in China's $18 Trillion State Company Sector," July 18; and Jennifer Hughes, 2017, "China's Communist Party writes itself into company law," *Financial Times*, August 15.

51 Emily Feng, 2016, "Xi Jinping Reminds China's State Companies of Who's the Boss," *The New York Times*, October 13.

52 Wei, "China's Xi Approaches a New Term" (see footnote 2 in this chapter).

53 Nicholas R. Lardy, 2018, "Prospects for Economic Reform and Medium-Term Growth in China," in Ha Jiming and Adam S. Posen (eds.), *US-China Economic Relations: From Conflict to Solutions*, Peterson Institute for International Economics, PIIE Briefing, June, chapter 6.

As Xi's second five-year term got under way in 2017-2018, so much of China's capital was being absorbed by inefficient SOEs that they were becoming a major drag on the nation's economic growth, according to both foreign and Chinese analysts.[54] The explanation for this seemingly irrational approach is that politics trumps economics. As scholar Minxin Pei puts it, "SOEs play a vital role in sustaining one-party rule, as they are used both to reward loyalists and to facilitate government intervention on behalf of official macroeconomic targets."[55]

One major reason for the shrinkage in the number of SASAC firms is that the agency has engineered many mergers in which strong SOEs took over weaker ones. These mergers included the combination of shipping groups COSCO and China Shipping, Baosteel Group and Wuhan Iron and Steel Group, textile equipment maker China Hi-Tech Group and China National Machinery Industry Corp., and mining conglomerates China Metallurgical Group and China Minmetals Corp.[56] The creation of ever-bigger national champions was evidently a Beijing priority, which SASAC managed with the help of a special fund.

Declarations from the leadership underscored that SASAC was expected to be a critical cog in the industrial policy machinery rather than devoting its efforts to maximizing return on investment. According to an August 2015 "Guiding Opinion," the assessment of SOEs "shall not only cover their business performance indicators and the preservation and appreciation of the value of their State-owned assets, but also focus on aspects such as their efforts to serve national strategies, safeguard national security and the operation of the national economy, [and] develop cutting-edge strategic industries."[57] A State Council notice in 2017 stated that for SASAC, it is vital to "promote the optimal allocation of State-owned capital by centering around the missions of serving national strategic objectives" and to "push State-owned capital to gravitate towards important sectors and key fields [including]... forward-looking strategic industries and enterprises with core competitiveness edges."[58]

54 For a rigorous study making this argument, see Nicholas R. Lardy, 2019, *The State Strikes Back: The End of Economic Reform in China?* Washington, DC: Peterson Institute for International Economics.

55 Minxin Pei, 2018, "China is Losing the New Cold War," Project Syndicate, September 5.

56 European Commission, "On Significant Distortions" (see footnote 12 in this chapter), chapter 5 .

57 "Guiding Opinions of the CPC Central Committee and the State Council on Deepening the Reform of State-owned Enterprises," adopted August 24, 2015, cited in European Commission, "On Significant Distortions" (see footnote 12 in this chapter), chapter 5.

58 State Council, 2017, "Notice on Forwarding the Plan of the State-owned Assets Supervision and Administration Commission of the State Council on Promoting the Transformation of Functions by Primarily Focusing on Capital Management," April 27.

Overcapacity with Chinese Characteristics

Mao predicted in 1958 that the Great Leap Forward would endow China with more steel production than Britain in 15 years. That didn't go so well, in part because of its reliance on the revolutionary enthusiasm of the masses to melt scrap metal in backyard furnaces. But by the time Xi rose to power, China's steel mills were producing almost as much as the rest of the world combined, and the story was much the same for aluminum and cement, given all the inputs needed for the nation's skyscrapers, bridges, homes, cars, roads and trains. The beneficiaries weren't only Chinese; they also included Australians, Brazilians and citizens of other countries where economies boomed as a result of supplying China's voracious appetite for iron ore and other raw materials.[59]

The problem was a surfeit of steel supply, much of which was unloaded on global markets as post-crisis government spending on infrastructure tailed off. From 2008 to 2015, China's annual steel exports more than doubled, to 112 million metric tons — an amount exceeding the yearly steel consumption of the United States. Although Washington and Brussels imposed anti-dumping and other duties on Chinese steel, world steel prices sank, leading to mill closings and layoffs in the West. To the fury of China's trading partners, many Chinese mills continued to operate at high levels, even when they were losing money, with help from financing by state-owned banks.

Chinese officials repeatedly sought to cut capacity — the leadership in Beijing took no pleasure in the debts that bloated, half-idle steel companies were accumulating, nor in the smog they were emitting, which ordinary citizens viewed with growing intolerance. But these efforts usually came to naught, because provincial and municipal authorities, who were evaluated based on their localities' GDP and stability, kept mills open to avoid costly closures and social unrest.

Steel was hardly the first Chinese industry to generate so much excess due to distortions in domestic market conditions. Makers of solar panels and other solar energy equipment, incentivized by government subsidies for installation costs and tens of billions of dollars worth of loans from state-owned banks, ramped up production in 2010 and 2011 that rapidly outstripped domestic demand, and the exportation of the surplus led to an 80 percent decline in international prices from 2008 to 2013. Again, governments abroad raised

---

59 Information on China's steel overcapacity can be found in *The Economist*, 2016, "Xi Jinping is a strongman. That does not mean he gets his way," October 22; U.S.-China Economic and Security Review Commission, 2016, "2016 Report to Congress," November, chapter 1, section 2; and Michael Schuman, 2016, "A Steel Mill Lives Again, in a Setback for China," *The New York Times*, November 9.

duties but not quickly enough to stave off disaster for foreign solar energy firms, mostly in the United States and European Union, which suffered 86 bankruptcies and closures from 2009 to 2015.[60]

"The Great Leap Backward" was the term humorously applied to a decree issued by the State Council in early 2016 aimed at slashing steel capacity by 100 million to 150 million metric tons by 2020, with similar targets for aluminum, cement and coal. Despite skepticism that this time would be different, it was — thanks, perhaps, to the fear Xi had struck in Party cadres with his anti-corruption campaign. By the second half of 2017, authorities reported surpassing the interim targets set by Beijing.[61] "We have reduced our work force and shed extra capacity, all while maintaining our social and economic stability," the party secretary of the northeastern city of Tangshan, a major steel-producing centre, assured a Party Congress.[62] (Inspectors had been sent from Beijing to Tangshan to check on false reporting of mill closures.) It helped that the government provided massive amounts of funds to compensate and resettle workers laid off in the iron, steel and coal sectors, who reportedly numbered more than one million.[63] Exports of Chinese steel declined by 30 percent in 2017 compared with the same period a year earlier, and the removal of that surplus from global markets helped to fuel a smart rebound in steel and other commodity prices worldwide.

The cutbacks, however welcome, were responses to diktats from above rather than price signals from the market. They involved arbitrary and inflexible mandates, such as limits on the number of days that coal mines could operate in a year. More systematic forces that lead to overcapacity — Beijing's backing for SOEs, subsidized credit for industries and projects deemed to be national priorities — were left unaddressed. That raised the obvious question of whether the next global glut would come in advanced sectors, such as robotics or semiconductors, targeted in Made in China 2025.

---

60 U.S.-China Economic and Security Review Commission, 2017, "2017 Report to Congress," November, chapter 4.

61 Information on China's capacity reductions can be found in *The Economist*, 2017, "Capacity cuts in China fuel a commodity rally and a debate," September 7; *The Economist*, 2017, "Making sense of capacity cuts in China," September 9; and Reuters, 2018, "China aims to meet 2020 target for steel capacity cuts this year," February 7.

62 Emily Feng, 2017, "Local Chinese leaders promise to make cuts," *Financial Times*, October 29.

63 According to the Ministry of Human Resources and Social Security, during 2016, a total of 726,000 employees in the coal, iron and steel sectors were resettled. In addition, the minister stated that the estimated number of employees in the three sectors that would be laid off in 2017 was around 500,000. Cited in Zhiyao (Lucy) Lu, 2017, "China's Excess Capacity in Steel: A Fresh Look," Peterson Institute for International Economics, China Economic Watch, June 29.

"Going Out" — For Profit, or National Strategic Purposes?

How fatuous it all seems now, the furour that arose in the United States during the late 1980s and early 1990s over the purchases by Japanese companies of US assets such as New York's Rockefeller Center, film studios Columbia and MCA, and Pebble Beach golf course. Hand-wringing over the prospect that Tokyo would snap up America's most prized patrimony turned out to be grossly excessive, as did the prices paid by the Japanese buyers in many cases.

Overseas acquisitions by Chinese companies likewise burgeoned in step with the nation's financial might. "Going out" is the term that leaders in Beijing used to encourage it, and Chinese enterprises responded with outward FDI valued at $146 billion in 2015 and $196 billion in 2016, up sharply from the 2006 level of $21 billion.[64] The outcomes were rightly viewed in many instances as exemplars of how such cross-border flows can serve as an elixir of growth and jobs. Chinese companies bearing chequebooks have provided much-needed capital for struggling European firms including Volvo, the Swedish automaker and Pirelli, the Italian tire maker; the sale of American meat giant Smithfield to China's Shuanghui International in 2013 for $4.7 billion is another benign case.

But Chinese FDI is often state-funded and appears to be state-guided, rather than driven by market factors that determine how other countries' companies choose their investments abroad. The result has been a backlash in the United States and Europe, especially against efforts by Chinese companies to buy firms with cutting-edge technologies. It would be going too far to suggest that Chinese FDI has closely tracked all of the government's industrial policy initiatives, but in at least one sector — semiconductors — the correlation is striking.

Following Beijing's announcement in mid-2014 of its "Guidelines for the Development and Promotion of the Integrated Circuit Industry" (see page 179), "private [Chinese] investors and government funds have embarked on an unprecedented buying spree of assets along semiconductor production chains in Asia, Europe, and North America," noted Daniel Rosen and Thilo Hanemann of the Rhodium Group, a research firm that specializes in monitoring investment flows. "Before the strategy was announced, outbound activity in this industry was low, never exceeding $1 billion in a single year," but by 2015, the figure rose to $35 billion; moreover, "most of these transactions

---

64 "MOFCOM, NBS, and SAFE Jointly Issue Statistical Bulletin of China's Outward Foreign Direct Investment," http://hzs.mofcom.gov.cn/article/date/201612/20161202103624.shtml (in Chinese), cited in USTR Section 301 technology transfer report (see footnote 22 in this chapter), section IV, C-1.

include funding from strategic finance vehicles set up by China's central government with an industrial policy mandate."[65]

A war chest fattened by state money can make a difference, especially if a bidding war erupts. One example was the purchase by Uphill Investment Co., a Chinese investment consortium, of Integrated Silicon Solutions (ISSI), a Milpitas, California-based chip designer and developer. Although Cypress Semiconductor Corp. of San Jose ardently pursued ISSI, it was outbid by Uphill's winning offer of $730 million, or $23 a share, a substantial premium over its initial proposal of $19.25 a share. Among Uphill's backers was a network of state-connected funds such as SummitView Capital, which manages a Shanghai government-owned fund established in response to the central government's 2014 semiconductor initiative.[66]

The highest-profile "national champion" in semiconductors — and one of the most adventurous international investors — is Tsinghua Unigroup, affiliated with the elite Tsinghua University, whose head, Zhao Weiguo, has declared, "Our goal is to build a Pacific fleet for China's information technology industry."[67] Controlled by a wholly state-owned parent company, with an equity investment from the National Integrated Circuit Fund, Tsinghua Unigroup made a $23 billion offer in mid-2015 to buy Micron, an Idaho-based company that is the last US-based manufacturer of dynamic random access memory chips and also has large chip-fabrication facilities in Taiwan and Singapore. The deal would have been the largest Chinese takeover of a US firm by far, but Micron scotched it on the grounds that it would surely run afoul of the Committee on Foreign Investment in the United States (CFIUS), a powerful inter-agency group centred in the US Treasury that scrutinizes foreign purchases of domestic companies for potential national security implications, with the right to block them or reshape the terms.[68]

Anticipation that government regulators would stiffen their opposition to such takeovers proved prescient. Another bid later in 2015 by a Tsinghua-affiliated unit to pay $3.78 billion for a 15 percent stake in Western Digital, a San Jose-based industry leader in hard-drive disks, was also abandoned when

---

65 Daniel H. Rosen and Thilo Hanemann, 2017, "Submission [for] Section 301 Investigation: China's Acts, Policies and Practices Related to Technology Transfer, Intellectual Property, and Innovation," September 28, www.regulations.gov/document?D=USTR-2017-0016-0031.

66 USTR Section 301 Report on Technology Transfer (see footnote 22 in this chapter), section IV, C-2-b.

67 Bloomberg News, 2016, "Western Digital Urges China to Tread Carefully on Chip Ambitions," September 8.

68 Liana B. Baker and Greg Roumeliotis, 2015, "Exclusive: Micron does not believe deal with Tsinghua is possible — sources," Reuters, July 21.

CFIUS launched an investigation.[69] (The two companies settled for a China-based joint venture.) And European attitudes toward Chinese acquisitions also hardened, especially in Germany, as realization sank in that China Inc. was using its deep pockets to acquire high-technology expertise in Germany's open markets even though foreign investors were constrained from operating freely in many of China's own advanced sectors. In mid-2016, when a Chinese appliance maker offered $5 billion to buy Kuka AG, a robotics firm, Berlin tried to stave the deal off by seeking counterbidders in Europe, reluctantly allowing the transaction to go through only after alternative buyers failed to emerge.[70]

Then came a $735 million Chinese bid in late 2016 for Aixtron, a German maker of advanced equipment and systems needed for the manufacture of chips and light-emitting diodes — and this time Chancellor Merkel really put her foot down.[71] US intelligence officials warned their German counterparts that chips produced using Aixtron's equipment could be used in China's nuclear program, so Berlin withdrew approval for the purchase by state-affiliated Fujian Grand Chip Investment Fund. Moreover, since nearly one-fifth of Aixtron's 700 employees were based in the United States, CFIUS intervened to block the takeover of Aixtron's US assets. Anxious to ensure that it could stop similar deals in the future, the Merkel government unveiled plans for new EU rules that would allow member states to rebuff Chinese approaches for companies in strategic sectors, especially when the prospective buyers were state-linked, as was the case in roughly 70 percent of the largest Chinese takeovers of German firms.

German officials stressed that they would continue to welcome foreign investment, including from China, but would not stand idly by in the case of state-directed acquisitions. Deputy Economics Minister Matthias Machnig told the *Financial Times*: "We need to have the powers to really investigate deals when it is clear that they are driven by industrial policy or to enable technology transfers."[72]

69 Arash Massoudi, James Fontanella-Khan and Shawn Donnan, 2016, "Tsinghua kills $3.8 bn investment plan in Western Digital," *Financial Times*, February 24.

70 William Wilkes and Andrea Thomas, 2016, "Germany Cools to Chinese Investors After Record Year for Takeovers," *The Wall Street Journal*, November 1.

71 Information about the attempted takeover of Aixtron can be found in Paul Mozur, 2016, "Showdown Looms as U.S. Questions Chinese Deal for German Chip Designer," *The New York Times*, November 19; and Eyk Henning, 2016, "CFIUS Again Objects to a China-Europe Deal," *The Wall Street Journal*, November 20.

72 Guy Chazan and Stefan Wagstyl, 2016, "Berlin pushes for EU-wide rules to block Chinese takeovers," *Financial Times*, October 28.

Officials like Machnig might have been more tolerant of Chinese takeovers if it hadn't been for other danger signs.

Appropriation of Foreign Technology: A Persistent Problem

Considering that China had no intellectual property laws four decades ago, its progress in protecting patents, trademarks and copyrights is an achievement for which it deserves much more credit than it usually gets abroad. The counterfeiting of brand-name goods, sales of pirated movies and software and copying of product designs — although by no means absent — are no longer the scourges that they used to be, and Beijing's record improved even further in the years since Xi became paramount leader. The government established specialized courts and tribunals in Beijing, Shanghai, Guangzhou and other cities to handle patent infringement and other such complaints involving intellectual property misappropriation; by many accounts, foreigners who bring cases in these courts often win.[73] Moreover, payments of licensing fees and royalties for the use of foreign technology rose to almost $30 billion in 2017, a four-fold increase over the previous decade.[74] Ensuring intellectual property rights, after all, is in the interest of a country that wants its best and brightest to innovate in fields such as artificial intelligence, where China has already moved far beyond the stage of imitating foreign inventions.

But multinational companies operating in China have continued to face demands for their technology — less rampantly and more subtly than before, but with an element of coercion in at least some cases. In certain sectors, Made in China 2025 and associated initiatives included almost blatant requirements for technology transfer by foreign firms. New energy vehicles again provide a particularly noteworthy example. Beijing promulgated laws requiring automakers to manufacture a substantial number of electric cars in China if they want to continue selling gasoline-powered vehicles there — a laudable move from an environmental standpoint. But to qualify as Chinese makers of new energy vehicles, companies would have to demonstrate mastery in key technologies, including battery production; this means that foreign automakers

---

73 Information about Chinese progress in protecting intellectual property can be found in the hearings held on October 17, 2017, by the USTR for the Section 301 investigation regarding "China's Acts, Policies, and Practices Related to Technology Transfer, Intellectual Property and Innovation." See, in particular, testimony by Scott Partridge of the American Bar Association and William Mansfield, director of intellectual property for ABRO Industries, https://ustr.gov/sites/default/files/enforcement/301Investigations/China%20Technology%20Transfer%20Hearing%20Transcript.pdf. See also Anton Malkin, 2018, *Made in China 2025 as a Challenge in Global Trade Governance: Analysis and Recommendations*, CIGI Papers No. 183, Waterloo, ON: CIGI, www.cigionline.org/publications/made-china-2025-challenge-global-trade-governance-analysis-and-recommendations, 11–16; and Charles Clover, 2018, "Chinese courts curb IP theft as US sees bigger threat," *Financial Times*, May 30.

74 State Administration of Foreign Exchange of China, cited in Nicholas R. Lardy, 2018, "China: Forced Technology Transfer and Theft?" Peterson Institute for International Economics, China Economic Watch, April 20.

participating in joint ventures would need to hand over their battery-making technology to their Chinese partners, rather than importing batteries made abroad. Failure to go along would risk being shut out of the world's largest car market.[75]

The problem has abated somewhat as Beijing has loosened requirements for foreign investors to form joint ventures with local partners. The vast majority of foreign firms operating in China do not complain, even in confidential surveys, about having been coerced; in the US-China Business Council's 2017 survey, a little less than one-fifth of the member companies said they had been asked to transfer technology over the previous year. And among those, two-thirds said the request came from their Chinese partners rather than government officials.[76] Even so, foreign executives are keenly aware that resisting such requests puts their operations at heightened risk of regulatory interference. Recounting his numerous interviews with managers of technology-intensive multinationals based in China, Lee Branstetter, an economics professor at Carnegie Mellon University, stated: "I have heard personal and detailed accounts of the lengths to which Chinese companies and the Chinese government have gone in their collective efforts to extract technology from foreign multinationals," and although the transactions might technically be "voluntary," they are "only voluntary in the sense that the business transactions engaged in by the fictional gangster of the *Godfather* series, Vito Corleone, were voluntary. China is effectively making an offer multinationals cannot refuse."[77]

An even more egregious form of technology transfer is the kind that would put Don Corleone to shame.

Five-fingered Technology Acquisition
Operating from four large networks in Shanghai, a ring of cyber spies, labelled "Advanced Persistent Threat 1" (APT1), had "systemically stolen" hundreds of terabytes of data from at least 141 companies and organizations spanning 20 major industries since 2006. The companies targeted by APT1's intrusions "match industries that China has identified as strategic" to its growth, and 115 were US based. "Once APT 1 has established access, they periodically revisit the victim's network over several months or years and steal broad

---

75 European Union Chamber, "China Manufacturing 2025" (see footnote 11 in this chapter), section 7.1.3.

76 US-China Business Council, 2017, "USCBC 2017 China Business Environment Member Survey," www.uschina.org/reports/uscbc-2017-china-business-environment-member-survey.

77 Lee Branstetter, 2017, written testimony to the USTR for the Section 301 Investigation on China's Acts, Policies and Practices Related to Technology Transfer, Intellectual Property, and Innovation, September 28, www.regulations.gov/document?D=USTR-2017-0016-0048.

categories of intellectual property, including technology blueprints, proprietary manufacturing processes, test results, business plans, pricing documents, partnership agreements, and emails and contact lists from victim organizations' leadership."

So said a bombshell report issued in February 2013 by Mandiant, a Washington-based internet security firm, that had investigated the intrusions over seven years for its clients.[78] Suspicions that APT1 was authorized or backed by Chinese government entities had been difficult to substantiate for a long time. But after painstakingly tracing the group's "attack infrastructure, command and control, and modus operandi," Mandiant said it had determined that APT1 activity "appears to originate…in precisely the same area" — a compound on Datong Road in Shanghai's Pudong district — where an intelligence component of the PLA, known as Unit 61398, was also partially located. Since this operation involved "one of the most prolific cyber espionage groups in terms of the sheer quantity of information stolen," its personnel would have to include "at least dozens, but potentially hundreds of human operators" and infrastructure "conservatively" estimated at more than 1,000 servers. "The sheer scale of duration and sustained attacks against such a wide set of industries from a singularly identified group based in China leaves little doubt about the organization behind APT1," Mandiant concluded. "We believe the totality of the evidence we provide…bolsters the claim that APT1 is Unit 61398."

Mandiant's revelations, the first ever to level such specific allegations against Chinese government-sponsored hackers, sparked a firestorm in Washington. Here was the clearest indication yet of the skullduggery to which Beijing would resort in its quest to siphon know-how from foreign companies. Notwithstanding heated disputation by Beijing of the report's validity, members of Congress and Obama administration officials vowed action that would go beyond strengthening the nation's cyber defences, including using all possible methods to punish the Chinese malefactors.[79]

A couple of months later, however, the United States lost the moral high ground on this issue, with the even more explosive information leaked by Edward Snowden, the former contractor for the US National Security Agency (NSA), about the NSA's worldwide surveillance apparatus. Among

78 Mandiant, 2013, "APT1: Exposing One of China's Cyber Espionage Units," February, www.fireeye.com/content/dam/fireeye-www/services/pdfs/mandiant-apt1-report.pdf.

79 Geoff Dyer, Kathrin Hille and Patti Waldmeir, 2013, "China military linked to hacking attacks," *Financial Times*, February 20.

the many disclosures to emerge was an NSA program that infiltrated the servers of a Chinese telecommunications company few Westerners had heard of — Huawei.[80]

Huawei's spectacular ascent had long attracted attention from the US intelligence community. Founded in 1987 by Ren Zhengfei, a former technical researcher for the PLA, the company was one of China's proudest private sector success stories. Rising from the entrepreneurial hub of Shenzhen, Huawei elbowed aside a rival national champion, ZTE, and by 2013 was well on its way to becoming the world's largest manufacturer of networking equipment, such as base stations, switches, modems and routers as well as mobile phones, as its dedicated army of engineers and technicians won contract after contract to supply gear in Asia, Africa and Europe. Based on classified briefings, the House Intelligence Committee issued a report in 2012 concluding that companies like Huawei and ZTE "cannot be trusted to be free of foreign state influence." If permitted to build US network infrastructure, the report warned, Huawei might install "malicious implants" that could serve as a "back door" for routing sensitive information to China, or perhaps even shut down power plants or the whole US communications system.

In fact, the Snowden documents showed American spies were doing to Huawei almost exactly what they feared Huawei would do to the United States. Under the code name "Shotgiant," an NSA cyber operation had been burrowing since at least 2010 into Huawei's headquarters. One goal was to discern whether Huawei was a front for the PLA or another Chinese intelligence service, which the company had always vehemently denied. Although proof of such links was evidently not forthcoming, the NSA program had another aim — to embed US surveillance capacity in equipment sold around the world. "Many of our targets communicate over Huawei-produced products," one NSA document noted. "We want to make sure that we know how to exploit these products."

Embarrassing as the Snowden documents were, US officials brushed aside accusations of hypocrisy. NSA spying, they maintained, was purely for national security purposes — and therefore qualitatively different from China's use of state-run intelligence assets to obtain commercial secrets for the benefit of individual companies. In Washington's view, governments should desist from the kind of snooping Unit 61398 had conducted, and in May 2014, the Justice

---

80 David E. Sanger and Nicole Perlroth, 2014, "N.S.A. Breached Chinese Servers Seen as Security Threat," *The New York Times*, March 22. For a full account of early US suspicions about Huawei and the revelations about the NSA's cyber operations against the company, as well as Mandiant's detection of hacking by APT1, see David E. Sanger, 2018, *The Perfect Weapon: War, Sabotage, and Fear in the Cyber Age*, New York, NY: Crown, chapters 3 and 5.

Department unsealed an indictment of five of the unit's members, including a couple of its most audacious hackers, who went by the pseudonyms of "UglyGorilla" and "KandyGoo."[81] Although nobody in the US government expected Beijing to extradite the defendants for prosecution, the indictment drove home Washington's argument about the acceptable boundaries for government spying.

Hard-fought progress materialized in the early fall of 2015, when Xi was scheduled to make his first state visit to Washington. The trip gave leverage to the US side because Chinese diplomats, with their acute sensitivity to protocol, were anxious to avoid any developments that might dampen the perception of a successful summit. Prior to Xi's arrival, American officials therefore let it be known, via press leaks and other channels, that they were ready to impose sanctions on Beijing for the offences committed by Unit 61398 and other Chinese hackers — and the only way to avoid such a blemish on the summit, they told their Chinese counterparts, was a non-aggression pact for economic cyber espionage.[82] In the event, the Chinese side agreed; Xi and Obama jointly committed that "neither country's government will conduct or knowingly support cyber-enabled theft of intellectual property, including trade secrets or other confidential business information, with the intent of providing competitive advantages to companies or commercial sectors."[83]

To the pleasant surprise of US officials, the accord appeared to work. Breaches of US companies' computer networks by Chinese organizations like APT1 plummeted by around 90 percent, according to a report issued in June 2016 by Mandiant (or more precisely by cyber security firm FireEye, which had acquired Mandiant).[84] "Since mid-2014, we have seen a notable decline in China-based groups' overall intrusion activity against entities in the U.S. and 25 other countries," the report stated, adding that the Obama-Xi pact formalized a trend that was already occurring because of "ongoing military reforms, widespread exposure of Chinese cyber operations, and actions taken by the U.S. government." Not that China-based hacks of US firms ceased altogether, but "they've been careful to go after targets where you can't clearly say what they're taking, or where they can defend what they're taking as permissible"

81 Michael S. Schmidt and David E. Sanger, 2014, "5 in China Army Face U.S. Charges of Cyberattacks," *The New York Times*, May 19.

82 Sanger, *The Perfect Weapon* (see footnote 80 in this chapter), chapter 5.

83 White House, 2015, "Fact Sheet: President Xi Jinping's State Visit to the United States," September 25, https://obamawhitehouse.archives.gov/the- press-office/2015/09/25/fact-sheet-president-xi-jinpings-state-visit-united-states.

84 FireEye, 2016, "Redline Drawn: China Recalculates Its Use of Cyber Espionage," June, www.fireeye.com/content/dam/fireeye-www/current-threats/pdfs/rpt-china-espionage.pdf.

under the terms of the Obama-Xi agreement, said Chris Porter, FireEye's chief intelligence strategist, in an article published by the magazine *Wired*.[85] The article quoted former US government cyber security experts agreeing that Beijing's thinking and behaviour had significantly shifted; even though attacks still occur, it is unfair to blame the nation's officialdom. "The Chinese government doesn't have complete and total control over all these Chinese hacker groups," J. Michael Daniel, the Obama White House's cyber security coordinator, told *Wired*. "Some of that activity may not be the Chinese government, but the companies that it would benefit, hiring those hackers to conduct these operations."

Garden-variety intellectual property theft has continued, to be sure — and it can be brazen. Criminal cases in Taiwan, where two-thirds of the world's semiconductors are produced, suggest that Chinese chipmakers used bribery to extract information from engineers and executives employed by Taiwanese units of Micron after the Idaho-based firm spurned Tsinghua Unigroup's purchase offer.[86] One of the cases brought by Taiwanese prosecutors involves allegations that Tsinghua Unigroup was the intended beneficiary of an internal document heist that occurred in late 2016. In another case, specifications and details about Micron's advanced memory chips were allegedly passed via a Taiwanese company to Fujian Jinhua Integrated Circuit, which was building a $5.7 billion chip factory in the Fujian Province city of Jinjiang with backing from its state-affiliated owners.

These cases are ongoing, and many of the accused have denied the charges. The issue of Chinese economic espionage and the outcome of the Obama-Xi agreement will be explored further in chapter 10. But one development in the Fujian Jinhua case deserves special attention for what it shows about the fuzzy lines between state and private enterprise that make China Inc. so impenetrable. In January 2018, Fujian Jinhua sought to turn the tables on Micron by filing a lawsuit against the US firm for patent infringement — and the court where the suit is being tried is in Fujian Province, whose government is one of the investors in Fujian Jinhua.[87]

---

85 Andy Greenberg, 2017, "China Tests the Limits of Its US Hacking Truce," *Wired*, October 31.

86 Information about the Taiwan cases can be found in Paul Mozur, 2018, "Inside a Heist of American Chip Designs, as China Bids for Tech Power," *The New York Times*, June 22; Lauly Li, 2017, "Five Former Inotera employees indicted for trade espionage," *Taipei Times*, September 26; and Chuin-Wei Yap, 2018, "Taiwan's Technology Secrets Come Under Assault from China," *The Wall Street Journal*, July 1.

87 Mozur, "Inside a Heist of American Chip Designs" (see footnote 86 in this chapter).

Cyber Controls — For National Security, and More

A famous saying of Deng's — "If you open a window for fresh air, some flies will blow in" — was the inspiration for China's Ministry of State Security when it announced an initiative in 2000 to prevent Chinese netizens from viewing web content deemed offensive or threatening to the government. The "Golden Shield Project," as it was called, mostly involved the blocking of sites discussing independence for Taiwan or Tibet, or the Tiananmen Square protests or Falun Gong's spiritual beliefs. It was a relatively modest start for a series of measures, commonly known as "the Great Firewall," that today keep Chinese cyberspace insulated from the rest of the world. Under Xi, state control over digital technology has been drastically tightened, with national security the ostensible purpose, but Chinese companies as the clear beneficiaries and foreign companies bemoaning what they perceive as discriminatory restrictions.[88]

Westerners who once dreamt of the internet as an unstoppable force for personal and political liberty in China got a shock in 2009 when Beijing cut off access within the country to Facebook, Twitter and YouTube, all of which were seen as potential transmitters of seditious content. The following year, Google abandoned the market rather than continuing to censor its Chinese search engine. The biggest blows to foreign tech firms, however, came after the 2013 Snowden leaks about the NSA's worldwide hacking activities. Whereas the Great Firewall had previously been grounded in political and ideological considerations, the Chinese authorities now had reason for worry about the risk of espionage arising from exposure to US technology and equipment — an unhappy development for tech companies that depended on China as their most rapidly growing market. State media accused eight firms, including Microsoft, Cisco and Intel, of serving as Washington's "guardian warriors" by penetrating China's digital infrastructure.[89]

This gave Xi all the justification needed for policies aimed at making Chinese cyberspace "secure and controllable" — the buzzwords that cropped up repeatedly in regulations, standards and other official promulgations. A cyber security law enacted in 2016 required extensive security checks on companies

---

88 Information on China's cyber security controls and the problems they pose for foreign companies can be found in Emily Rauhala and Elizabeth Dwoskin, 2016, "Behind the Firewall: How China tamed the internet," *The Washington Post*, December 22; *The Economist*, 2016, "China adopts a tough cyber-security law," November 12; Jane Perlez and Paul Mozur, 2015, "Mutual Suspicion Mars Tech Trade With China," *The New York Times*, February 27; and U.S.-China Economic and Security Review Commission, "2016 Report to Congress" (see footnote 59 in this chapter), chapter 1, section 1.

89 Daniel H. Rosen, 2013, "Eight Guardian Warriors: PRISM and Its Implications for US Businesses in China," Rhodium Group, July 18, http://cim.rhg.com/notes/eight-guardian-warriors-prism-and-its-implications-for-us-businesses-in-china-2.

in tech-heavy industries, such as finance and communications, and mandated the in-country storage of data — all designed to fortify local networks against hacking, but raising alarm abroad about the risks of giving the Chinese government access to networks, encryption keys, source code and other valuable technology. For foreign cloud-computing companies, the new law — in particular the data storage requirements — presented impediments to their businesses that didn't afflict their Chinese competitors.

In response to objections that China was using security concerns as a pretext for protectionism, Chinese regulators have eased a few rules. But such complaints rang hollow in Beijing, given America's treatment of China's own "guardian warriors." As early as 2008, US policy makers blocked a Huawei investment in a California-based digital electronics manufacturer, and since 2012, Washington virtually banned Huawei and ZTE from doing business in the US market. (More on Huawei and ZTE in chapter 10.)

The difficulty of discerning the true intent of China's policies in the digital realm — is it national security, or promoting national champions? — is another testament to the depth of the state's presence in the economy, especially the cyber economy. The Chinese internet is not only more heavily censored than ever, it is increasingly becoming an instrument of omniscient control, as the vast amount of data at Beijing's disposal enables its monitors to identify people deemed anti-social and inflict disadvantages (credit downgrades, travel restrictions and the like) on them. That is the price for the incredible convenience that hundreds of millions of Chinese enjoy as they shop, bank, text and browse the Web using applications such as WeChat and Alipay on their phones.

Whether the leadership was initially motivated by politics or economics in its approach to digital governance, the results cannot be displeasing to the nation's economic planners. Home-grown internet companies — Alibaba, Tencent, Baidu, Xiaomi, to name a few — dominate the domestic market; even when foreign Web-based firms (LinkedIn, for example) managed to gain footholds in China, they have struggled to compete. By 2018, nine of the 20 largest internet companies in the world (by market value) were Chinese, compared with only two half a decade earlier.[90]

90 Rani Molla, 2018, "Mary Meeker: China now has nine of the world's biggest internet companies — almost as many as the U.S.," Recode, May 30.

Is China a market economy? That might sound like a facetious question, especially in view of the Xi-era developments enumerated above — Made in China 2025, the 13th Five-Year Plan, the growing clout of SASAC and the Communist Party, SOEs' increasing heft, chronic overcapacity in state-supported sectors, continuing pressure for technology transfer, the state's role in overseas investment and so on. But it is a serious *legal* question that rose to the fore on December 11, 2016, exactly 15 years after China became a WTO member.

Rewind to that morning in November 1999 when, as recounted in chapter 3, Zhu Rongji went to the Commerce Ministry for the negotiating session with Charlene Barshefsky that finally sealed the US-China agreement on Beijing's WTO accession. Among the last issues the pair settled was how long a period after accession China's trading partners would be entitled to deem it a non-market economy — an important consideration in anti-dumping cases. They compromised on 15 years, and once that 15 years had elapsed, Chinese officials were insisting "time's up!" — China's non-market economy status must be revoked; the nation must henceforth be treated as a market economy when dumping complaints are lodged. Moreover, any trading partner that didn't do so would be hauled before a WTO tribunal.

In the period leading up to that anniversary, China waged a diplomatic campaign to obtain market economy status from WTO members and dozens had agreed (in some cases as conditions for bilateral free-trade pacts), including Argentina, Australia, Brazil, New Zealand, Russia and Switzerland.[91] But the Obama administration declared its determination to stick with the non-market economy designation, and among the other unmoved trading partners were Japan, Canada, India and Mexico; the European Union was trying to fudge the issue but failed to satisfy Beijing.

In economic terms, the question of whether China gets market economy status matters some, although not hugely. Remember from previous chapters that in anti-dumping cases, the products of a non-market economy are treated more severely than other countries' goods — that is, accusations of dumping are easier to prove, and the duties that result tend to be very high. As the world's most frequently accused dumper, Beijing obviously prefers for its products to be treated more gently. On the other hand, most Chinese exports

---

91 Jacob Schlesinger, 2017, "How China Swallowed the WTO," *The Wall Street Journal*, November 1; and Mark Magnier, 2016, "5 Things About China and World Trade," *The Wall Street Journal*, December 9.

are sold under normal conditions, with only a modest fraction impeded by anti-dumping duties involving non-market economy status.[92]

Beyond the considerations of dollars, euros and RMB are matters of political principle. In Chinese minds, the United States and the other governments that agreed with it are guilty of bad faith; China honoured the text of its accession protocol, so its trading partners should too — including the relevant provision on market economy status, which was contained in Article 15 of the 102-page protocol.[93] Even some non-Chinese legal experts have told me privately that they view the wording of the text as unequivocally in Beijing's favour, and on December 12, 2016, the day after its fifteenth anniversary of WTO membership, China carried out its threat to file complaints against the United States and the European Union. An eloquent condemnation of Washington and Brussels' stance came from Zhang Xiangchen, China's WTO ambassador, who quoted the Latin maxim *pacta sunt servanda* — "agreements must be kept" — in the opening panel hearing of the EU case.[94]

But applying the term market economy to a system such as China's, which had become much more distorted than originally anticipated, was more than the Obama administration could stomach. And the wording of the protocol didn't *guarantee* the conferral of such status after 15 years, in the opinion of some scholars.[95] This dispute now looms as one of the WTO's most incendiary.

Denying market economy status to China was just one of many actions the Obama administration took during the Xi regime to counter Beijing's trade policies. As noted above, Washington blocked some Chinese acquisitions

---

92 As of 2015, only about seven percent of Chinese exports to the United States — in categories such as steel, solar panels, paper, furniture, shrimp and some others — were affected by anti-dumping restrictions involving non-market economy status, according to estimates by Chad Bown of the Peterson Institute for International Economics. Moreover, even if Washington were prohibited from invoking non-market economy status for China, a flood of Chinese imports wouldn't ensue, because US officials have readied other trade remedies that they could use. See Chad P. Bown, 2016, "Trump says China is not a market economy. That's a big deal," *Monkey Cage* (*Washington Post* blog), December 12, www.washingtonpost.com/news/monkey-cage/wp/2016/12/12/trump-says-china-is-not-a-market-economy-heres-why-this-is-a-big-deal/?utm_term=.0eb9ccb0d06b.

93 The clause states: "In any event, the provisions [allowing trading partners to deem China a non-market economy] shall expire 15 years after the date of accession."

94 See Henry Gao, 2018, "Broken Promises set a bad example for China in the WTO," East Asia Forum, March 9, www.eastasiaforum.org/2018/03/09/broken-promises-set-a-bad-example-for-china-in-the-wto/.

95 According to adherents of this view, WTO members would no longer have the right, after the 15-year deadline, to *automatically* declare China a non-market economy in every anti-dumping case that comes along. But government officials investigating dumping complaints involving Chinese products could subject China to the same sorts of examination as other countries, and if the evidence supported a non-market economy designation, the rules for such status might apply. Mark Wu, 2016, "The China Inc. Challenge to Global Trade Governance," *Harvard International Law Journal* 57 (2): 261–324.

of US businesses and took strong measures to end cyber theft of data for commercial purposes. In addition, the Obama team mobilized international pressure on Beijing to reduce excess capacity in industrial sectors such as steel and brought a number of WTO cases against China — involving discriminatory taxation on aircraft; export restrictions on copper, tin and other raw materials (beyond those previously litigated); excess government support for farmers; duties on exports of US vehicles; and subsidies to aluminum producers. Meanwhile, anti-dumping and other trade remedies continued to be employed liberally against Chinese imports.

None of those measures, however, held much promise of fundamentally changing the direction China had taken. The arcade game of "Whac-a-Mole" was often invoked in Washington trade policy circles as a metaphor for the difficulty US trade warriors faced, because every time they managed to beat down one problematic Chinese initiative or policy, another seemed to pop up.

If only a more systematic approach were available. Obama and his aides thought they had one.

CHAPTER 9

TRANS-PACIFIC DELUSIONS

onsidering the small size of the economies involved and the vast distances separating them, the "Trans-Pacific Strategic Economic Partnership" was a grandiose name for the trade pact struck in 2005 by New Zealand, Chile, Singapore and Brunei. But this little band of countries harboured dreams of expanding, and in the spring of 2008, Susan Schwab, the US trade representative, was pondering whether the United States ought to participate in negotiations for joining the group. The Bush administration had previously launched talks with 16 countries for 11 separate free trade agreements — that is, accords that eliminate most trade barriers between the participating countries, reducing tariffs even below the levels allowed under WTO commitments. Most of those agreements had been completed and ratified. Now, with Bush's presidency winding down, the opportunity to start the process of striking yet another deal had arisen.

China was one of the factors on Schwab's mind — but only one of several — as she weighed the pluses and minuses of embarking on negotiations. She concluded it would be a good idea, for a variety of reasons. Southeast Asian countries were negotiating several accords with their neighbours, including China, and US firms were concerned about being put at a disadvantage in some of the region's markets. Also, both Democratic candidates for president,

Hillary Clinton and Barack Obama, were decrying the impact of trade on American workers, and with the Doha Round languishing, the Bush team liked the idea of ensuring that the next administration, whoever led it, would inherit a trade-liberalization initiative promoting US open-market values among like-minded countries. Based on Schwab's recommendation, the president formally notified Congress in September that Washington would participate in the talks. Australia, Vietnam and Peru joined a couple of months later. "It was never a geopolitical or geoeconomic strategy primarily vis-à-vis China," Schwab told me.

The name was shortened, with the words "strategic" and "economic" omitted. But when trade ministers shook hands on the terms in October 2015, the TPP had morphed into a "mega deal," encompassing 12 nations that produced 37 percent of global GDP, making it the most sweeping trade and investment agreement since the creation of the WTO. And it had morphed into something else as well — an alliance of China's neighbours and trading partners agreeing that the commerce they conducted among themselves would be governed by rules divergent from, and even antithetical to, Chinese policies.

By the time of the ministerial agreement's signing, the TPP was routinely described by Obama administration officials and many experts in trade and international relations in China-centric terms. The president himself hailed the event by stating: "We can't let countries like China write the rules of the global economy. We should write those rules."[1] When the TPP came under attack during the 2016 election, warnings resounded that critics were endangering the most effective instrument for combatting Chinese industrial policy; the deal "would set in stone the rules of engagement that China would have no choice but to follow," as one prominent commentator put it.[2] Trump's decision to withdraw shortly after his inauguration in January 2017 prompted similar lamentations about the folly of forgoing a pact that, in the words of various pundits and experts, "was set up as a bulwark against China,"[3] was "the single most valuable tool America had for...pressuring China to open its markets,"[4] and would have given the president "the biggest piece of leverage he had to deal with the biggest challenge in the world of trade, which is

---

1   The White House, 2015, "Statement by the President on the Trans-Pacific Partnership," October 5, https://obamawhitehouse.archives.gov/the-press- office/2015/10/05/statement-president-trans-pacific-partnership.

2   Edward Luce, 2016, "US-led globalism is dying with the TPP," *Financial Times,* July 28.

3   Jim Tankersley (quoting David Autor), 2018, "Economists Say U.S. Tariffs Are Wrong Move on a Valid Issue," *The New York Times,* April 11.

4   Thomas L. Friedman, 2017, "Trump is China's Chump," *The New York Times,* June 28.

the increasingly troubling behavior by the world's second largest economy, China."[5]

In its morphing process, in other words, the TPP came to be widely touted as a potential nemesis of China's economic model. Unfortunately, it has been oversold in that regard — that is the central contention of this chapter.

Was China a major impetus for the TPP's formation, and would the pact have induced much change in Beijing's policies? As the anecdote about Schwab's decision indicates, different reasoning lay behind Washington's initial considerations. And as this chapter will further show, a look back at the TPP's history reveals that its expansion to mega-deal status stemmed mainly from governments jockeying over membership in a club that they feared being excluded from, with domestic and commercial issues topping their list of reasons rather than China-related ones. The most contentious wrangling involved issues that didn't concern Beijing at all.

To be sure, as the TPP evolved, it dovetailed neatly with US strategy in Asia, commonly known as "the pivot" — the Obama administration's decision to expend more diplomatic effort and military resources in the region with the aim of preventing China from displacing American power and influence. Moreover, several of the TPP's major provisions, notably the ones involving SOEs and digital commerce, would require a substantial overhaul of China Inc. — if Beijing were a member. Suppose it joined? Much speculation about such an eventuality has arisen, but to believe that would happen requires making some dubious assumptions. Pleasant as it might be to think that Xi would undertake a major market-liberalization campaign for TPP membership, the imperatives for doing so are nowhere near as strong as they were for Zhu when he was pressing for WTO entry.

An oft-expressed opinion in trade policy circles — it might even be called conventional wisdom — is that US abandonment of the TPP was a staggeringly misguided act of unilateral disarmament in the battle against Chinese mercantilism.[6] Closely associated with this conviction is the argument that Washington could greatly improve its chances of bringing China's technonationalists to heel by rejoining its 11 former TPP partners, which in 2018 struck a new pact among themselves called the Comprehensive and

---

5   Edward Alden, 2017, "Trump and the TPP: Giving Away Something for Nothing," *Renewing America* (Council on Foreign Relations blog), January 23, www.cfr.org/blog/trump-and-tpp-giving-away-something-nothing.

6   This is not just a criticism of Trump; prospects for US ratification appeared highly tenuous even before the 2016 election, both because of congressional opposition and Clinton's declaration during the campaign that she couldn't accept the terms as drafted.

Progressive Agreement for Trans-Pacific Partnership (CPTPP). An example, by Bloomberg columnist Noah Smith: "In his struggle to win the U.S. a more favorable negotiating position relative to China, a new TPP would be Trump's most potent weapon."[7]

With the aim of scrutinizing the validity of these claims, this chapter will concisely review the TPP's evolution[8] and examine the case for its efficacy on the China trade front.

The TPP was almost consigned to obscurity in the early months of the Obama administration, thanks to the dismissive view of National Economic Council director Larry Summers, who argued that the economic benefits were too minimal for the United States to continue participating in the negotiations. It is easy to see why: Not only were the GDPs of the partner countries at the time modestly proportioned, their trade barriers, based on the tariffs they applied on an MFN basis to products from other WTO members, were already low — a mere 0.2 percent on average for Singapore and 2.0 percent for New Zealand, which was even lower than the United States' 3.4 percent (which, in turn, was roughly the same as Australia and Peru). Vietnam had by far the highest average tariffs, at 9.5 percent, but it was not yet a full participant, holding only "associate member" status at that point.[9] Moreover, the United States already had free trade accords with Australia, Chile, Singapore and Peru, meaning that almost all US exports could enter the biggest TPP economies duty free.

But the Obama team decided that Washington should stay involved in the TPP, in part to demonstrate US commitment to the region and also because the White House wanted to show it had an active trade agenda; the TPP appeared easier to sell to Congress than other agreements. In any event, an unexpected development helped instill the grouping with some potential economic heft.

---

7   Noah Smith, 2018, "The Best Way Trump Can Squeeze China on Trade," Bloomberg News, October 17.

8   The historical material in this chapter is based in part on interviews with former trade officials who were involved in the negotiations. Many of those sources spoke on a deep background basis, so not all of the details can be footnoted without violating confidentiality.

9   WTO Tariff Profiles, cited in Ian F. Fergusson, Mark A. McMinimy and Brock R. Williams, 2015, "The Trans-Pacific Partnership (TPP): Negotiations and Issues for Congress," Congressional Research Service, March 20.

Among the many summits the US president is expected to attend is the annual APEC forum, which in November 2010 took place in Yokohama, Japan. As hosts, Japanese diplomats were distraught to learn of plans afoot for a mini-summit on the sidelines among the nine leaders from TPP nations (Malaysia had joined a few weeks earlier), and they insisted that if such a gathering was to take place on Japanese soil, Prime Minister Naoto Kan ought to be included. Obama aides retorted that the mini-summit was limited to leaders whose countries had clear intentions of opening their markets wider to each other's goods and services, to which a surprising answer was forthcoming: Japan's leadership was contemplating the possibility that the TPP might help foment desirable liberalization in Japanese markets, even in the most heavily protected of all, rice. That sufficed to gain Kan's admission to the mini-summit; the prime minister issued a statement announcing that, "regarding the Trans-Pacific Partnership, Japan will launch consultations with relevant countries" and "push forward with agricultural reform…With the aging of Japan's agricultural practitioners, there can be no bright prospects for this sector…if we simply continue on as is."[10]

Japan was still undecided about becoming a full-fledged member, and a debate ensued among US policy makers, as well as their Australian and New Zealand counterparts, about whether overtures from Tokyo should be welcomed. Japan's agriculture lobby constitutes a powerful voting bloc that has long ensured the maintenance of high tariffs and other obstacles to protect the nation's small, inefficient farms from foreign competition. Veterans of past trade battles cited their recollections of endless foot-dragging by Japanese negotiators. But given Japan's $5.7 trillion GDP, the prospect of adding it to the TPP member rolls was enticing, and if doing so helped spark a healthy discussion in Tokyo about freeing farm trade, so much the better as far as Washington was concerned.

By the following year's APEC summit, which was held in Honolulu, Chinese officials were taking much greater notice of the TPP, thanks in large part to an October 2011 article in *Foreign Policy* titled "America's Pacific Century" by Secretary of State Clinton. "As the war in Iraq winds down and America begins to withdraw its forces from Afghanistan, the United States stands at a pivot point," she wrote. "One of the most important tasks of American statecraft over the next decade will therefore be to lock in a substantially increased investment — diplomatic, economic, strategic, and otherwise — in

---

10 Government of Japan, 2010, "Remarks by H.E. Mr. Naoto Kan, Prime Minister of Japan, at the APEC CEO Summit 2010 Yokohama," November 13.

the Asia Pacific region."[11] That article heralded the policy, variously dubbed the "pivot" or the "rebalancing," which included new deployments and rotations of US troops in Australia and Singapore, plus pledges to maintain high levels of spending on the Navy's Pacific fleet and other military assets. The TPP was the pivot's main economic element — by enhancing conditions for American companies' exports and investments in Asia, the pact would bolster confidence in the US commitment to preserving regional peace and stability, in particular the reliable and safe transport of goods in the Indian and Pacific Oceans.

Understandable though it was for China to regard the pivot as intended to thwart its ambitions for regional dominance, US officials were taken aback by a surge in Chinese hostility toward the TPP. The pact was depicted in official media as a scheme to corral Pacific nations in an economic encirclement against China and thereby suppress its growth and development. Chinese academics also chimed in, an example being an article titled "TPP: A Serious Challenge for China's Rise," by Li Xiangyang, director of Asia-Pacific Studies at the Chinese Academy of Social Sciences.[12]

"The Chinese were telling me, 'This is your plot to contain China's economy,'" recalls Tim Stratford, who was practising law in Beijing after leaving his top-level position at the trade representative's office in 2010. "I said, 'That's factually not true. I was in the meetings, and there wasn't a single word about containing China.'" But Chinese officials were not assuaged by soothing suggestions that their country might aspire to TPP membership at some point in the future provided it accepted the terms. Instead, China accelerated efforts to form a trade grouping that pointedly excluded the United States, called the Regional Comprehensive Economic Partnership (RCEP), which would include the 10 members of the Association of Southeast Asian Nations (ASEAN) plus the half-dozen countries that had free trade agreements with ASEAN — Australia, China, India, Japan, New Zealand and South Korea. Beijing also stepped up talks for a trilateral trade deal with Tokyo and Seoul.

Meanwhile, the TPP bulked up. Once again, the charged atmosphere of a summit would provide a milieu conducive to enlisting new members.

---

11 Hillary Clinton, 2011, "America's Pacific Century," *Foreign Policy*, October 11.

12 For references to Chinese views about the TPP at this juncture, including the Li article, see Wen Jin Yuan, 2012, "Freeman Briefing: The Trans-Pacific Partnership and China's Corresponding Strategies," CSIS, June 20.

Canadian and Mexican factories and farmers already enjoyed preferential access to the US market under NAFTA. But in Ottawa and Mexico City, concern was growing that American competitors would gain an edge in Asia, especially Japan, if Washington struck a TPP deal that included Tokyo. Officials of the two countries' governments therefore tentatively approached the TPP negotiating table in 2012.

For the White House, the prospect of bringing Canada and Mexico into TPP negotiations was appealing, because it afforded an ideal vehicle for achieving a trade goal that otherwise looked unattainable — "fix[ing] a lot of what was wrong with NAFTA in the first place," as Obama later put it.[13] Although philosophically inclined toward free trade, the president shared the view among leftist critics that trade pacts must include strong provisions on labour rights and environmental protections, lest more American jobs move to countries where unions are oppressed and pollution laws ignored. US trade negotiators therefore admonished their Mexican counterparts that joining the TPP would entail agreement to new, more rigourous labour and environmental rules to replace NAFTA's relatively weak ones. And they told Ottawa that Canada would also be obliged to pay a stiff price for entry into the TPP, such as an opening-up of Canadian dairy markets, which even under NAFTA had been kept tightly shut.

The decisive summit this time was a June 2012 gathering of leaders from the Group of Twenty major economies, in Los Cabos, Mexico. On the eve of the summit, the Mexican hosts informed Michael Froman, Obama's top aide on international economic issues (he later became US trade representative), that Mexico would join the TPP negotiations. According to an account in *Politico Magazine*:

> Froman notified Canadian trade officials [about Mexico's decision] just as Prime Minister Stephen Harper was boarding his plane to the summit, but they said they weren't ready to follow suit. Froman said he understood but warned that Mexican President Felipe Calderón would make a splashy commitment to TPP in Los Cabos. As soon as Harper landed, the Canadians called back and said they were ready to join as well. TPP felt like the next big platform, and they didn't want to be left out.

---

13 Michael Grunwald, 2017, "The Trade Deal We Just Threw Overboard," *Politico Magazine,* March/April.

"It's hard to put a dollar value on that desire to be part of the club, but it's real and it's important," Froman says.[14]

Japan finally took the plunge as well in March 2013, soon after the electoral victory of Shinzo Abe, leader of the old-guard Liberal Democratic Party, who won on a platform of revitalizing the nation's stagnant economy. Whereas his predecessors had dithered, the new prime minister seized on the TPP as a lever for advancing "Abenomics," his signature strategy that combined monetary and fiscal stimulus with structural reforms in Japan's hidebound services and agricultural sectors. Abe also saw the pact as helpful in boosting security ties with Washington, and although Japanese farmers would undoubtedly have to make some sacrifices, transition rules could protect them against sudden onslaughts of imports.[15]

At that point, all of the 12 countries whose trade ministers would negotiate the TPP were represented in the talks. China's trade policies were not a major motive for joining for any of them. But the pact's status as an anyone-but-China club could hardly escape notice. "No one will say it out loud," David Pilling of the *Financial Times* wrote in May 2013, "but the unstated aim of the TPP is to create a 'high level' trade agreement that excludes the world's second-biggest economy."[16]

To widespread surprise, China executed an about-face by indicating its openness to the TPP shortly before Xi's first summit with Obama in California in June 2013. In comments posted by a spokesperson on its website, the Commerce Ministry said it "will analyze the pros and cons as well as the possibility of joining the TPP, based on careful research and according to principles of equality and mutual benefit."[17] Chinese academics had been analyzing the possible losses to the nation's exporters should the TPP-12 forge a preferential accord, and although conclusions varied, some scholars were worried.[18] By no coincidence, the Chinese tone-softening came during the time that Xi appeared to be moving in a pro-reform direction (see previous chapter).

When the Chinese leadership proclaimed later in 2013 that market forces would play a "decisive" role in allocating resources, a reciprocal gesture materialized in a speech by Susan Rice, Obama's national security adviser: "We

---

14 Ibid.

15 Reiji Yoshida, 2013, "Abe declares Japan will join TPP free-trade process," *The Japan Times*, March 16.

16 David Pilling, 2013, "It won't be easy to build an 'anyone but China' club," *Financial Times*, May 23.

17 Reuters, 2013, "China to study possibility of joining US-led trade talks," May 31.

18 Yuan, "Freeman Briefing" (see footnote 12 in this chapter).

welcome any nation that is willing to live up to the high standards of this agreement and join and share in the benefits of the TPP, and that includes China."[19]

Any notions of incorporating China into the TPP were for the distant future at best, however. The Obama team was insistent that the pact would exceed even the "gold standard" deals struck during the Bush administration, which went well beyond erasing tariffs to include rules on behind-the-border issues such as investment, intellectual property and regulatory transparency. This entailed round after round of meetings every few weeks among trade ministers and deputy ministers to haggle over "non-papers," often drafted in Washington borrowing language from previous US trade accords. Inviting Chinese negotiators to the table would have risked endless delays regarding provisions that Beijing was nowhere close to being ready to accept. Three TPP chapters (the final total was 30 when the text was released in late 2015) stood out in particular for imposing requirements inimical to the thrust of Chinese policy as it was evolving under Xi.[20]

SOEs (Chapter 17)

The TPP wouldn't bar SOEs (even the United States has some, the best known being the passenger rail company Amtrak), but it aimed to eliminate advantages that SOEs have over private firms. In their buying and selling of goods and services, SOEs would be prohibited from discriminating against companies from other TPP member countries. They couldn't give or receive subsidies or favouritism — such as loans, or special prices on purchases or sales — if doing so caused "adverse effects" on domestic firms of other TPP members. Local courts would have jurisdiction over disputes involving SOEs' commercial decisions and would be required to rule impartially. Member countries would also have to disclose information about their SOEs — including the percentage of government ownership, involvement of government officials and programs providing any non-commercial assistance — to other TPP member governments, or post the information on public websites.

Those rules mainly affected Vietnam, which still had many elements of a socialist command economy including more than 3,000 SOEs that employed about 1.5 million people. The Hanoi government, eager for its textile and

---

19 The White House, 2013, "Remarks as Prepared for Delivery by National Security Advisor Susan E. Rice," November 21, https://obamawhitehouse.archives.gov/the-press-office/2013/11/21/remarks-prepared-delivery-national-security-advisor-susan-e-rice.

20 For a detailed account of the TPP's provisions, see Cathleen Cimino-Isaacs and Jeffrey J. Schott (eds.), 2016, *Trans-Pacific Partnership: An Assessment*, Washington, DC: Peterson Institute for International Economics, July.

apparel industry to gain preferential access to the US market, grudgingly acquiesced. Helping to smooth agreement was the fact that the rules had some big loopholes, notably an exception for SOEs owned by sub-central governments.

Electronic Commerce (Chapter 14)

Member countries agreed to allow the free flow of data across borders and to eschew data "localization" — that is, laws or regulations (such as ones that China was enacting) requiring the storage of data in a country as a condition for operating in its market.

Competition Policy (Chapter 16)

Antitrust laws should be aimed strictly at the objective of promoting "economic efficiency and consumer welfare," TPP member countries agreed. This chapter also bound them to ensure procedural fairness in enforcing these laws, by requiring strict standards of transparency and impartial review of decisions — a different approach, in other words, from that which foreign companies in China complained they were enduring at the hands of the authorities.

Those chapters could aptly be called the TPP's "anti-China Inc." provisions. But the biggest battles — and the areas where the negotiators devoted most of their attention — concerned other issues. These included esoteric matters such as whether to use the "yarn-forward rule" or "cut-and-sew rule" in determining whether an apparel product could qualify as coming from within the TPP area and therefore be deemed eligible for preferential treatment.[21] Another bone of contention concerned intellectual property, with Washington pushing for maximum stringency in protection and others resisting, notably on "biologics" (medical preparations derived from living organisms). A major clash also occurred between the United States and Australia over whether the TPP's investor-state dispute settlement system, which allows private companies to sue governments for alleged discrimination, should apply in the tobacco industry.[22]

One key reason the talks took so long, and were so hard-fought, was that the United States, with Froman serving as US trade representative, was unwilling

---

21 The yard-forward rule was used in previous US free trade agreements, and is generally favoured by the US textile industry because it requires the entire manufacture of an apparel product, from the spinning of the yarn to final assembly, to occur within the countries that are parties to the agreement. The cut-and-sew rule is less restrictive; it allows products made from materials outside the free-trade area to benefit from preferential tariffs.

22 Australia bans logos and colours from cigarette packages for public health reasons and did not want to risk exposure to a suit by multinational tobacco giants under terms of the TPP.

to offer much in the way of concessions in its own market.[23] For example, American automakers have long prized the 25 percent US tariff on pickup trucks, one of Detroit's most profitable product lines, and Froman rejected demands from Japan to lower it in the foreseeable future; this barrier would be kept at its current very high level for 29 years and eliminated only in year 30. US negotiators also held fast against modifying the federal program that shelters America's politically powerful sugar cane and sugar beet farmers from foreign competition. Relations between Froman and Akira Amari, his Japanese counterpart, became so tense that their deputies schemed to keep them from encountering each other in person, aides recall; each man walked out of meetings at different junctures. To be sure, Tokyo was also stiff-arming demands from its trading partners, especially on beef and rice.

Symbolically mid-Pacific, a Maui resort was where the deal was supposed to be sealed when trade ministers from TPP countries gathered there in July 2015. But the luxurious accommodations and breathtaking scenery could not compensate for the pressures that kept key players from compromising. Harper was fighting for his political life, facing national elections in October, and Canadian negotiators would not budge on opening their dairy market more than a tiny crack. Froman, too, was hemmed in by threats from lawmakers that Congress would reject any deal falling short of the pharmaceutical, sugar and auto industries' requirements. After a late-night session punctuated by high-decibel eruptions, the meeting ended in failure, with the media deriding claims of "significant progress" as spin and many fingers pointing at Washington.[24] "The TPP died in Hawaii because the US offer was too miserable to survive," wrote Australian journalist John Garnaut.[25]

Reports of the TPP's death turned out to be premature. In the early morning hours of October 5, 2015, a meeting in Atlanta produced enough budging for all parties to agree at last. So intense was the round-the-clock wheeling and dealing that Darci Vetter, the chief US agricultural negotiator, went three nights with no sleep whatsoever. Canada was continuing to take a hard line on dairy, to the fury of the team from New Zealand, which depends heavily on exports of cheese, butter and milk products; as for American dairy farmers, they wanted access to Canadian markets but were anxious to keep New Zealand imports at bay. Again, from *Politico's* account: "At 5:30 a.m., Canada finally agreed to accept imports of about 4,000 tons of butter, 14,500 tons

23 This point is trenchantly made in Richard Katz, 2016, "Trading Down," *Foreign Affairs*, September 21.
24 Grunwald, "The Trade Deal We Just Threw Overboard" (see footnote 13 in this chapter).
25 John Garnaut, 2015, "In TPP talks, Barack Obama loses battle against traditional trade powers," *The Sydney Morning Herald*, August 1.

of cheese and 50,000 tons of milk — the first real incursion into its market, even though it amounted to just over 3 percent of its sales. The United States agreed to a similarly modest opening, and everyone shook hands — except for New Zealand's negotiator, who was too angry to shake hands with Vetter."[26]

<hr>

With the TPP's terms agreed and released, sales pitches and policy analyses abounded, from both supporters and opponents. This book is not the place to examine the many arguments that were advanced about the pact's likely impact on member countries' GDPs, or on specific sectors or aspects such as technological innovation or the advantages allegedly bestowed on multinational corporations at the expense of workers. Rather, the focus shall remain on the implications for China and the rules-based trading system. And on that score, even some of the US negotiators who worked on the TPP admit to having winced when they heard the rhetoric emanating from the White House.

Assertions that the TPP meant "America will write the rules of the road in the twenty-first century" (as Obama stated in November 2015[27]) might make good talking points for selling the accord to Congress and the public, especially since China was held out as the alternative rule maker. But the high-handedness of such claims grated on trade-savvy diplomats. Global rules are WTO rules, and other WTO members are involved in writing them.

A more modest formulation often cited by TPP boosters was that the deal would prevent China from writing the rule book in the Asia-Pacific region. But this too was quite a stretch. The China-led RCEP, and Beijing's other free-trade agreements, are mostly about cutting tariffs; they make no pretense to "gold standard" rule making. Although the TPP would undoubtedly draw Vietnam further from its socialist past — a worthy achievement — Hanoi is pretty much unique in that regard; other major economies in the region are in no danger of succumbing to the lure of Chinese-style statism.

Ultimately, the soundness of contentions about the TPP's far-reaching rules comes down to the questions posed at the beginning of this chapter: Would the deal have eventually engendered reform in China itself, presumably by incentivizing Beijing's membership? And would rejoining the other 11 countries in the CPTPP give Washington an indispensable tool for effectuating such a result?

<hr>

26 Grunwald, "The Trade Deal We Just Threw Overboard" (see footnote 13 in this chapter).

27 The White House, 2015, "Here's the Deal: the Trans-Pacific Partnership," November 6, https://obamawhitehouse.archives.gov/blog/2015/11/06/heres-deal-trans-pacific-partnership.

Those who believe the answer is "yes" tend to cite the exports and other commercial activity that China stood to lose to a fully fledged TPP because of the preferential treatment the member countries planned to accord each other. Experts at the Peterson Institute for International Economics have estimated the potential "trade diversion" at $100 billion[28] — an appreciable loss for Beijing, obviously. The most sophisticated version of this argument is based on the importance of supply chains that today's multinational corporations use to spread their research, design, engineering, component-making, final assembly and product marketing across a multitude of countries depending on the competitive advantages of each. Many TPP enthusiasts maintain that the agreement would foster a massive network of supply chains within the bloc, which China would find too lucrative to resist and too costly to ignore.

That sounds logical, but it's unconvincing. China is no longer the country of Zhu Rongji or even Hu Jintao or even the early Xi years. Joining a club whose rules Washington boasts of writing is hardly in keeping with "Xi Jinping thought," especially since some of the rules (such as those on free data flows) would pose a threat to the Party's control. It would be another matter if China stood to reap huge benefits by gaining preferential access to TPP markets. But even studies touting the economic importance of the TPP, such as the Peterson Institute's, have acknowledged that Beijing could offset much of the TPP's effects on Chinese exporters by concluding the RCEP or other free-trade pacts.

Among those who have poured cold water on the economic cruciality of the TPP for China are John Whalley, former CIGI distinguished fellow, and Li Chunding, deputy director of the international trade department at Beijing's Institute of World Economics and Politics. Six TPP members already have free-trade agreements with the United States, Li and Whalley noted in a 2016 paper and wrote: "Liberalization is apt to be phased in gradually. Therefore, it is expected that trade may be a bit freer between the TPP members, but [not much more than before]. This means that the negative impacts of the TPP on China will be limited." An economic modelling exercise that they had conducted in 2014, they noted, showed that the TPP would be a net minus for the Chinese economy, "but these effects are relatively small."[29]

---

28 This estimate is based on the assumption that other Asia-Pacific countries, such as Indonesia and South Korea, would also join the TPP but not China. See Jeffrey J. Schott, 2016, "Overview: Understanding the Trans-Pacific Partnership," in Cathleen Cimino-Isaacs and Jeffrey J. Schott (eds.), *Trans-Pacific Partnership: An Assessment* (see footnote 20 in this chapter).

29 Li and Whalley note that they favoured China's entry into the TPP, and pursuing more reform, but they said TPP by itself would not have a major impact. Li Chunding and John Whalley, 2016, *China and the Trans-Pacific Partnership Agreement*, CIGI Papers No. 102, Waterloo: ON, CIGI, www.cigionline.org/sites/default/files/paper_no.102.pdf.

Even more devastating to the pro-TPP case is an analysis by Harvard's Mark Wu. "The economic threat to China of being excluded from the TPP... appears to be grossly over-exaggerated," Wu concluded in a 2017 paper.[30] The "general equilibrium" models that have been used by economists to estimate the effects of trade pacts are increasingly useless in an era of global supply chains, according to Wu, and that is particularly true for the modelling that has been done of the TPP. Instead of relying on such models, Wu conducted a deep dive into individual product markets to examine how Chinese exports might be affected. His results should put to rest claims about the "leverage" the TPP would provide against Beijing if Washington were to rejoin it.

China already holds such a dominant position in many of the goods that it exports to TPP countries that its competitive position could barely be dented, Wu's analysis showed. "Of China's top 500 exports to the U.S., in nearly half (233) of these product markets...China accounts for 50% or more of the total share of imports of that product," he wrote. "Furthermore, for more than half (268) of the top 500 products, the collective share of imports from [TPP countries that would newly gain tariff-free access to the United States] is less than 5%." Looking at the Japanese, Canadian and Mexican markets, Wu found a similar pattern, which led him to conclude: "Because China's position in these product markets is so entrenched and its competitors' capabilities are non-existent or so under-developed, it is unlikely that any firm would shift its production away from China, even with the tariff advantages arising out of the TPP."[31]

As for products where there is some competitive overlap, Wu also found that the TPP's impact would probably be "immaterial" for China. That is because "many of these top export products are already not subject to tariffs due to existing WTO commitments. For example, of China's top 25 exports to Japan, more than two-thirds already enter the country tariff-free." The only Chinese exporters that *would* be threatened turn out to be mainly concentrated in "sunset" industries — clothing and footwear, for example — that China is trying to transition away from anyway as the result of rising labour costs and the national strategy of moving into more advanced manufacturing. "Outside of these already-shrinking sectors, Chinese exporters face little competitive threat from the TPP," Wu contended, so "even had the TPP been

---

30 Mark Wu, 2017, "Rethinking the Rise and Fall of the TPP," Draft for Cambridge-INET Brexit Conference," www.inet.econ.cam.ac.uk/our-events/copy7_of_DraftonlyRethinkingtheRiseand FalloftheTPPWhytheAnalysisofTradeAgreementsRequiresanOverhaul.pdf/view.

31 Wu's analysis was based solely on the impact of the TPP, without incorporating estimates about the effects of unilateral tariffs that the Trump administration has imposed on Chinese goods, which is a separate issue.

ratified, it would not have succeeded in pressuring China to adopt a posture more beneficial to the U.S."

None of this is to imply that the TPP is lacking in value or relevance with regard to China. When Ashton Carter, Obama's defense secretary, said approving the TPP was "as important to me as another aircraft carrier,"[32] he was expressing a widely held view about the need for the "pivot" to include a salient economic component. When Singapore Prime Minister Lee Hsien Loong warned that "ratifying the TPP is a litmus test of [America's] credibility and seriousness of purpose" in Asia,[33] he reflected the opinion of many in the region. But those geopolitical arguments have little bearing on whether China alters its trade policies, or whether failure to ratify the TPP deprived Washington of a heavy-duty trade weapon.

If the TPP is reinvigorated with the United States rejoining, its advocates could be proven right someday about China's response. Even if Beijing were not a member, it would "live in a TPP world," as Froman put it to me in an interview, and the attractiveness of neighbouring countries for investment — with solid rule of law, in particular — may impel Chinese policy makers to clean up their act with regard to treatment of foreign companies. More countries, such as South Korea and Indonesia, may join the TPP; the pact could be merged with another mega-deal between North America and the European Union and eventually presented to the whole WTO as the basis for new global rules. Given lengthy enough transition times, reform-minded Chinese might go along, with an eye to rectifying weaknesses in their state-led system.

How lovely if such a scenario were to materialize. Wishful thinking, however, is a poor substitute for strategy. This much can be said in the TPP's defence: at least it would be more likely to produce desirable outcomes than the approach taken by the president who withdrew the United States from the agreement.

---

32 Helene Cooper, 2015, "U.S. Defense Secretary Supports Trade Deal With Asia," *The New York Times*, April 6.

33 Lee U-Wen, 2016, "Ratifying TPP a litmus test of US's credibility: PM Lee," *The Business Times* (Singapore), August 3.

CHAPTER 10

MIGHT UNMAKES RIGHT

The mood in China was upbeat, almost giddy, in the aftermath of Donald Trump's victory in the 2016 US presidential election. A European who travels often to Beijing recalled that on the day after the election, he heard the following from a Chinese trade official: "In China we have all these plans — five-year plans, 10-year plans and a 25-year plan to become the world's leading nation. We are now shortening the 25-year plan to five years." That was a joke, of course, but it reflected the view that China could stop worrying about effective US resistance to its ambitions now that American democracy had produced a president whom state-run media dismissed as an "egomaniac" and a "blowhard."[1] Moreover, Trump had expressed isolationist views about the US military role in Asia and showed every sign of giving the Chinese leadership a free pass on human rights. Sure, he had lambasted China on the trade issue, but if he were so foolish as to start a trade war, Beijing would counterpunch. "A batch of Boeing orders will be replaced by Airbus. U.S. auto and iPhone sales in China will suffer a setback, and U.S. soybean and maize imports will be halted," warned the *Global Times*, a strident Party mouthpiece.[2]

---

1   Hannah Beech, 2016, "Donald Trump's Victory Is Some of the Best Foreign News China Could Have Hoped For," *Time*, November 10.

2   Cited in Eduardo Porter, 2016, "A Trade War Against China Might Be a Fight Trump Couldn't Win," *The New York Times*, November 22.

In Geneva, by contrast, a funereal atmosphere pervaded the Centre William Rappard when I arrived three weeks after the election to conduct interviews for this book. The men and women who worked at WTO headquarters, after all, had special reason to dread the impending Trump presidency. The country largely responsible for creating and guiding the institution they served would henceforth be led by a man who, based on his campaign rhetoric, held that institution — and the rules-based system that it protected — in disdain; he had called the WTO "a disaster" and suggested that he might well withdraw US membership.[3] Moreover, he clung to the conviction that trade is a zero-sum game, with the US trade deficit signifying a "loss of money" to countries running surpluses. One of the Geneva veterans I spoke with, WTO Deputy Director-General David Shark, recalled that eight years earlier, when Obama was inaugurated, "the US mission held a big reception, with huge monitors in different rooms. It was the hottest ticket in town." No such festivities would accompany Trump's inauguration.

As people in Geneva were quick to remind me, the WTO was in rocky shape even prior to Trump's election. Thanks to the failure of the Doha Round, WTO rules had gone more than two decades without an update of the sort that had occurred every few years when multilateral rounds were completed during the second half of the twentieth century. Thus, the rules in place were designed for an era before the advent of smartphones, digital commerce, cloud computing and other major technological innovations of the past 20 years. In another sign of the system's enfeeblement, numerous bilateral and regional free trade agreements had gone into effect — the total identified by the WTO was nearly 450 in 2016, more than quadruple the number in 2001.[4] This trend reflected countries' frustration with the lack of progress in the Doha Round and detracted from the WTO's centrality in the trading system.

But Trump's victory laid the WTO even lower, evincing as it did the depth of popular disillusionment with economic globalization. Whereas Bill Clinton's rhetoric had a ring of credibility at the turn of the century when he rhapsodized about the potential for the embrace of US-style capitalism to spread freedom and democracy around the globe, no major politicians — including Democratic presidential candidate Hillary Clinton — were echoing such predictions in 2016. To some extent the 2008 financial crisis was responsible for throwing economic globalization on the defensive, but the political atmosphere also stemmed in no small part from China-related developments covered in this book.

---

3   NBC News, 2016, "Meet the Press," July 24, www.nbcnews.com/meet-the-press/meet-press-july-24-2016-n615706.

4   See http://rtais.wto.org/UI/PublicMaintainRTAHome.aspx.

The China shock turned out to be more than just an economic phenomenon — it was a political one as well, according to research published in 2016 by the same economists who authored the original paper documenting the impact of Chinese import competition on US blue-collar regions.[5] In congressional districts that were most exposed to that sort of import penetration, this research showed, electorates were disproportionately "polarized" — that is, substantially more likely to remove moderate representatives from office in favour of very conservative Republicans or very liberal Democrats, even before the 2016 campaign.

That polarization was part of a deep reservoir of sentiment, especially among white working-class Americans, that their country's trading partners had taken it for a ride — and no trading partner offered a greater target for such excoriation than China. In his quest for the White House, Trump gained an enormous boost by tapping into that vein of opinion. The election result turned on many issues, of course; they included immigration, race, identity politics and a host of others. But trade appears to have played a big role in putting Trump over the top, based on analyses of voting patterns showing how he won the industrial states that provided his Electoral College margin of victory — Michigan, Wisconsin and Pennsylvania (none of which had gone Republican since the 1980s) and Ohio (which hadn't gone Republican since 2004).[6] "Build the wall" may have been one of Trump's biggest applause lines, but he also struck a chord with his claim that in its trade relations with the United States, China was guilty of "rape."

Even among China experts who recoil at such language, a drastic reassessment of fundamental assumptions regarding China's evolution had taken place by the time of Trump's election. A rough consensus was once held in government ministries, corporate boardrooms and think tanks around the world that greater economic interdependence between the Chinese economy and the West would foster a convergence of interests and an easing of trans-Pacific tensions. But that consensus has disintegrated, not only because of the trade issues covered in this book but for other reasons as well: internally, China has regressed toward authoritarianism and a cult of personality for Xi Jinping. More than almost any time since the end of the Mao era, activists and dissidents are subjected to intolerance and intimidation, the most notorious example being the extra-legal detention of Muslims in the

---

5   David Autor, David Dorn, Gordon Hanson and Kaveh Majlesi, 2016, "Importing Political Polarization? The Electoral Consequences of Rising Trade Exposure," NBER Working Paper No. 22637, September.

6   Gerald F. Seib, 2016, "Trade, Not Immigrants, May Have Been Key Motivator of Donald Trump's Voters," *The Wall Street Journal*, November 10.

far-western province of Xinjiang. In its foreign policy, Beijing has thrown its weight around by building up military bases on disputed islands in the South China Sea and defiantly rejecting an international tribunal's ruling in July 2016 against its expansive territorial claims. On occasion, Chinese assertiveness toward its neighbours has verged on the thuggish, as in a dispute with South Korea over US missile placement when Korean businesses underwent a financial battering at Beijing's hands — dozens of Lotte department stores in Chinese cities, for example, were cited in 2017 for "fire hazards" and closed.[7] Rather than bolstering existing international institutions, China has shown a distinct preference for establishing new ones that it can control, such as the Belt and Road Initiative, Xi's signature program for building infrastructure projects in Asia and Africa that are funded with massive sums from state-owned banks.

Citing those developments, as well as economic trends, two Asia specialists who served in top Obama administration positions authored a 2018 *Foreign Affairs* article titled "The China Reckoning" that lucidly conveyed the shift in the policy community's consensus. The reckoning's first step, they argued, should be "doing away with the hopeful thinking that has long characterized the United States' approach to China."[8]

As this book has shown, the trade realm is where the gulf is particularly gaping between initial hopes and current reality — that is, between expectations at the time of China's WTO accession and the policies adopted since by Beijing. For a benchmark, consider the state of affairs at the time of my visit to Geneva in late 2016, before Trump had taken office. This also happened to coincide with the fifteenth anniversary of China's accession. As noted in previous chapters, China's accession protocol envisioned that Beijing would attain "market economy status" 15 years after joining the WTO, and a dispute was under way over the implications for the treatment of Chinese products in anti-dumping cases.

Never mind the legal spat over anti-dumping — let's focus on the term "market economy" in the broad sense, as it is commonly used, and contemplate why the 15-year deadline was set. The answer is that the US officials negotiating China's accession were working on the assumption that the Chinese economy would surely merit such a description after a decade and a half, and

---

7   Tom Hancock and Wang Xueqiao, 2017, "South Korean consumer groups bear brunt of China's Thaad ire," *Financial Times,* August 20.

8   Kurt M. Campbell and Ely Ratner, 2018, "The China Reckoning: How Beijing Defied American Expectations," *Foreign Affairs,* March/April.

Zhu Rongji gave every reason to believe that he shared that view. Instead, when that fifteenth anniversary arrived in December 2016, the myriad ways in which the party-state influenced the Chinese economy's inner workings presented the global trading system with its single greatest problem. The implications, both for the economic futures of China's trading partners and for the trading system's continued viability, should not be underestimated.

Even though China's top-down industrial policies may flop at nurturing companies that surpass foreign rivals in fields such as civil aviation, semiconductors and robotics, the potential for deleterious effects on economies and industries abroad is undeniable. The massive subsidization of priority sectors, if unchecked, is likely to generate excess capacity in world markets for many technologically advanced products in ways similar to what happened in steel, aluminum and solar panels. State-backed financing and other incentives have shown a marked tendency to spur waves of investment by Chinese companies leading to surfeits of global supply over demand, with the resulting suppression of prices destroying the profitability of healthy and weak firms alike. It is easy to conceive of such a fate befalling cutting-edge companies outside of China that cannot depend on the state helping them endure downturns as their Chinese competitors can. Worries are already mounting that electric vehicles may be the next global industry to be adversely affected by Chinese overproduction.[9]

As for the impact of China's trade practices on WTO rules, let's stipulate that it is unfair to assume the truth of every single accusation against Beijing — the ones involving forced technology transfer and the funnelling of state subsidies to national champions, for example. But nobody should doubt that such practices occur and are probably common, given the power of SASAC, the NDRC and the Party to influence decisions by major Chinese companies; and the responses of foreign multinationals to confidential surveys. A similarly functioning "Ethiopia Inc." or even "Vietnam Inc." might be tolerable from a systemic standpoint; when it's China Inc., the impact is corrosive.

Does this mean the approach taken in dealing with China during the accession negotiations and in subsequent years was fundamentally misguided? Has the WTO proven to be so helpless in countering China's industrial policies that unilateral measures antithetical to WTO principles are in order? Is China such a flagrant rule violator, and do its policies so direly menace

---

9   David Stanway, 2018, "Chinese electric car makers, nurtured by state, now look for way out of glut," Reuters, October 17; Scott Kennedy and Qiu Mingda, 2018, "China's Expensive Gamble on New-Energy Vehicles," *Caixin*, November 8.

its trading partners' prosperity, as to justify putting the rules-based system at risk? The evidence presented in previous chapters has furnished readers with the information needed to draw their own conclusions. My belief is that the answer to those questions should be "no" — sometimes an emphatic "no," sometimes a qualified one.

To the extent China could have been prevented from evolving as it has, the failures by the United States and its allies were attributable less to a lack of toughness than a lack of imagination. The accession negotiations, in particular, took hard-nosed confrontation with Beijing to the practical limit. Looking back on the events chronicled in chapters 2 and 3, it is impossible to conclude that Chinese negotiators believed they were getting WTO membership on easy terms. They were not play-acting when they lost their tempers. They were beside themselves, for example, about the April 1999 release of the 17-page paper listing their concessions — which turned out to be a ruthlessly clever US ploy. Within the Politburo, hardliners who hated the idea of going too far in submitting to WTO rules lost out to Zhu's insistence that there was little laxity in the position of Barshefsky and her fellow negotiators.

What the supporters of China's WTO accession *really* got wrong was correctly identified by Robert Lighthizer in 2010 when he derided their hubris for assuming that WTO membership would lead Beijing to adopt a Western economic, political and legal model. As we saw in chapter 3, some specialists, such as Robert Herzstein, foresaw that China would likely cling to a state-led approach, to the detriment of foreign companies trying to penetrate its market. Even so, it defies logic to believe that Beijing would have been a better trading partner outside the WTO than in, considering all the tariff lowering, barrier removing and reform implementing that took place in the five years after 2001.

Suppose the US government and its allies had, in effect, said to China: "Sorry, we can't let you in the WTO because we believe you are incapable of fully abiding by the international rules-based system." That would almost surely have led to much worse tribulations with Beijing than anything the world currently faces. China would still be a manufacturing juggernaut, and there would have been endless confrontations over trade disputes involving threats of unilateral sanctions, instead of resorting to mediation by international tribunals. For the Chinese, nationalistic demons would have been stirred up about foreign powers conspiring to keep their country down. Integrating China into the global economy presented an immense challenge to the international community, and although the WTO has been far from perfect, the process has gone much more smoothly from a global standpoint than it would have otherwise.

The main failings came after China's WTO accession. During the five-year post-accession period when Beijing was fulfilling its market-opening commitments, Bush administration policy makers wisely gave their Chinese counterparts breathing space as reforms were implemented. But Washington should have been much quicker and more aggressive in addressing the cheap RMB. Using the IMF made sense, and US officials pushed the Fund hard. As seen in chapter 5, Treasury demands for IMF action were characterized behind the scenes with phrases such as "take no prisoners" and "blackmail." But the Bush team passed up the opportunity to use the special China safeguard as an extra tool to incentivize Beijing, as noted in chapter 6 — and that, I believe, was a serious mistake in retrospect. A threat that the White House would start approving US companies' requests for safeguard duties, delivered *sotto voce* to the Chinese leadership so as to minimize damage to overall Sino-US relations, might well have achieved significantly faster RMB appreciation. Although the China shock still would have occurred, it might have been less brutal, and Chinese competition would have been fairer.

The "sharp elbows" that China was throwing around in the trade arena — which Obama rightly exhorted his aides to combat — became much sharper in the Xi era. The Obama administration deserves credit for filing numerous WTO cases against Beijing, confronting Chinese officials at countless bilateral meetings over complaints raised by foreign firms and demanding an end to cyber spying for commercial purposes. But by 2015, the direction of Xi's economic policy had become clear, as witnessed by the litany of interventionist measures and initiatives recounted in chapter 8 — and a more comprehensive approach was needed. Unfortunately, the Obama team put its chips on the TPP at that point, on the assumption — misplaced, as I argued in chapter 9 — that China would be obliged to change its ways in response to this "mega-regional" trade pact.[10]

During the years following its accession to the WTO, China implemented the vast majority of the commitments it undertook at the time it joined. To be sure, implementation was not always in the spirit of its trading partners' expectations; the resulting economic system diverged markedly from what was widely envisioned in 2001. But when Chinese policies were clearly shown to abrogate WTO rules, especially when tribunals issued rulings to that effect, Beijing respected its legal obligations. Nearly all of the major complaints

---

10 The Obama administration also tried to negotiate a bilateral investment treaty with China, which would have covered many of the most contentious issues concerning Beijing's treatment of foreign multinationals, and the talks made impressive progress in some areas. But the two sides weren't able to reach final terms, and even if they had, the pact would have faced major difficulties in Congress, in part because of a reluctance to relax restrictions on some Chinese investments in the United States.

about China's trade regime involve practices where the applicability of WTO rules is uncertain or where proof of violation is effectively impossible. Can those complaints be addressed by invoking the rules in new and imaginative ways to induce further alterations in Chinese policies? As shall be seen in the next chapter, some promising possibilities exist for doing so.

Two overarching principles should thus govern the approach that the United States and other concerned countries take in their efforts to modify China's trade practices. First, the WTO should be the chief policy instrument for dealing with Beijing. The trade body remains the best way of inducing China to play by the rules, and its authority should be nurtured to the maximum extent possible; steps that undermine it should be avoided. Second, China should be treated as the trading system's single biggest problem, meriting a concerted campaign in which Washington rallies like-minded countries to its side and builds a broad alliance.

Regrettably, the Trump administration has taken an almost diametrically opposite approach. The negotiations that the president has pursued with China, backed by the imposition of tariffs, may conceivably yield a widely lauded accord; since this book is going to press before any deal is struck, the terms are a matter of speculation. But whether the negotiations "succeed" or not, Washington has degraded the WTO by flouting its rules, crippling its adjudicative system and blatantly bullying trading partners. As a result, the dubious distinction of "the trading system's biggest single problem" now belongs to the United States. To fully absorb the deplorability of this outcome, the events that led to it merit detailed retrospection.

Call it "the year of the paper tiger." At first, Trump's presidency was remarkable for its failure to produce much more than tweets and other forms of fulmination on the trade issue. The only major trade-related campaign promise that the president fulfilled during his first year in office was withdrawal from the TPP. Especially with regard to China, the Trump administration was prone to lurching from pugnacious demands to extravagant boasts about the progress it was making.[11] Adding to the shambolic quality of his diplomacy,

---

11 For example, when Washington and Beijing agreed in May 2017 on a 10-point plan that included greater access for US beef in the Chinese market, Commerce Secretary Wilbur Ross told reporters, "This is more than has been done in the whole history of US-China relations on trade," even though the accord consisted mainly of adding new deadlines or details to pacts already reached during the Obama administration. See William Mauldin, 2017, "U.S.-China Trade Plan Marks Key First Step," *The Wall Street Journal,* May 12; and Keith Bradsher, 2017, "U.S. Strikes China Trade Deals but Leaves Major Issues Untouched," *The New York Times,* May 11.

Trump publicly stated that if China helped pressure North Korea to denuclearize, he would adopt a much more lenient stance toward Beijing regarding trade matters.[12] A mainstream group of Trump advisers, dubbed the "globalists," appeared to be winning internal battles over a hawkish faction known as "economic nationalists" and keeping Trump's protectionist proclivities in check — much to the frustration of the president himself. "China is laughing at us," he told his newly installed chief of staff, John Kelly, in August 2017, according to an account provided by administration insiders to the media website Axios. "I want tariffs. And I want someone to bring me some tariffs."[13]

More months would pass before Trump's tariff fantasy came true — but when it did, with two major US actions in March 2018, the foundations on which WTO rules rest were upended. Historians may well look back at that month as the point in time when the postwar trading system suffered mortal wounds.

On March 1, the president basked in the approving smiles of 10 steelworkers who had been hastily summoned to the White House to witness him signing a directive imposing tariffs of 25 percent on imported steel and 10 percent on imported aluminum. The globalists were caught flatfooted; unbeknownst to them, the economic nationalists had secretly drafted the order, circumventing the normal policy process in which the president was supposed to hear a variety of arguments before making a major decision.[14] Trump was sick of listening to naysayers urging caution, and the leading naysayer, National Economic Council Director Gary Cohn, resigned in a huff.

The steel and aluminum tariffs affected only about two percent of US imports, so taken in isolation the economic impact was minimal. But the justification that was cited — protecting America's national security — marked a historic deviation in US trade policy and risked an endless loop of retaliation and counter-retaliation. The obscure, rarely invoked provision of US law used by the White House, known as section 232, accords the president virtually unchecked power to impose trade restrictions on national security grounds — a desirable tool to have in the event of war or other genuine security threat. In this case, the invocation of the law was a mere pretext for action Trump was lusting to take. US steelmakers produced roughly two-thirds of the steel

---

12 On April 11, 2017, for example, the president tweeted: "I explained to the President of China that a trade deal with the U.S. will be far better for them if they solve the North Korea problem!" Donald J. Trump, Twitter post, April 11, 2018, 4:59 a.m., https://twitter.com/realdonaldtrump/status/851766546825347076?lang=en.

13 Jonathan Swan, 2017, "Exclusive: Trump vents in Oval Office, 'I want tariffs. Bring me some tariffs!'" Axios, August 28.

14 Jenna Johnson, Seung Min Kim and Josh Dawsey, 2018, "Trump rolls out tariff policies like a reality show — complete with cliffhangers," The Washington Post, March 8.

the nation consumed in 2017, with nearly all the rest coming from allies such as Canada, the European Union, South Korea, Mexico and Japan.[15] (Chinese steel imports were already subject to high anti-dumping duties.) As for aluminum, the national security claim was equally bogus given the fact that the United States was totally dependent on imports of bauxite, an essential raw material for aluminum manufacturing.[16] Tellingly, Defense Secretary James Mattis saw no reason for concern about the adequacy of secure steel and aluminum supplies for the US military; his memo to that effect was shrugged off by the White House. The Trump administration's argument — that a healthy steel and aluminum sector is essential to the economic strength that America's security requires — was a rationalization that tortured the definition of national security.

One obvious problem with using such a flimsy excuse for protectionism is that other countries will feel free to follow suit by concocting their own national security rationales for raising tariffs when it is politically expedient to do so. Another serious drawback is imperilment of the WTO. The trade body's rules dating back to the GATT include a national security exception stating that a member nation can take "any action," such as raising tariffs, "which it considers necessary for the protection of its essential security interests." Although this rule has been presumed to be "self-judging," meaning that each country gets to determine when its security is threatened, the exception explicitly applies only during war or an international emergency or in cases related to nuclear or arms trade. It was easy to imagine what would happen if a WTO tribunal were to find Trump's steel and aluminum tariffs to be an abuse of the rules — the president might well quit the trade body in fury over foreign judges passing judgment on where America's security interests lie.[17] On the other hand, a giant loophole in WTO rules would open up if a tribunal were to accept the Trump argument.

Ironically, the steel and aluminum tariffs were supposedly aimed at China — the villain in the worldwide glut of those metals — but China's steelmakers were little affected because, as noted above, Chinese imports were already restricted by high anti-dumping duties. If anything, Trump's action diminished his ability to confront Beijing, because it alienated many US allies who shared Washington's concerns about China's economic policies and might

15 US International Trade Administration, 2018, "Global Steel Trade Monitor," June, www.trade.gov/steel/countries/pdfs/imports-us.pdf.

16 Greg Ip, 2018, "The Flaw in Trump's National Security Tariffs Logic," *The Wall Street Journal*, March 9.

17 A presidential order of a US withdrawal from the WTO would surely be challenged in court, but in any event, the White House has other ways of wreaking havoc on the trade body, as shall be seen later in this chapter.

have made common cause with Washington on the issue. Retaliation came the day after Trump's announcement, with the European Union, Canada, Mexico and other trading partners announcing that they were prepared to slap tariffs on quintessential American goods such as Kentucky bourbon, Harley-Davidson motorcycles and blue jeans, as well as pork and cheese. Those retaliatory tariffs also contravened WTO rules, which oblige countries to refrain from such actions unless they have been authorized by a tribunal based on proper adjudicative procedure. But WTO propriety was going up in flames, upon which Trump poured more fuel. He declared that if Brussels persisted, he would counter-retaliate by imposing tariffs on European automobile imports, based on the same national security provision of US law that he used for steel and aluminum.[18]

The trade wars of 2018 were just getting started. Bigger guns were about to be fired from Washington, and this time they would be aimed squarely at Beijing, from which a return fusillade would be forthcoming.

On March 22, the US administration announced that it was readying restrictions on imports from China, with Trump stating vaguely that levies of 25 percent would apply to "about $60 billion [of imports] but that's really just a fraction of what we're talking about."[19] Unlike the chaotic decision on metals tariffs, this move was the culmination of a months-long process masterminded by Lighthizer, who had been quietly accumulating power in his position as US trade representative. The legal basis was Section 301, which had fallen into disuse since the mid-1990s; the dusting off of this provision of trade law was another sign of the Trump administration's readiness to operate outside WTO rules.

Lighthizer was no novice at wielding unilateral sanctions — and he was far from squeamish about doing so.[20] During his tenure as deputy US trade representative in the Reagan administration, he employed such tactics often against Japan, the main target during the 1980s of US complaints about unfair trade practices. Using America's economic muscle to maximum advantage made

18 Shawn Donnan and Robin Wigglesworth, 2018, "Trump fires back at EU tariff retaliation threats," *Financial Times,* March 4.

19 White House, 2018, "Remarks by President Trump at Signing of a Presidential Memorandum Targeting China's Economic Aggression," March 22, www.whitehouse.gov/briefings-statements/ remarks-president-trump-signing- presidential-memorandum-targeting-chinas-economic-aggression/.

20 Information about Lighthizer can be found in Shawn Donnan, 2017, "Trump trade tsar wields power over WTO destiny," *Financial Times,* December 11; Ana Swanson, 2018, "The Little-Known Trade Adviser Who Wields Enormous Power in Washington," *The New York Times,* March 9; Bob Davis, 2018, "The Architect of Trump's Threatened Trade War," *The Wall Street Journal,* April 6; and James Bacchus, 2018, *Might Unmakes Right: The American Assault on the Rule of Law in World Trade,*" CIGI Paper No. 173, May, www.cigionline.org/publications/might-unmakes-right.

sense, he believed, and he was loath to see Washington lay down unilateral weapons, especially 301, when multilateral negotiations began devising the WTO's binding dispute settlement system in the 1990s. From the WTO's outset, Lighthizer was leery of its potential for infringing on US sovereignty and, as noted in chapters 6 and 7, he became a prominent critic of rulings by the trade body's tribunals and its difficulties in handling China.

In support of the 2018 China tariffs, Lighthizer's office released a 200-page report alleging numerous "unreasonable" and "discriminatory" Chinese actions and policies (including Made in China 2025 and others detailed in previous chapters of this book) that harmed US intellectual property rights and deprived US industry of the fruits of its technological innovations.[21] Importantly, the rationale for unilateral action this time was that Beijing's transgressions fell outside WTO rules. Indeed, at a meeting in Geneva of representatives from WTO countries on March 27, US ambassador Dennis Shea defended his government's policy: "The United States made no findings in the Section 301 investigation that China breached its WTO obligations."[22] To the extent any Chinese policy appeared to violate the trade body's rules, he added, the United States would duly follow multilateral principles by filing a complaint (and on one issue, involving the licensing of technology, Washington did so). But the Trump administration contended that imposing sanctions for Chinese behaviour not covered by WTO rules was within US rights.

Although based on a much more elegant legal foundation than the tariffs on steel and aluminum imports, the brandishing of these anti-China tariffs was another example of Washington setting itself up as prosecutor, jury and judge. That, in turn, raised the question of how WTO rules could retain their authority if individual member countries felt entitled to establish and enforce rules on their own.

⎯⎯⎯

At 12:01 a.m. on July 6, 2018, the US-China trade war was officially under way, negotiations having failed to bridge the large gaps separating the two sides. At US ports, customs agents began assessing duties of 25 percent on $34 billion worth of Chinese imports containing "industrially significant

21 USTR, 2018, "Findings of the Investigation Into China's Acts, Policies, and Practices Related to Technology Transfer, Intellectual Property, and Innovation Under Section 301 of the Trade Act of 1974," March 22.

22 Simon Lester, 2018, "Forced Technology Transfer and the WTO," *International Economic Law and Policy Blog*, March, http://worldtradelaw.typepad.com/ielpblog/2018/03/index.html.

technologies," and another $16 billion worth on August 23. Beijing responded by imposing tariffs "of equal scale and equal strength" on $50 billion of US goods.[23] The Trump administration dismissed concerns that China, with its authoritarian government and resolve to rebuff foreign pressure, was much better suited politically to withstand whatever economic suffering might ensue. The president and his advisers voiced confidence in victory for the simple reason that US imports from China, at $505 billion in 2017, were so much greater than the $130 billion of Chinese imports of American goods, which meant that Washington could inflict more pain on Beijing than vice versa. But the world was soon treated to a teachable moment about the problems of twenty-first-century trade conflict. Especially when the adversaries are two giant and interconnected economies, it is difficult for one side to penalize the other without incurring self-harm.

Supply chains were facing unprecedented disruption. In contrast to the popular image of trade involving products made from start to finish in one country and shipped to another, most of the Chinese imports targeted by the Trump administration consisted of intermediate goods, which were assembled in China at subsidiaries of US multinationals or their contract manufacturers, then exported to the United States for use in final products. Examples included circuit boards, injection-moulded plastics and semiconductors for the electronics industry; and brake rotors, crankshafts and windshield-wiper blades for the auto industry. In many cases, the value added during the Chinese manufacturing stage was minor, involving as it did simple assembly or other repetitive tasks, such as testing discs from which semiconductors are cut.[24] Even so, the fact that such goods were shipped directly from, say, Shanghai to Seattle meant that levies would be imposed and paid by the US firm importing them. "The result is actually counterproductive for US technological competitiveness," noted Mary Lovely and Yang Liang of Syracuse University in a detailed analysis. "Manufacturers from other advanced economies, such as Germany, Japan, or South Korea, will be able to purchase their capital goods and supplies from China untaxed and use them to build final goods that compete directly with American producers thus disadvantaged by the Trump tariffs."[25]

---

23 Bob Davis, Vivian Salama and Lingling Wei, 2018, "China Issues Retaliatory Tariffs as Trade Fight Heats Up," *The Wall Street Journal*, June 15.

24 Richard Waters, 2018, "Trump tariff salvo triggers anxiety for US chipmakers," *Financial Times*, July 4.

25 Mary E. Lovely and Yang Liang, 2018, "Trump Tariffs Primarily Hit Multinational Supply Chains, Harm US Competitiveness," Peterson Institute for International Economics, Policy Brief 18-12, May, https://piie.com/system/files/documents/pb18-12.pdf.

The news media was soon full of stories about companies in heartland America that were being adversely affected exactly as the study predicted. Indiana-based Cummins Engine, already paying higher prices for steel as a result of the tariffs on that metal, was now forced to pay more for components such as turbochargers that it imported from its own Chinese plants to put into engines sold in the US market. "The company said tariffs will make its products less competitive with foreign rivals," reported *The Wall Street Journal*.[26] A similar tale of woe about the impact of tariffs levied on components from its Chinese affiliates came from Husco International, a company whose Wisconsin and Iowa plants make hydraulic and electro-mechanical gear for autos and construction vehicles. "The people it helps most of all are my competitors in Germany and Japan, who also have large parts of their supply chain in Asia but don't have these tariffs," CEO Austin Ramirez told *The New York Times*.[27]

The damage stemming from supply chain breakage was not limited to individual companies. Substantial benefits accrue from supply chains, including to overall living standards and purchasing power, if business enterprises operate at their most efficient scale and countries specialize in the goods and services for which they hold comparative advantage. Despite the wide acceptance of that perspective among economists, Trump and his advisers were unsympathetic to US companies that had, in their view, turned into rootless multinationals outsourcing American jobs in quests for profit maximization. Bringing those jobs back home remained Trump's most cherished goal.

That goal, however, stood no chance of being achieved. In hearings held by the US trade representative's office, business chieftains and industry representatives emphasized that as much as they would like to employ more American blue-collar workers, tariffs wouldn't help.[28] Replacing their China-based supply chains with US production would entail inconceivably high capital investment, given that shuttered factories had long since been converted to offices, apartments and retail establishments; suppliers were out of business; and labour markets were already tight. Even in towns that had been hit by the China shock, such as the furniture-making centres of the Carolinas, scant hope could be found for a resurrection of labour-intensive manufacturing.

---

26 Bob Tita and Patrick McGroarty, 2018, "Cummins Will Pay Tariff to Import Engines From Its Own Plants in China," *The Wall Street Journal*, June 22.

27 Ana Swanson, 2018, "Trump's Trade War Against China Is Officially Underway," *The New York Times*, July 5.

28 Alan Rappeport, 2018, "Companies Warn More China Tariffs Will Cripple Them and Hurt Consumers," *The New York Times*, August 20; see also Bob Davis and Andrew Duehren, 2018, "U.S. Moves Toward New Tariffs on China Despite Fresh Round of Trade Talks," *The Wall Street Journal*, August 20.

"The theory is you turn (imports) off, the jobs come back. That's not really true," Alex Bernhardt Jr., chief executive of Bernhardt Furniture, told Reuters reporter Howard Schneider. "The buildings don't exist. The people don't exist. The machinery does not exist" for making furniture of the sort now coming from China and Vietnam.[29]

Chinese officials, meanwhile, imposed tariffs mainly on US agricultural products, such as soybeans, sorghum and pork, to the dismay of American farmers who effectively lost one of their biggest markets overnight. (The farm belt received limited relief in the form of emergency subsidies that Trump ordered the Agriculture Department to provide.) Another US product hit by China's tariffs was autos, which were shipped to the Chinese market from plants in South Carolina and Alabama owned by German automakers BMW and Daimler-Benz, as well as some made by Ford and Tesla. Moreover, Beijing cut hundreds of its MFN tariffs, the idea being to ease the overall financial stress of higher import costs while squeezing US producers. By reducing the MFN levy on imported autos to 15 percent, for example, while raising duties on American cars to 40 percent, policy makers gave incentives for Chinese consumers to buy vehicles made in Japan, South Korea and Germany instead of in US facilities.[30]

Not that China was escaping unscathed. Although its $12 trillion GDP was continuing to expand at a six percent-plus rate in the third quarter of 2018, growth was slowing and the Shanghai and Shenzen stock markets dropped sharply in the summer and fall (a period when US share prices, buoyed by Trump's corporate tax cuts, hit record highs). The trade war was at least partly responsible; according to one survey of 200 China-based companies with significant export business, 125 reported a decline in orders, and among those, 23 percent said they laid off staff while 27 percent slashed capital expenditures.[31] To circumvent US tariffs, some multinational firms were shifting their Chinese production to low-wage countries, such as Vietnam, Thailand, Cambodia and India, or acknowledging the likelihood of doing so. But many were staying put, because their supply chains could not function efficiently without the numerous benefits of China-based facilities. Even though Chinese factory workers commanded higher wages than their counterparts in many neighbouring countries, China boasted far superior roads, rail lines,

29 Howard Schneider, 2018, "In a U.S. manufacturing hub, no illusions about tariffs and jobs," Reuters, September 26.

30 Trefor Moss, 2018, "U.S. Car Makers Left in the Dust as China's Tariff Cut Boosts Europe, Japan," *The Wall Street Journal*, August 10.

31 Xiaoqing Pi, 2018, "Chinese Factories Cut Prices, Lay Off Workers in Trade War: UBS," Bloomberg News, December 17.

skilled engineers, logistics and networks of vendors for all manner of parts and services that needed to be sourced locally.[32]

Undeterred, Trump escalated the battle in late September 2018, adding $200 billion of Chinese goods to the list that would be subject to tariffs (10 percent immediately, 25 percent starting on January 1, 2019). This time, lots of consumer goods would be affected — travel bags, computers, lamps, furniture and vacuum cleaners, among others. Beijing likewise refused to back down, levying duties on $60 billion worth of US goods. That defiance elicited fresh threats from Trump that tariffs would be slapped on all $500 billion of Chinese imports.

A prolonged, two-way test of mettle loomed. Then, in the fall of 2018, a new US strategy began to emerge. As incoherent as the administration's initial moves toward China had appeared, the new approach would involve the formation of an international alliance. Although Washington's allies were appalled at Trump's trade strategy, the White House had a plan for bringing them around — or so it seemed, for a while at least.

Nice little auto industry, Canada — what a shame if something happened to it. That was the gist of a presidential warning, posted on Twitter on August 10, 2018, exhorting Ottawa to accept US demands in negotiations for revising NAFTA. "Will tax cars if we can't make a deal!" Trump tweeted — meaning he would again invoke national security as a rationale for tariffs, this time on the vehicles produced in Ontario factories.[33] Having already taken umbrage when Canadian steel was hit with US tariffs on national security grounds, the government of Prime Minister Justin Trudeau stood fast against Washington's most offensive terms, backed by popular fury at this fresh threat against the Ontario auto plants, which are a mainstay of the Canadian economy. But the Trudeau government struck a compromise on October 1 for the creation of an agreement to replace NAFTA, the Canada-United States-Mexico Agreement (CUSMA, or as it is known in the United States, USMCA).

Taken in isolation, the CUSMA was a source of relief to free traders; it differed only in modest ways from NAFTA. The same was true of an accord reached

---

32 Samantha Vadas, Adam Jourdan and Anne Marie Roantree, 2018, "Trade war puts new strains on America Inc's factories in China," Reuters, August 20; Liza Lin and Dan Strumpf, 2018, "A Twist in the U.S. Tariff Battle: 'It's Helping China Be More Competitive," *The Wall Street Journal*, September 17; and Alexandra Stevenson, 2018, "Trump's Tariffs May Hurt, but Quitting China Is Hard to Do," *The New York Times*, September 24; *The Economist*, 2018, "China's grip on electronics manufacturing will be hard to break," October 11.

33 Donald J. Trump, Twitter post, August 10, 2018, 4:12 p.m., https://twitter.com/realdonaldtrump/status/1028056640422068225?lang=en.

around the same time to revise Washington's free-trade pact with South Korea. For all his shrillness about "horrible deals," Trump appeared willing to replace them with rebranded versions as long as he could trumpet them to his political base as more advantageous for America. But the duress to which he was subjecting trading partners was another matter. The president took unbridled glee in it, in particular with regard to Japan, which agreed to start negotiating a bilateral trade accord after resisting for months. "Without tariffs we wouldn't be talking about a deal," Trump told reporters shortly after the CUSMA pact was struck. "I said [to Prime Minister Abe], 'You don't have to negotiate, but we're going to put a very, very substantial tax on your cars if you don't....So because of the power of tariffs and the power that we have with tariffs, we, in many cases, won't even have to use them. That's how powerful they are, and how good they are."[34] The European Union was likewise discussing Washington's complaints about its trade policies with the understanding that national security tariffs would be suspended while talks proceeded.[35]

All these bouts, White House officials explained, would serve as mere preliminaries for the main event — China. Once the allies had been softened up in negotiations for trade agreements that required only modest concessions, they would combine forces with Washington in a phalanx of nations united by abhorrence of Chinese industrial policies. "We are talking to the European Union again, we are talking to Japan again, and we are moving to what I have characterized as a trade coalition of the willing to confront China," said Larry Kudlow, the director of the National Economic Council.[36]

The plan to isolate China using a "trade coalition of the willing" coincided with a related series of policies and statements coming out of Washington evincing a readiness — indeed, a determined effort — to deepen the schism with China's economy.

Trump administration officials began leaking word that US tariffs weren't a mere ploy aimed at extracting concessions from Beijing but might be maintained for a long time. Among the administration's most hawkish factions, the tariffs were reportedly seen as serving a broader purpose, namely an economic "decoupling" that would reduce the exposure of US industry to Chinese theft

---

34 Kyodo News, 2018, "Trump brags auto tariff threat forced Japan into trade talks," October 1.

35 Alan Beattie, 2018, "Donald Trump's global trade offensive gathers speed," *Financial Times*, October 1; Jacob M. Schlesinger and Josh Zumbrun, 2018, "Trump Aims to Model New Trade Deals on Revised Nafta," *The Wall Street Journal*, October 4.

36 Neil Irwin, 2018, "The Trump Trade Strategy is Coming Into Focus. That Doesn't Necessarily Mean It Will Work," *The New York Times*, October 6.

and coercion.[37] Disrupting China-based supply chains and reversing the process that had led to the coining of the term "Chimerica" was therefore desirable from the hawks' standpoint rather than regrettable. In a more concrete step toward reducing Sino-American economic interaction, Trump signed legislation in August 2018 that tightened restrictions on Chinese takeovers of US businesses, requiring more vetting for security risks. That was one reason such investment plunged in 2018 to a seven-year low of $5 billion.[38]

In an indication that the hawks were prevailing, Vice President Mike Pence delivered a speech on October 4 that was widely viewed as heralding a "new Cold War" against China. The vice president assailed Beijing for persecuting religious minorities, for building "an Orwellian system premised on controlling virtually every facet of human life," for seeking to "push the United States of America from the Western Pacific" and for using "stolen technology" to "turn plowshares into swords on a massive scale."[39] Many of the issues raised in Pence's speech are beyond the scope of this book, but one passage stood out for its schismatic tenor. "More business leaders are thinking beyond the next quarter, and thinking twice before diving into the Chinese market if it means turning over their intellectual property or abetting Beijing's oppression," Pence declared. "But more must follow suit."

Second thoughts about Chimerica's allure were also occurring to Beijing, especially after the near-death of a major Chinese company at American hands in the spring of 2018. The company was ZTE, China's second-largest maker of smart phones, which was found guilty by Washington of violating US laws against doing business with Iran and North Korea and failing to comply with the terms of its initial punishment. For those offences, the US Commerce Department banned ZTE in April from buying US components, effectively forcing the firm to cease operations and start laying off its 75,000 employees because it would no longer be able to obtain high-end chips and software from Qualcomm, Intel, Google and other American suppliers. A reprieve from execution came from Trump himself, who stunned many of his aides in May when he directed Commerce to reconsider the ban — as a favour to Xi,

---

37 Greg Ip, 2018, "An Economic Cold War Looms Between the U.S. and China," *The Wall Street Journal*, September 26; Uri Friedman, 2018, "Trump May Seek More Independence from China," *The Atlantic*, October 4.

38 The legislation, the Foreign Investment Risk Review Modernization Act, was billed as an update of the law regarding national security implications of US asset purchases by all foreigners, but it was clearly drafted with China in mind. See Thilo Hanemann, Daniel H. Rosen, Cassie Gao and Adam Lysenko, 2019, "Two-Way Street: 2019 Update, US-China Investment Trends," Rhodium Group and National Committee on U.S.-China Relations, May.

39 White House, 2018, "Remarks by Vice President Pence on the Administration's Policy Toward China," October 4, www.whitehouse.gov/briefings-statements/remarks-vice-president-pence-administrations-policy-toward-china/.

according to his tweeting on the subject. (The president had ample motives for beneficence; he may have been seeking Xi's help with North Korea, and he was presumably also concerned also about the big hit that ZTE's US suppliers would suffer from the loss of an important Chinese customer.) For the Chinese establishment, the episode was likened to a "Sputnik moment" as realization sank in about China's dependence on technologically superior foreign rivals — and the distance the country would have to go to break free.

"The recent ZTE incident made us see clearly that no matter how advanced our mobile payment is…without microchips and operating systems, we can't compete competently," Pony Ma, the CEO of internet giant Tencent, told a science forum[40] — a problem that would be all the scarier for China if the world's advanced countries banded together against it as Kudlow had suggested.

In any event, the "trade coalition of the willing" strategy was shelved not long after it surfaced. It soon gave way to bilateral negotiations with Beijing, in which US officials would demand that China import large quantities of American crops, natural gas and other products on preferential terms. That approach would presumably leave Washington's "coalition" partners in the lurch, and it would presumably mean more US-China coupling, at least in some sectors, rather than decoupling.

But the iniquity would be the same, whichever of these two routes the Trump administration took. Insouciance — indeed, reckless disregard — was the administration's order of the day concerning the institutional degradation that its trade wars were inflicting. Didn't it matter that the imposition of unilateral tariffs — and threats to impose more — made such a mockery of WTO rules as to impair the trade body's authority irreparably, leading to the replacement of international rule of law with a system of "might makes right?"

Other measures taken by the Trump regime were also propelling the global trading system in a might-makes-right direction.

Like most members of the WTO Appellate Body, Shree Baboo Chekitan Servansing, a 63-year-old Mauritian diplomat with degrees from British and Australian universities, hoped to serve two four-year terms on the WTO's equivalent of the Supreme Court. But as his first term neared its end in the summer of 2018, Servansing became the latest WTO jurist to be denied

40 Li Yuan, 2018, "ZTE's Near-Collapse May Be China's Sputnik Moment," *The New York Times,* June 10.

reappointment by the United States. This time, unlike in previous cases, Washington had no specific objections to Servansing. Rather, under a policy started in the fall of 2017, Trump administration officials were refusing to allow the filling of *any* Appellate Body vacancies, by exercising the legal right of a single member country to block consensus.[41]

That posed a potentially lethal threat to WTO dispute settlement, because retirements and resignations had left only four Appellate Body members to consider appeals in 2018 as a backlog of cases mounted. And once Servansing was gone, only three would remain, the bare minimum required for a division (WTO-speak for a group of jurists who hear and rule on appeals, as noted in chapter 7).

In Geneva legal circles, never-before-contemplated scenarios were circulating: suppose no new members were named and insufficient numbers were available for divisions — circumstances that could arise after other members' terms ended in late 2019, or perhaps even earlier for other reasons, such as recusals. Appeals can't proceed in the absence of a division, so any country that lost a case at the panel level could legally block the ruling by insisting that its right to an appeal had been denied.

In effect, the United States was holding the WTO's dispute settlement system hostage by preventing the Appellate Body's replenishment, and the longer this went on the more likely the system would be rendered dysfunctional. In such a situation, "every case potentially becomes a trade war," Alan Wolff, a WTO deputy director-general, noted in an October 2018 speech. "The natural consequence of dispute settlement becoming inoperative is to return trade relations…to a state of nature — combat without rules."[42]

What was Washington trying to accomplish? Lighthizer's office was studiously vague about what would be required for appointments to proceed, but he had long been forthright regarding his dissatisfaction with the Appellate Body, whose jurisprudence had also raised hackles during prior US administrations. As noted in chapter 7, the Appellate Body stands accused of judicial overreach — "inventing" rules by applying its own interpretations to parts of WTO agreements where the wording is ambiguous — and being overly rigid in adhering to previous rulings that have come under attack as faulty.

41 Jan Dahinten, 2018, "U.S. Blocks WTO Judge Reappointment Amid Looming Trade Crisis," Bloomberg News, August 28.

42 Alan Wolff, 2018, "The WTO and the Future of the Global Trading System," speech delivered to the Council on Foreign Relations, Washington, DC, October 15, www.wto.org/spanish/news_s/news18_s/ddgra_15oct18_s.htm.

US criticism of the Appellate Body is viewed sympathetically in some other countries' trade ministries, but the blockage of new appointments evoked a mixture of hand-wringing and horror, especially after Trump levelled a rhetorical blast on television against the trade body: "The WTO...was set up for the benefit for everybody but us. They have taken advantage of this country like you wouldn't believe.... We lose the lawsuits, almost all of the lawsuits in the WTO.... Because we have fewer judges than other countries. It's set up as you can't win."[43]

The president went even further in an interview with Bloomberg News. "If they don't shape up, I would withdraw from the WTO," he said, adding that "we rarely won a lawsuit except for last year," but "in the last year, we're starting to win a lot. You know why? Because they know if we don't, I'm out of there."[44]

Those comments imply that Trump believes in an American entitlement to control WTO tribunals and win victories. Worse yet, he shows no compunction about menacing the trade body with effective annihilation in order to obtain rulings to his liking — a bald-faced assault on judicial impartiality. Putting aside his imperiousness, his claim about US losses in WTO cases contradicted a report issued by his own economic advisers, which cited research showing that the United States actually fares better in disputes than most WTO member countries.[45]

Fortunately, Lighthizer holds a more reality-based view of the WTO than his boss. He has acknowledged the trade body's value,[46] and during his tenure as trade representative the United States has filed several cases, indicating a desire to maintain the institution's viability. One relatively benign explanation for Lighthizer's strategy on Appellate Body appointments is that he is playing a game of brinkmanship, aimed at forcing changes in the way the body works.

The question of whether any reasonable reforms will satisfy the Trump administration is a source of anxiety-ridden conjecture, however. Lighthizer

---

43 ValueWalk, 2017, "Trump with Dobbs [Full Transcript]," Interview with host Lou Dobbs on Fox Business, October 25, www.valuewalk.com/2017/10/trump-dobbs/.

44 John Micklethwait, Margaret Talev and Jennifer Jacobs, 2018, "Trump Threatens to Pull U.S. Out of WTO If It Doesn't 'Shape Up,'" Bloomberg News, August 31.

45 The White House, 2018, *Economic Report of the President, Together with the Annual Report of the Council of Economic Advisers*, February, chapter 5, page 251. The report cites Andrew Mayeda, 2017, "America Often Wins With Trade Referee That Trump Wants to Avoid," Bloomberg News, March 27. See also Louise Johannesson and Petros C. Mavroidis, 2016, "The WTO Dispute Settlement System 1995–2016: A Data Set and its Descriptive Statistics," European University Institute, Robert Schuman Centre for Advanced Studies, Working Paper RSCAS 2016/72.

46 USTR, 2017, "Opening Plenary Statement of USTR Robert Lighthizer at the WTO Ministerial Conference," December, https://ustr.gov/about-us/policy-offices/pressoffice/press- releases/2017/december/opening-plenary-statement-ustr.

has waxed nostalgic on occasion about the GATT system,[47] which had less-binding, more power-based adjudication than the WTO, and it is possible that he will contentedly allow the Appellate Body to slide into dysfunctionality. The most sinister interpretation of all is that the Trump team intends to foster the WTO's well-being only to the extent that the trade body allows the president to impose tariffs as he sees fit. If big rulings go against Washington — on issues such as the national security tariffs — there may be no let-up in the US throttling of the Appellate Body.

In ordinary times, the Appellate Body's impending membership shortage would have been perceived as the gravest danger facing the trading system. But times were not ordinary in the autumn of 2018, as the trade wars were raging at heightened intensity levels. By that point, some of the repercussions finally began to rattle the White House.

A 90 percent fall in Chinese purchases of American soybeans was leading to widespread hardship in states such as North Dakota and Iowa, where farmers were storing their crop in silos or piling it in tarp-covered mounds, risking spoilage rather than sell at heavy losses.[48] General Motors, suffering from a profit squeeze partly caused by steel tariffs, announced on November 26 that it was idling several North American plants and laying off thousands of workers. The Dow Jones Industrial Average sank by nearly 2,000 points in the middle two weeks of November, and although Federal Reserve policy was probably the main factor, the president — who obsessively followed market fluctuations — was reportedly anxious to buoy investor sentiment by showing that the US-China trade battle was under control.[49]

Serendipitously, an opportunity to lower tensions materialized — a G20 summit in Buenos Aires, Argentina, where Trump could meet Xi in person. The US president seized the chance.

On December 1, over dinner featuring grilled Argentine sirloin, the two leaders agreed on a truce scheduled to last three months. Trump postponed his threat to increase tariffs on $200 billion in Chinese goods (although existing

47 See, for example, Lighthizer's remarks in an interview with John J. Hamre at CSIS on September 18, 2017, www.csis.org/analysis/us-trade-policy-priorities-robert-lighthizer-united-states-trade-representative.

48 Binyamin Appelbaum, 2018, "Their Soybeans Piling Up, Farmers Hope Trade War Ends Before Beans Rot," *The New York Times,* November 5; Demetri Sevastopulo, 2018, "Farmers round on Donald Trump as demand for soyabeans dries up," *Financial Times,* November 6; Shruti Singh, Isis Almeida and Mario Parker, 2018, "Frozen Out of China, American Farmers Refuse to Sell Their Soy," Bloomberg News, November 12.

49 Mark Landler, Glenn Thrush and Keith Bradsher, 2018, "Trump Could Seek a China Trade Truce at G-20, Despite Tough Talk," *The New York Times,* November 27.

tariffs would remain), and Xi vowed to lift punitive barriers to imports of American food, energy and cars. A deadline of March 1, 2019, was set for the two sides to negotiate an agreement on a range of deeply divisive issues; if by then no deal was struck, the higher US tariffs would go into effect, presumably along with Chinese retaliation resuming as well.

"Relations with China have taken a BIG leap forward," Trump tweeted.[50] But on the very day of his dinner with Xi, a development 11,000 km north suggested otherwise.

Vancouver airport was supposed to be a mere transit stop for Meng Wanzhou when she landed there on December 1, 2018, to change flights en route to Mexico. Instead, the 46-year-old Meng, chief financial officer of Huawei, was arrested by Canadian authorities at the request of the US government, which sought her extradition on charges of fraudulently violating US sanctions on Iran. So explosive was the plan to detain Meng that Trump was kept in the dark about it until after his dinner with Xi, according to his aides[51] — an understandable precaution, because as well as being a top-level Huawei executive, Meng is the eldest daughter of the company's legendary founder, Ren Zhengfei.

Meng's arrest was just one among a flurry of actions by law enforcement and national security officials in the United States and other countries against Chinese individuals and companies in late 2018 and early 2019. Underpinning these actions was the assessment, spelled out in Pence's speech, of China's growing strategic threat. Washington's legal strategy for countering the peril came one month before Meng's arrest with the announcement by Attorney General Jeff Sessions of a "China Initiative" that would include investigations and prosecutions for trade secret theft, espionage and other crimes endangering US economic and national security.

Although the alleged malefactions varied widely, they raised a common question about whether globalization is compatible with rapid advances in the cyber realm. Thanks to China's Great Firewall, a "splinternet" already divides the world's netizens into those who use Google, Facebook and Twitter versus those who use WeChat, Weibo and Alibaba. The US crackdown has accentuated the probability that something akin to a Digital Iron Curtain is in the

---

50 Donald J. Trump, Twitter post, December 3, 2018, 4:54 a.m., https://twitter.com/realdonaldtrump/status/1069575605199482881?lang=en.

51 Louise Lucas, Demetri Sevastopulo, James Kynge and David Crow, 2018, "China demands release of Huawei CFO held on US charges," *Financial Times,* December 7.

offing, which would mean companies in a variety of tech sectors — telecommunications, artificial intelligence, semiconductors and so on — operating in separate ecosystems, with some obliged to choose between China and the United States.

In his speech unveiling the China Initiative,[52] Sessions also announced one of the initiative's first big cases — indictments over the alleged stealing of proprietary information from Idaho-based Micron. As noted in chapter 8, this case, originally filed by Taiwanese prosecutors, involved allegations that individuals in Micron's Taiwan affiliates had passed specifications and details about Micron's advanced memory chips to Fujian Jinhua, a Chinese SOE start-up, in 2016. The charges levelled against Fujian Jinhua in the United States led to sanctions on the company barring it from buying US componentry, software and other technology goods — a virtual death sentence of the sort that had been imposed earlier on ZTE, but this time there was no presidential reprieve, and the company soon thereafter had to halt production.

In addition, the attorney general accused China of reneging on promises concerning the purloining of technology. "In 2015, China committed publicly that it would not target American companies for economic gain," Sessions declared. "Obviously, that commitment has not been kept." That was a factual distortion; as also noted in chapter 8, the 2015 pact struck by Xi and Obama involved a highly specific pledge that both governments would refrain from state-sponsored hacking — defined as "cyber-enabled theft of intellectual property" — for the purpose of boosting the competitiveness of commercial firms. And it was hardly "obvious" that Beijing was cheating on the terms. Even when US and UK authorities announced another round of indictments on December 20, 2018, against a Chinese hacking ring called Advanced Persistent Threat 10, or APT10, many of the targets that were hacked — government agencies and laboratories, as well as private companies — were involved in military and national security work, or the intrusions took place prior to the 2015 accord.[53] It may well be, of course, that China did go beyond the agreed-upon bounds by resuming some state-sponsored cyber espionage for economic purposes; a number of government and private

---

52 US Department of Justice, 2018, "Attorney General Jeff Sessions Announces New Initiative to Combat Chinese Economic Espionage," November 1, www.justice.gov/opa/speech/attorney-general-jeff-sessions-announces-new-initiative-combat-chinese-economic-espionage.

53 Dustin Volz, Kate O'Keeffe and Bob Davis, 2018, "U.S. Charges China Intelligence Officers Over Hacking Companies and Agencies," *The Wall Street Journal,* December 20.

cyber security experts stated in late 2018 that evidence indicated as much.[54] One theory was that Chinese officials had abided by the Obama-Xi deal at first, then concluded that their commitment no longer applied once the trade war had commenced.

Overshadowing all of these charges and counter-charges were the suspicions about Huawei. The company, whose worldwide revenue in 2018 topped $100 billion, had vaulted into a dominant position in the race to supply equipment and software for fifth-generation (5G) networks, which will revolutionize mobile telecommunications with enormously faster uploads and downloads of data. This achievement was a stunning testament to the dynamism of China's private sector relative to the sclerosis of many SOEs. But it unnerved the US government, which had not changed its view of Huawei from that noted in chapter 8 — that is, as a potential conduit for spying and perhaps even sabotage of US infrastructure. Having long barred Huawei products from all but a few networks in rural America, Washington embarked on a concerted campaign to persuade allied countries that their 5G systems should be Huawei-free. That was the main topic at a secret meeting in Halifax, Nova Scotia, in July 2018 of spy chiefs from the "Five Eyes," an elite intelligence-sharing network that includes Canada, the United States, Britain, Australia and New Zealand.[55]

The depth of Washington's anxiety was evident in a leaked memo and slide presentation, apparently produced in early 2018 by a senior official of the National Security Council. "While '4G' was an evolution of '3G,' simply promising faster speeds, '5G' is by no means simply a 'faster 4G,'" stated the memo's author, who described 5G as "a change more like the invention of the Gutenberg Press." Therefore, "Whoever leads in technology and market share for 5G deployment will have a tremendous advantage towards...commanding the heights of the information domain...everything from automated cars and aircraft to advanced logistics and manufacturing to true [artificial intelligence] enhanced network combat." Currently, "we are losing," the official warned, and if the United States fails to build a secure system that overcomes Huawei's advantage, "China will win politically, economically, militarily."[56]

54 David E. Sanger and Steven Lee Myers, 2018, "After a Hiatus, China Accelerates Cyberspying Efforts to Obtain U.S. Technology," *The New York Times*, November 29; Adam Segal and Lorand Laskai, 2018, "A New Old Threat: Countering the Return of Chinese Industrial Cyber Espionage," Council on Foreign Relations, December 6, www.cfr.org/report/threat-chinese-espionage.

55 Chris Uhlmann and Angus Grigg, 2018, "Secret meeting led to the international effort to stop China's cyber espionage," *Financial Review* (Australia), December 13.

56 Jonathan Swan, David McCabe, Ina Fried and Kim Hart, 2018, "Scoop: Trump Team considers nationalizing 5G network," Axios, January 29, www.axios.com/trump-team-debates-nationalizing-5g-network-f1e92a49-60f2-4e3e-acd4-f3eb03d910ff.html.

A double blow against Huawei came on January 28, 2019, when the Justice Department unsealed two indictments — one that formally charged Meng with evading Iran sanctions, and another that accused the company of stealing information in 2013 from the wireless carrier T-Mobile about a phone-testing robot called "Tappy." Among the most damning revelations in the "Tappy" indictment was an internal Huawei program, also launched in 2013, that apparently offered employees bonuses for obtaining confidential information from competitors. The filing of these criminal cases posed a dire threat to Huawei because Washington might impose the same punishment as it did on Fujian Jinhua, blocking the company's access to US components, including the high-end chips on which it depended. Powerful members of Congress were clamouring for just such a measure, but it had an obvious downside — a huge loss of business for a number of US firms with cutting-edge technology, including Intel, Seagate and Qualcomm.[57]

From a Chinese viewpoint, and even some Western ones, the US assault on Huawei smacked of protectionism aimed at thwarting China's high-tech ambitions.[58] Accusations that Huawei owed its success to theft didn't square with evidence of the company's high levels of investment in research and development and record of obtaining international patents.[59] The "Tappy" indictment in particular drew criticism as a weaponization of criminal law, based as it was on a six year-old episode that had already been the subject of a civil lawsuit in Seattle.[60]

To keep such criticism in perspective, it is important to remember, as seen in chapter 8, that China also uses laws, regulations and other government restrictions — the Great Firewall being the best-known — to hinder foreign technology companies in the name of protecting China's national security. But the most glaring evidence of hidden US motives came from Trump himself. When asked by Reuters reporters in a December 11, 2018, interview whether he might intervene in Meng's case (as he had with ZTE), the president gave a reply that undercut his government's claims to be following rule of law: "If I think it's good for what will certainly be the largest trade deal

---

57 *The Economist*, 2018, "America Unseals Its Indictment against Huawei," January 31.

58 Pankaj Mishra, 2018, "Attacking Huawei Will Backfire," Bloomberg Opinion, December 11.

59 Keith Johnson and Elias Groll, 2019, "The Improbable Rise of Huawei," *Foreign Policy*, April 3.

60 Chuin-Wei Yap, 2019, "U.S. Weaponizes Its Criminal Courts in Fight Against China and Huawei," *The Wall Street Journal*, January 17; *The Economist*, America Unseals Its Indictment against Huawei" (see footnote 57 in this chapter).

ever made, which is a very important thing, what's good for national security, I would certainly intervene if I thought it was necessary."[61]

Whether Huawei officials committed the crimes of which they are accused, and whether the company maintains secret links to the Chinese military as is often claimed, are arguably irrelevant to the big question: should Huawei and other Chinese firms be banned as vendors to 5G networks in the United States and allied countries? Those who favour a ban cite ample grounds for erring on the side of prudence. Although no "backdoors" have been detected in Huawei equipment, and even though Ren and other executives swear they would refuse orders to help spy in foreign countries, China's authoritarians do not brook disobedience, and the lines are all too blurry between the party-state and private sector. At some Chinese internet companies, which are ostensibly private, the police maintain embedded cells to facilitate monitoring of users' behaviour.[62] An illuminating example of the problem was uncovered when the Polish government arrested a Huawei employee and his Polish handler for spying in January 2019; although the company promptly fired and disavowed its employee, the case showed how easy it would be for Beijing's intelligence agencies to plant agents among Huawei personnel.

Still, as US officials pressed the case in foreign capitals for a Huawei ban from 5G in early 2019, others — including some highly respected names in cyber security — pushed back. Decrying the "growing hysteria over Chinese tech," Robert Hannigan, former director of Britain's signals intelligence and cryptography agency, argued in a *Financial Times* op-ed that he and his colleagues had gained unique insight into how to manage the risks.[63] In Britain, where Huawei was a long-time supplier to telecom networks, the government had established a special London-based laboratory, the National Cyber Security Centre (NCSC), that rigorously analyzes Huawei's hardware and code as well as its internal processes, and had not found evidence that the company's system was used for malicious Chinese activity. Although the NCSC was well aware of attacks by Chinese hackers on targets around the world, including Britain, "the fact that these attacks did not require the manipulation of Chinese sovereign companies such as Huawei merely underlines how ineffective a blanket security ban based on company national flags is likely to be," Hannigan wrote. A similar assessment came from Ciarin Martin, head of the

61 Jeff Mason and Steve Holland, 2018, "Trump says he could intervene in U.S. case against Huawei CFO," Reuters, December 11.

62 Liza Lin and Josh Chin, 2017, "China's Tech Giants Have a Second Job: Helping Beijing Spy on Its People," *The Wall Street Journal*, November 30.

63 Robert Hannigan, 2019, "Blanket bans on Chinese tech companies like Huawei make no sense," *Financial Times*, February 12.

NCSC, who contended that the focus on Huawei was misplaced. "The supply chain, and where suppliers are from, is one issue, but it is not the only issue," Martin said in a speech, and noting that some major incursions on UK networks had come from Russia, he added: "As far as we know, those networks didn't have any Russian kit in them, anywhere."[64]

For those reasons, a number of governments have rejected US exhortations for the exclusion of Huawei from 5G development plans — as of the date this book was finalized for printing, they included Britain, Germany, India, Turkey and the United Arab Emirates. However, Australia and Japan have declared their intention to follow Washington's lead.[65]

Whatever judgment security officials reach about the manageability of the Huawei risk — and I have no cyber wisdom to impart — the case is shaping up as a sobering object lesson in the potential costs of a deep schism in the trading system. Even Huawei's critics have acknowledged that its 5G hardware, network development capacity and service are superior to rivals such as Nokia and Ericsson, and cheaper to boot. In early 2019, one scenario that appeared likely to materialize was the following: Huawei would be blocked from the US and some allied markets, causing the world to bifurcate into two cyber realms affecting trillions of dollars' worth of goods and services. Using a variety of carrots and sticks, Washington and Beijing would jockey for supremacy to secure adoption of their preferred 5G systems in as many countries as possible. Assuming Huawei was able to maintain its edge, the US-led sphere would stagger under the handicap of a slower and more expensive 5G rollout while the Chinese-led one exploited the benefits of network hyper speeds. Companies in the Chinese-led sphere would therefore have first-mover advantages in developing "Internet of Things" applications including driverless vehicles, automated machinery, Web-enabled health devices (pacemakers, for example), as well as drones and other military technologies.

Perhaps the United States and China can reach some accommodation that will limit the extent of this bifurcation. But the schismatic forces appear inexorable. Having been repeatedly hacked by Chinese spies, Washington is understandably averse to allowing Huawei into the American telecommunications network, and Beijing — having seen how vulnerable Huawei and ZTE are to cutoffs of American technology — has newfound incentive to nurture indigenous suppliers. If the result is a world in which 5G and other sectors or markets are carved into zones of influence, Sino-US tensions will be all the more inflamed,

---

64 NCSC, 2019, "Ciarin Martin's CyberSec speech in Brussels," February 20, www.ncsc.gov.uk/speech/ciaran-martins-cybersec-speech-brussels.

65 Julian E. Barnes and Adam Satariano, 2019, "U.S. Campaign to Ban Huawei Overseas Stumbles as Allies Resist," *The New York Times*, March 17.

and innovative companies on both sides of the Pacific will lose major opportunities to develop their business.

For countries and businesses caught in the middle, uncomfortable predicaments are already arising, even with 5G years away from operation in most parts of the world. US officials have publicly warned that they may not share sensitive intelligence with counterparts in nations using Chinese 5G equipment, while China is evidently resorting to its distinctive form of thuggery. Shipments of Australian coal to Chinese ports have been slowed at customs,[66] and in apparent retaliation over the detention of Meng, Canada has endured the arrest by Chinese police of two Canadian citizens on dubious grounds, followed by a stoppage in Chinese imports of Canadian canola seeds based on alleged contamination.[67] Despite valiantly adhering to a principled position that rule of law must apply to Meng's extradition case, Canada was effectively betrayed when Trump suggested anew that the criminal charges against Meng and Huawei might be used as a bargaining chip in the trade talks. "We'll be talking to the U.S. attorneys. We'll be talking to the attorney general. We'll be making that decision," the president told reporters on February 22, 2019 — reinforcing the Chinese belief that the prosecutions were political.[68]

Fortunately for Trump, China's anger over Meng's arrest did not translate into truculence in trade negotiations. The Chinese leadership proved ready to compartmentalize and keep talks going with the United States to end the trade war. Like their US counterparts, Chinese officials had reason to be rattled about economic developments.

Among his many distinctions, which include a master's degree in public administration from Harvard, Liu He was a classmate of Xi Jinping at Beijing 101 Middle School. That was the beginning of an association that would lead to Liu becoming one of China's top economic policy makers under Xi's presidency, with the rank of vice premier. When Xi needed an emissary to lead his trade negotiating teams with the Trump administration, the 66-year-old Liu was the logical choice — not only because he was a long-time Xi confidant, and not only because of his genial demeanour, but because he was widely known to be one of the most pro-market figures in the nation's leadership.[69]

66 Bloomberg News, 2019, "China Will Continue Slowdown in Australian Coal Until After Election," April 24.

67 Josh Wingrove and Peter Martin, 2019, "China's Canola Ban Adds to Trudeau's Woes in Bitter Huawei Feud," Bloomberg News, March 28.

68 Steven Overly, 2019, "Trump says Huawei charges on the table in China trade talks," *Politico*, February 22.

69 Tom Mitchell, 2019, "China's 'pragmatist' Liu He is hemmed in on both sides," *Financial Times*, January 30.

It was impossible to pinpoint where Liu stood in the internal deliberations of Zhongnanhai, which were as secrecy-shrouded as ever. But in the fall of 2018, he was in the thick of a debate under way about the need to roll back some of the government intervention that had advanced during the Xi regime. Recall from chapter 8 that shortly after Xi became president, a report issued jointly by the World Bank and Development Research Center of the State Council urged that China pursue a more market-oriented approach, and a Party congress endorsed a "decisive role" for the market in allocating resources. The forces that supported those positions were evidently staging an insurgency in late 2018. Online comments were surfacing, carefully couched to avoid direct criticism of the leadership but strongly favouring a course change. "The private sector is experiencing great difficulties right now," wrote Hu Deping, a retired senior official and son of a former top Communist leader, in an online essay posted in September. "We should try not to replicate the nationalization of private enterprise in the 1950s and [the trend toward] state capitalism."[70]

The impetus was easy to discern: a variety of indicators were signalling trouble for the Chinese economy, with auto sales in 2018 declining year-over-year for the first time since 1991, hiring and wages slowing and factory shutdowns spreading. Although not in recession, the economy was expanding at a much more modest pace than before, and many private analysts reckoned that the reality was significantly worse than the official data showed. Trump's tariffs were one cause, but deeper and more systemic ills were almost certainly at play. The pendulum had swung too far in the direction of party-state control; economic growth had become too dependent on debt-fuelled construction; and the SOE sector was hogging an excessive amount of credit and capital.[71] Small wonder that reformers were piping up to argue that for the sake of sustaining healthy growth, China should depend more on liberating its private sector, which had produced not only Huawei but other success stories in industries such as e-commerce.

Cynics might well scoff that in Xi's China, people espousing such opinions lack clout or only feign favouring reformist policies so as to gull foreigners. But even Lighthizer, no naïf when it comes to Beijing's intentions, said in a media interview: "I think you have to start with the proposition that there

70 Li Yuan, 2018, "Private Businesses Built Modern China. Now the Government is Pushing Back," *The New York Times*, October 3.

71 Nicholas R. Lardy, 2019, *The State Strikes Back: The End of Economic Reform in China?* Washington, DC: Peterson Institute for International Economics, offers an authoritative analysis of these reasons for China's slowdown.

are people in China who believe that reform is a good idea. And you have to believe that those people are at a very senior level."[72]

Therein lies the most plausible explanation for the headway that Liu, Lighthizer and their respective negotiating teams made after the truce struck by Trump and Xi in December 2018. Beijing was willing to move in market-oriented directions that were in its self-interest — not with steps that might loosen the Party's grip on power (allowing the free flow of data across Chinese borders, for example), but in other ways. Rather than lash out at Washington and stoke nationalistic passions, the Chinese leadership opted for a series of measures that would help end the trade war while also benefiting the nation's own economic prospects.

In mid-December, Chinese officials — who had stopped mentioning Made in China 2025 in public remarks for several months — began soft-pedalling it even more, leaving it off a list of mandates for local governments.[73] Later in the holiday season came measures the media dubbed "Christmas gifts." The first was a report in state media on December 24 that Beijing would draft a new foreign investment law banning forced technology transfer — that is, requiring that any negotiation involving the sharing of intellectual property be strictly voluntary. A second "gift" was the State Council's endorsement on December 26 of a principle called "competitive neutrality," which would oblige SOEs to make purchasing and other business decisions without regard to the preferences of the party-state.[74] To further improve the negotiating atmosphere, Beijing also dropped its punitive tariffs on politically sensitive US goods, such as cars and soybeans.

These "concessions" were replete with question marks about whether China's treatment of foreign companies and goods would really become fair. The power of the party-state was just as overwhelming as before, and rule of law just as subject to the Party's whim. For the most part, Beijing was proposing merely to codify what it had long insisted — that Made in China 2025 was not intended to establish hard targets, that multinationals seeking access to the Chinese market are never "forced" to transfer technology and that SOEs always act according to market incentives. Even if such principles were

---

72 National Public Radio, 2019, "U.S. Trade Representative Robert Lighthizer Discusses Ongoing Trade Negotiations with China," March 25.

73 Lingling Wei and Bob Davis, 2018, "China Prepares Policy to Increase Access for Foreign Companies, *The Wall Street Journal*, December 12; and Keith Bradsher, Alan Rappeport and Glenn Thrush, 2018, "A Weakened China Tries a Different Approach with the U.S.: Tread Lightly," *The New York Times*, December 12.

74 Tom Mitchell, 2018, "China's Christmas gifts are unlikely to ease trade war tension," *Financial Times*, December 31.

enshrined in law, industrial policy could continue to work, with pressure being subtly exerted to bolster national champions and other favoured competitors.

No better exemplification of the difficulty in discerning China's true intentions could be found than a speech to China's legislature by Premier Li Keqiang on March 5, 2019, in the Great Hall of the People. Absent from Li's remarks were any references to Made in China 2025, which he had highlighted in speeches delivered on the same occasion in previous years. But the premier's comments nevertheless showed that the leadership hadn't lost its penchant for economic heavy-handedness. He asserted that the government would "work faster to make China strong in manufacturing," and would "encourage more domestic and foreign users to choose Chinese goods and services." A report issued the same day by the NDRC said Beijing would help develop "a number of clusters of strategic emerging industries." In a *Wall Street Journal* article on Li's speech, an anonymous local official was quoted as saying: "We're told not to talk about 'Made in China 2025' anymore because the Americans don't like it. But of course the government will continue to provide support to important industries."[75]

To the dismay of hardliners in Washington, who remained deeply skeptical of Beijing's gestures, Trump repeatedly signalled a strong desire to close a deal. His keenness was attributable in large part to Chinese promises to buy hundreds of billions of dollars' worth of American products — corn, sorghum, soybeans, petroleum, chemicals, semiconductors and airplanes, among others. "That's going to make our farmers very happy. That's a lot of soybeans," Trump exulted to reporters at a White House meeting on January 31 during which Liu presented an offer to ramp up China's soybean purchases from US suppliers.[76]

The shamelessness of this stratagem on both sides was mind-boggling. Pledges by Beijing to buy US products would accomplish little in the way of changing fundamental Chinese behaviour — if anything, they would buttress China's use of state power to achieve economic goals. Moreover, countries whose exports were discriminated against by China would presumably have grounds for a WTO complaint based on MFN principles. A further drawback was that the United States would become more vulnerable than before to a capricious cutoff by Beijing; orders of US goods by government fiat could easily be reversed if doing so suited China's leadership.

75 Lingling Wei, 2019, "Beijing Drops Contentious 'Made in China 2025' Slogan, but Policy Remains," *The Wall Street Journal*, March 5.

76 Shawn Donnan and Jenny Leonard, 2019, "Trade Hawks Quietly Bristle as Trump's Deadline Approaches," Bloomberg News, February 5.

But in his eagerness to obtain terms that would shrink the bilateral US trade deficit with China, buoy the stock market and provide relief to the farm belt, Trump sent one conciliatory message after another, including a willingness to extend negotiations past the agreed-upon March 1 deadline. Knowledgeable insiders were quoted as expecting a deal to be wrapped up in time for Trump and Xi to seal it at a summit by the end of March; although that goal slipped to April, then to May or June, the signals remained upbeat. A 100-strong Chinese delegation, led by Liu, was due to arrive in Washington on May 8 for what was billed as the deal's closing phase.

It was at this juncture, as noted in chapter 1, that the talks broke down. In retrospect, nobody should have been surprised. All along, Lighthizer had been unwavering in insisting that the agreement must go far beyond Chinese purchases of US goods, to address the full gamut of complaints, including technology transfer, intellectual property theft, favouritism toward national champions, requirements for foreign companies to form joint ventures with Chinese partners, subsidization of SOEs and discriminatory restrictions against foreign digital services firms.[77] Some US demands proved relatively easy for China to handle — regarding currency, for example, Beijing would pledge to refrain from depreciating the RMB's exchange rate for competitive reasons.[78] But on other issues, Washington's demands struck at the core of China's economic model. Although ready to reform to some extent, Beijing was unwilling to undergo root-and-branch change, and Liu — whatever his philosophical leanings — was in no position to override Xi's conservative instincts. For its part, the White House was anxious to protect itself against accusations of settling for superficial alterations in Chinese policies. Compromise was perforce difficult — much more so on the issues dear to Lighthizer's heart than on, say, soybean purchases.

Still, the belligerence of the tweets by @realDonaldTrump on May 5, three days before Liu's scheduled arrival in Washington, came as a shock to many in both nations' capitals. "Trade Deal with China continues, but too slowly, as they attempt to renegotiate. No!" the president thundered,[79] adding that starting the following Friday, he would order an increase from 10 percent to 25 percent in the tariffs already in effect on $200 billion worth of Chinese

---

77 Ana Swanson, 2019, "As U.S. and China Near Trade Deal, Enforcement Is Key," *The New York Times,* April 11.

78 This provision was necessitated by the fact that China still maintained an opaque mechanism for setting the RMB's value rather than leaving it to market supply and demand. See William Mauldin and Josh Zumbrun, U.S.-China Pact Takes Aim at Currency Manipulation," *The Wall Street Journal,* April 12.

79 Donald J. Trump, Twitter post, May 5, 2019, 9:08 a.m., https://twitter.com/realdonaldtrump/status/1125069836088950784.

imports. In an effort to appear reasonable and get the deal back on track, Liu flew to Washington anyway, but returned to Beijing with no breakthrough to report and Trump's tariff hikes were initiated. Although both governments emphasized that talks would resume, the omens did not bode well on Chinese internet sites, where Liu was being compared to a Qing dynasty official who is much maligned for having signed a humiliating treaty with Japan in the late nineteenth century.[80]

Tell me how this ends. In mid-May 2019, as final changes were being made to this book, economic hostilities were back in full swing.

Beijing struck back at Trump's tariff hike on Chinese goods by announcing plans to increase duties on $60 billion in US products, and Washington published a new list of nearly $300 billion in imports from China that could be taxed at 25 percent rates as early as the summer. The Trump administration went even further on May 15, infuriating Beijing by putting Huawei on a list of foreign companies that couldn't buy products and technology from US firms unless federal approval for such transactions was given first. Perhaps, as many in the business and financial communities fear — and some hawkish Americans hope — both sides will dig in, erecting even more barriers and decoupling further from each other. But the two governments left time to patch things up by postponing the implementation of their tariffs for a couple of weeks. So who knows? By the time this book is available for purchase, a US-China pact may have been agreed.

If and when that happens, great sighs of relief will emanate from many quarters. Financial markets may even get a boost from the end, or at least de-escalation, of the Sino-US trade war. Trump supporters will claim vindication for the strategy of enduring the short-term pain of tariffs for the long-term gain of altering some of China's techno-nationalistic practices. Criticism will also be in plentiful supply, from Democratic politicians, in particular, who will scorn the terms as insufficiently rigorous to ensure that China Inc. will truly change. Clichés about the devil being in the details, and the proof of the pudding being in the eating, will be cited ad nauseam — and aptly, because of the shadowy ways in which the Chinese party-state works its will.

Illusions about the durability and scope of any such accord should be cast aside; the truce will be fragile and limited. It could easily fall apart over new

---

80 Bloomberg News, 2019, "Memories of China's 1895 Shame Loom Over Envoy's High-Stakes Talks," May 9.

allegations, valid or not, that China is using informal obstacles to foil foreign businesses. With the 2020 election approaching, both major US parties will be seeking to position themselves as toughest — and their opponents as soft — on Beijing. (Trump has already claimed that Chinese leaders desperately crave a victory by former Vice President Joe Biden, who is seeking the Democratic presidential nomination.) And given ongoing geopolitical rivalry, nothing in a trade pact will halt the manoeuvring by both China and the United States to achieve technological independence at each other's expense — the United States in 5G, China in semiconductors and software.

Deal or no deal, one refrain is certain to echo loudly: that tariffs and trade wars may be terrible, but nothing else has worked with China in the past, so Trump was right to use such an approach as long as he sought meaningful concessions. This argument, or variations of it, was an oft-cited theme in commentary during the US-China faceoff of 2018-2019. The president's tactics were acknowledged to be "unorthodox" or "unconventional,"[81] and his execution as unskillful or even maladroit. But dispensing with conventionality was justified in China's case — or so it was said.

Without knowing the specifics of the US-China agreement, or even whether an agreement will be forthcoming, I contend that the above perspectives miss the big point. In its trade policy since March 2018, the Trump administration frequently and flagrantly resorted to Mafia-like tactics, for which terms like "unconventional" are euphemistic in the extreme. It strains credulity to conceive that China will submit to those tactics by agreeing to restructure its economic system in far-reaching ways, and even if the terms exceed expectations, the deal will not have been worth the costs.

By "costs," I am referring not only to the raised prices, lost jobs, disrupted supply chains and ruined livelihoods that have resulted from the trade wars, nor the fraying of US alliances and loss of faith in Washington's trustworthiness — although those costs are hardly trivial. The steepest cost arises from the trampling of WTO rules, which occurred in plain sight of every government in the world and every industry or interest group that might want protection from foreign competition. Having seen the trade body's biggest and most powerful member behave so high-handedly, other countries will be less constrained about violating the rules themselves in the future. Governments that lose WTO disputes and honour the trade body's judgment will risk being ridiculed as suckers, especially if the opposing disputant is a small trading

---

81 David King and John Stensholt, 2018, "Outlook conference: Trump taking an unconventional way to better tariff deal: PM," *The Australian*, October 11.

partner. The more countries succumb to the temptation to engage in Trump-style rule flouting, the further the trading system will descend into law of the jungle. Dollar signs cannot be attached to the prospective losses; economists' models cannot estimate the percentage decline in GDP resulting from the lessening of stability and predictability in international commerce. It stands to reason, though, that the world will be poorer than it would be otherwise, long into the future.

Policy makers and citizens of big countries, Americans in particular, may think they have little to lose economically from the absence of effective international rules because their market leverage will enable them to dictate the terms of trade to others. They should think harder. Smaller players are not defenceless in a global trade jungle. Consider, for example, the Trade-Related Aspects of Intellectual Property Rights accord (TRIPS), the WTO provisions that protect motion pictures, computer software, drug patents and the like from piracy abroad. A breakdown in adherence to TRIPS would be disastrous for Silicon Valley and Hollywood, with negative consequences as well for scientific advancement, technological innovation and artistic creativity worldwide.

To prevail upon China's leaders for the types of reforms they appear ready to take in 2019, much less injurious methods could and should have been employed. Suppose the clock could be rewound to the time of my visit to Geneva at the end of 2016. What wise and efficacious approach might have been devised for dealing with China Inc. before Trump's America surpassed it as problem number one for the global trading system?

CHAPTER 11

MAKE THE WTO GREAT AGAIN

On June 28, 2018, Wang Shouwen, China's vice minister of commerce, threw down the gauntlet to his country's critics. After presenting a staunch defence of China's trade practices at a news conference, he issued an icy suggestion to countries that believe Beijing has failed to open up as promised: "You can sue us at the WTO."[1]

This was a dare, meant to convey China's confidence that it fully complies with WTO rules and wouldn't be found in violation by impartial international tribunals. Smug as it may have sounded, Wang's certitude was consistent with a central theme of this book, seen in chapter after chapter: China's violations of the trade body's rules are less wanton than commonly thought, and to the extent rule-breaking occurs, substantiation is often elusive if not infeasible. The challenge lies deeper, in the problematic ways the Chinese economic system has evolved that the rulebook can't always address.

Wang's dare nonetheless ought to have been seized with alacrity by China's trading partners, with the United States in the lead. Doing so would have been an excellent way of implementing the principles mentioned on page 230 — focusing in unison on China as the trading system's main problem and

---

1   Agence France-Press, 2018, "China defends its post-WTO business record," June 28.

using the WTO as the main instrument for effecting change. Rooted as they are in multilateralism, those principles have none of Trumpism's downsides, and some measures based on them have surprising upsides, as this chapter will show. It's a pity that such measures weren't used in 2018, but they're still well worth considering since the world just might need good alternatives to a trade war, especially with China, in the future.

A number of proposals have been advanced for bringing WTO cases against China using the trade body's rules in novel, untested ways.[2] The most intriguing and exciting by far comes from Georgetown University Law Professor Jennifer Hillman — yes, the same Jennifer Hillman who, as we saw in chapter 7, was denied a second term as a judge on the WTO Appellate Body.

In her June 2018 testimony to a congressional commission on US-China relations, Hillman urged "a big, bold, comprehensive case at the WTO filed by a broad coalition of countries that share the United States' substantive concerns about China."[3] Examining in turn the main grievances about Chinese trade practices listed in the Trump administration's Section 301 report, she contended that various commitments China made — in its protocol of accession and the report by the working party handling the accession process — could be invoked in ways that haven't been tried before, along with other WTO rules. But the heart of the case she proposed involved Article XXIII of GATT/WTO rules, called "nullification or impairment."[4] Obscure and seldom used though it may be, this provision might be the perfect ace in the hole for playing against China Inc.

Under this provision, a WTO member can be found in violation of its obligations and subject to sanctions if its policies nullify or impair the legitimate expectations of its trading partners by violating the overall intent of the rules — even if no specific rules are being broken. Hillman acknowledged that such claims have been rare for good reason; the provision is explicitly drafted to be used only in exceptional circumstances, because countries should reasonably expect to be sued only for clear rule contraventions. However, she cited the preamble of the declaration establishing the WTO, which states that the

---

2   See, for example, James Bacchus, Simon Lester and Huan Zhu, 2018, "Disciplining China's Trade Practices at the WTO," Cato Institute Policy Analysis, Number 856, November 15, https://object.cato.org/sites/cato.org/files/pubs/pdf/pa856.pdf.

3   U.S.-China Economic and Security Review Commission, 2018, "Testimony of Jennifer Hillman, Hearing on U.S. Tools to Address Chinese Market Distortions," June 8, www.uscc.gov/sites/default/files/Hillman%20Testimony%20US%20China%20Comm%20w%20Appendix%20A.pdf.

4   As noted in chapter 5, this provision was considered, but not used, for addressing Beijing's currency policy.

global trading system would be "based on open, market-oriented policies," and she continued:

> The widespread concerns with China's economy and the difficulties it has raised for WTO members suggests that this is indeed time for an exceptional approach…China's economy is structured differently from any other major economy and is different in ways that were not anticipated by WTO negotiators.…It is exactly for this type of situation that the non-violation nullification and impairment clause was drafted. The United States and all other WTO members had legitimate expectations that China would increasingly behave as a market economy — that it would achieve a discernible separation between its government and its private sector…that subsidies would be curtailed…[and] that SOEs would make purchases based on commercial considerations.…It is this collective failure by China, rather than any specific violation of individual provisions, that should form the core of a big, bold WTO case.

Who would win such a case — China or the complainants? Obviously a victory over Beijing would be no certainty. But as a former Appellate Body member, Hillman has a well-informed idea of what might pass muster with WTO judges; Chinese officials would be foolish to dismiss the possibility of suffering a catastrophic loss. Perhaps the best outcome of a Hillman-style "big, bold" case is that China would be forced to consider a negotiated settlement in which it would pledge to dismantle some of its most objectionable practices and adopt reforms of a similar nature to the ones it was prepared to make in the Trump administration's bilateral negotiations. Better yet, perhaps Beijing would be even more forthcoming in such a multilateral forum, and sincere in undertaking reforms, than it would be in responding to American threats.

As Hillman pointed out in her testimony, such a case would stand a good chance of bearing fruit only if a wide array of countries joined in bringing it to the WTO. China needs to see that objections to its industrial policies are global in scope, and the arguments advanced by the complainants would be all the more powerful if companies and policy makers from a variety of nations provided evidence. Yet another reason for complainants to seek strength in numbers, Hillman noted, is to shield themselves from retaliation by Chinese officialdom.

Above all, she asserted, the international community has a collective interest at stake: "If the WTO can be seen to be able to either bend or amend its rules to take on the challenges presented by China's 'socialist market economy' framework, then faith in the institution and its rules-based system can be enhanced, for the good of the United States and the world."[5]

It would be risky, of course, for the United States and its allies to rely too much on the big, bold case that Hillman proposes. China might well litigate to the end and might win — and the process would be enormously time-consuming. Fortunately, there are other ways, not involving litigation, for China's trading partners to band together and use WTO rules to maximum advantage in countering the predatory effects of Beijing's policies. The most promising one might be called, for shorthand purposes, the "anti-glut" strategy. It comes courtesy of legal scholars Weihan Zhou, Henry Gao and Xue Bai, who have zeroed in on a provision in China's accession protocol that has gone underutilized.[6]

This provision gives countries significant leeway to restrict imports of subsidized Chinese products using countervailing duties. Normally government officials seeking to impose countervailing duties on subsidized imports must amass a lot of evidence to show the existence and amount of the subsidy. But recall from chapters 2 and 3 that in China's eagerness to join the WTO, it agreed to some unusual, discriminatory rules. One of them, section 15 (b) of the protocol, states that if distorted market conditions in the Chinese economy cause "special difficulties" to trading partners in estimating Chinese subsidies, the calculations can be made using prices and costs for comparable goods and inputs in other countries — which makes it much easier to conclude that subsidization is occurring and high duties are warranted.

This provision doesn't expire, unlike other discriminatory rules that China accepted (for example, the special China safeguard, which had a 12-year duration, and the non-market economy status for anti-dumping cases, which was supposed to last 15 years). It has gone unused partly because the United States, in particular, preferred anti-dumping duties; henceforth, US officials and their counterparts in other countries should view countervailing duties as their trade remedy of choice for China, given the ease of applying the "special difficulties" standard, according to Zhou, Gao and Bai.

---

5   U.S.-China Economic and Security Review Commission, "Testimony of Jennifer Hillman" (see footnote 3 in this chapter).

6   Weihuan Zhou, Henry S. Gao and Xue Bai, 2018, "China's SOE Reform: Using WTO Rules to Build a Market Economy," Society of International Economic Law, Sixth Biennial Global Conference, July, https://ssrn.com/abstract=3209613 or http://dx.doi.org/10.2139/ssrn.3209613.

If China's trading partners start availing themselves of this legal weapon, they needn't worry so much about lacking an effective defence against global over-capacity of goods produced by national champions benefiting from initiatives such as Made in China 2025. Together with Australia, Brazil, Canada, the European Union, Japan, South Korea and other advanced economies, the United States can warn Beijing that if subsidized Chinese companies begin exporting excess supplies of their products on global markets, countervailing duties will be imposed and China will be stuck with the glut in its domestic market. Here again, Washington would need to forge a coalition with all the countries that have major markets for such goods, to ensure that everyone would act in concert.

Crucially, this strategy, used in conjunction with a Hillman-style big-and-bold case, would help preserve and bolster the WTO rather than subverting its authority. Trade with many other countries besides China is governed by the WTO, so a WTO-centred approach is all the more preferable if it offers ways of significantly ameliorating the China Inc. problem.

The WTO was beset with troubles even before Trump took office, as noted in chapter 10, and it is now under unprecedented siege. Other restorative steps besides the ones above are therefore badly needed. The most urgent problem is to stave off paralysis of the Appellate Body, which will lose two of its three remaining members in December 2019, and it behooves WTO members to recognize the validity of some US gripes.

Among the sensible proposals to deal with the problem of excessive judicial activism, for example, is a procedure called a "legislative remand."[7] Under this approach, when the Appellate Body is faced with a dispute over WTO rules that aren't completely clear, the judges would stop short of issuing any decision that would effectively create new rules. Instead, the issue would be referred to the WTO membership to negotiate, and if consensus proves impossible, a three-fourths majority vote could resolve the ambiguity.

It isn't certain whether the Trump administration really wants an agreement that would allow the appointment of new members needed to keep the Appellate Body functioning. But an all-out effort should be made. As my CIGI colleague Robert McDougall sagely observed in a paper spelling out a comprehensive set of reforms: "Despite uncertainty about the United States' true end-game, addressing some of its longstanding systemic concerns — if

---

7   Tetyana Payosova, Gary Clyde Hufbauer and Jeffrey J. Schott, 2018, "The Dispute Settlement Crisis in the World Trade Organization: Causes and Cures," Peterson Institute for International Economics, Policy Brief 18-5, March, https://piie.com/system/files/documents/pb18-5.pdf.

this can be done while preserving the compulsory, impartial and enforceable nature of dispute settlement — would actually improve the system's legitimacy and effectiveness in the long run."[8]

The other WTO infirmity crying out for attention is its lameness at negotiating new rules. The most fruitful type of deal would be "plurilateral" — that is, an accord that doesn't require consensus among all 164 countries but rather just a "critical mass" of them, to liberalize trade or formalize rules in certain areas such as e-commerce, services, environmental goods and investment. These types of deals can be concluded on MFN terms, meaning the benefits apply to all WTO members, or they can be non-MFN, meaning that the benefits accrue only to the countries that accept the obligations. To Lighthizer's credit, he has endorsed the idea of the United States joining in plurilateral negotiations as the best way forward for WTO talks,[9] and in late January 2019, more than 70 countries, including the United States and China, agreed to start negotiating new rules for "trade-related aspects of electronic commerce."[10]

That's the good news. The bad news is that the participating governments have vastly different notions of what a final deal would look like, given their disagreements over key issues such as cyber security, privacy of personal data and freedom of cross-border data flows. Sadly, nobody is holding out any prospect for a comprehensive pact encompassing a wide range of issues of the sort concluded in the rounds of the last century. The flameout after flameout in the Doha Round talks put an end to such ambitions.

As for the conflicts regarding the security of next-generation telecommunications networks built by companies such as Huawei, the WTO is probably ill-suited to play much of a role. But one possibility for preventing, or at least limiting, the likely schism in global markets is the creation of a new multilateral body. A proposal for such a body — tentatively dubbed the "International Communications Infrastructure Integrity Inspector" — has been advanced by Geoff Mulgan, who heads the United Kingdom's National Endowment for Science, Technology and the Arts.[11] As Mulgan envisions it, this institution would be modelled on the International Atomic Energy Agency, which for decades has served as the world's trusted authority in ensuring that nuclear

---

8   Robert McDougall, 2018, *Crisis in the WTO: Restoring the WTO Dispute Settlement Function*, CIGI Paper No. 194, Waterloo, ON: CIGI, www.cigionline.org/publications/crisis-wto-restoring-dispute-settlement-function/.

9   Peter Ungphakorn, 2017, "MC11: Did Argentina break an impasse, or the WTO itself?" Agra Europe, December 18, https://iegpolicy.agribusinessintelligence.informa.com/PL214601/MC11-Did-Argentina- break-an-impasse-or-the-WTO-itself.

10   *The Economist,* 2019, "A new initiative aims to modernize global trading rules," January 31.

11   Geoff Mulgan, 2019, "Build a global body to oversee telecoms infrastructure," *Financial Times,* May 5.

power is used securely and for peaceful purposes. A new communications body would require a sizable staff with technical expertise, along with rights of inspection of software and hardware to credibly certify that networks are backdoor-free. That might be the least of its challenges. In Mulgan's words, "creative multilateralism…has become unfashionable in the age of Donald Trump."

It is almost certainly too late for the Trump administration to reverse course on its China trade strategy and adopt a WTO-centred approach like the one recommended in this chapter. For those who value the multilateral rules-based system, the only practical way forward may be to wait in the hope that Americans will sooner or later elect a president with a more enlightened trade policy than "my way or the highway." But if the US-China negotiations of 2019 fail to achieve a satisfactory outcome, and if Trump is so inclined — a long shot, to be sure — here's one way he could phrase an explanation for abandoning uniltaterally imposed tariffs in favour of reviving multilateralism:

> I've been saying for years that China is the worst offender on trade. And now everyone admits I was right. So I want to invite our allies to join us in filing a big suit against China at the WTO and coordinating our defences against Chinese subsidies. I'm not happy about the trade problems we have with our allies, but I'll make an offer to them: If they go along with this new strategy of mine, I'll terminate the steel and aluminum tariffs I imposed in 2018, and I'll also drop my threats to impose tariffs on cars. Just to show how serious I am, I'll even suspend the tariffs I've imposed on Chinese imports pending the outcome of this litigation, provided of course that China reciprocates in kind. I'm still skeptical of the WTO, and I'm not apologizing for anything — hey, those tariffs scared the hell out of everybody, didn't they? Just like in The Art of the Deal. But I'm a pragmatic guy, which means setting priorities. Nobody's better than me at setting priorities. And priority number one in trade is fixing our problems with China. What matters to me is results — good results for the American people. So I hope friends like Justin Trudeau, Shinzo Abe, Angela Merkel and Emmanuel Macron will agree that their countries also have a big stake in this issue and will take advantage of my proposal.

Even if, by some miracle, Trump were to utter words like those and shift his trade policy to something along the lines I've suggested, the result would be no panacea for the China Inc. problem. A big, bold WTO case will not diminish the influence of "Xi Jinping thought" on China's political economy;

the party-state will remain uber-powerful and continue to operate in a non-transparent manner; foreign companies seeking market access in China will remain fearful of lodging complaints that may anger the authorities. To some extent, therefore, the scales may remain tilted in favour of SOEs and national champions. But similar problems will haunt any conceivable deal resulting from the 2019 US-China negotiations. To reiterate a couple of points from chapter 1, conflict between China and its trading partners will be ongoing, and the best that can be expected from the WTO is that trade will be pretty free, pretty fair and pretty reciprocal — with the big bonus of a rule of law system that fosters stability and predictability.

Whoever succeeds Trump may take an even harder line toward Beijing, disdaining him for allowing China Inc. to remain intact. He or she would be well advised to use a WTO-compatible strategy rather than unilateral sanctions. And Beijing would be well advised to respond constructively rather than defiantly to such an approach.

All countries belonging to the WTO have benefited from membership, China most of all. China's state capitalism has eroded the organization's credibility and authority; Trump's unilateralism has bruised and battered it. Whether the rules-based trading system can survive the fracturing that has resulted is an open question; the danger of a full-fledged schism looms larger than ever. Working cooperatively, Beijing and Washington have it in their power to substantially reduce the risk of such a scenario and hopefully avert it altogether.

If only grounds for hope were in more bountiful supply. The system's fate is heavily dependent on the decisions of two men — Trump and Xi. For those assessing the merits and demerits of the outcome, this book has hopefully provided some enlightenment, but it can offer little if any comfort.